The Christian
in Complete Armour

THE CHRISTIAN IN COMPLETE ARMOUR

WILLIAM GURNALL

Abridged by Ruthanne Garlock, Kay King,
Karen Sloan and Candy Coan

Volume 2

THE BANNER OF TRUTH TRUST

THE BANNER OF TRUTH TRUST
3 Murrayfield Road, Edinburgh EH12 6EL
P.O. Box 621, Carlisle, Pennsylvania 17013, U.S.A.

*

First published in three volumens in 1655, 1658 and 1662
Revised and reprinted in 1864 by Blackie & Son, Glasgow, Scotland
The 1864 edition (unabridged) republished by the Banner of Truth
    Trust, Edinburgh, Scotland in 1964, 1974, 1979, 1983,
    1987 and 1990
The 1864 edition (Volume 2) revised and abridged, published by
    World Challenge, Inc., David Wilkerson Crusades, Lindale,
    Texas, U.S.A. in association with the Banner of Truth Trust, 1988
© World Challenge Inc., 1988
Reprinted 1990
Reprinted 1994
Reprinted 2000
Reprinted 2002
ISBN 0 85151 515 0

*

Printed and bound in Finland
by WS Bookwell

Contents

Chapter 8: *Seventh Consideration: The
Christian's Spiritual Shoe* 245

I. WHAT IS MEANT BY THE GOSPEL 245

The Several Pieces of the Whole Armour of God

6: *Fifth Consideration: The Christian's Spiritual Girdle*

Having your loins girt about with truth (Eph. 6:14).

W HAT is *truth* here? Some say it is Christ Himself, who is called 'the truth' in John's Gospel. But in this passage the apostle assigns distinct meanings to several pieces of armour, and Christ cannot be confined to any one of them. Instead, He is the whole in whom we are complete, compared to the entire suit of armour: 'Put ye on the Lord Jesus Christ' (*Rom. 13:14*).

Others think the apostle is implying *truth of doctrine* or *sincerity*, and indeed both are necessary to make the girdle complete. Neither one will work without the other. It is possible, of course, to have a kind of sincerity without truth. For instance, God did not sanction Saul's zeal when he persecuted the Christian church, although he earnestly believed he was doing God a favor. And neither is it enough to have truth on our side if it is not in our hearts. Jehu defiantly opposed idolatry but later tore down his testimony by hypocrisy. Both, then, are vitally essential – *sincerity* to set forth a right purpose and *knowledge of the word of truth* to direct us toward that end.

And what is meant by *loins*? Peter interprets Paul: 'Gird up the loins of your mind' (*1 Pet. 1:13*) – they are our spirit and mind which wear this girdle of truth. The loins are to the body as the keel is to the ship. Because the whole vessel is connected to this keel it is sustained by it. And the body is knit to the loins; if the loins fail, the entire body sinks. Even when we get tired physically, nature prompts us to support both hands on our loins as our primary strength. Thus to 'smite through the loins' is a phrase of destruction; weak loins make a weak man (*Deut. 33:11*).

Therefore as the actions of our minds and spirits are powerful or passive, so we are strong or weak Christians. If a person's understanding is clear in its hold on truth and his will is sincerely grounded in holy purposes, then he is a maturing Christian. But if the understanding is uncertain and the will is wavering and unsteady, the man is dull and his life is one of spiritual impotence.

Truth of doctrine for the mind, and *truth of heart* or *sincerity* for the will, unite and establish both these faculties. And this is exactly what happens when they are fastened firmly around the soul, as the girdle about the loins of the body. Although the loins are the strength of the body, they need help from the girdle to keep those parts inseparable in their force.

1. Truth of Doctrine as a Girdle for the Mind

We shall begin with *truth of doctrine*, called 'the word of truth' because it is the Word of God, who is Himself the God of truth (*Eph. 1:13*). Peter warned us to resist the devil, 'stedfast in the faith' (*1 Pet. 5:9*) – that is, in the truth. The word 'faith' is used here as the object of our faith, which is the truth of God. And in the following verse Peter earnestly prays for God to 'stablish, strengthen, settle you' (*v. 10*). The concentration of these different expressions all leading to the same purpose implies the dangerous, unsettling potential of Satan and the necessity of standing unshaken in the faith against him. In the volatile times of the early church it was impossible for Christians to keep the faith from being torn away from them without this girdle to hold it close.

Just as the devil has a double design to rob Christians of truth, so there are two sides of being girded with this grace. First, Satan comes as a *serpent* in the persons of false teachers to cheat us with error for truth. To defend ourselves against his conspiracy we must be girded with truth in our understanding and have established judgment in the truths of Christ. And second, Satan comes as a *lion* in the role of persecutors who strive to separate saints from the truth through fear of danger and death. The only way to defend ourselves against this lion is to be girded with truth and thus maintain our profession of faith in every circumstance.

ESTABLISHED JUDGMENT IN THE TRUTHS OF CHRIST

Since Satan comes as a serpent concealed in false teachers and tries to deceive us with error for truth, every Christian needs an established judgment in the truths of Christ. The Bereans studied Scripture to satisfy their judgments concerning the doctrine Paul preached. They refused to believe anything he had said before they 'searched the scriptures daily, whether those things were so' (*Acts 17:11*). They took the preacher's doctrine straight to the written word and compared it to that; and the result was 'therefore many of them believed' (*v. 12*). As the Bereans dared not believe before, they could not help but believe now.

Tertullian described the preaching of heretics like this: 'They teach by persuading, and do not by teaching persuade.' That is, they court the emotions of their hearers without convincing their judgment. For instance, it would be hard for an adulterer to convince his companion that her prostitution is lawful. Instead, he works another way: by romantic overtones and appeal to the flesh. The question of law is soon forgotten. Judgment is easily and quickly absorbed by burning lust.

Thus error, like a thief, comes in through the window; yet truth, like the owner of the house, enters at the door of understanding, and from there moves into the conscience, will, and affections. The man who finds and professes truth before he understands its excellency and beauty cannot fully appreciate the worth of its heavenly birth and descent. A prince travelling in disguise is not honored because people do not realize who he is. Truth is loved and prized only by those who recognize it and know it personally.

If we do not desire to know truth we have already rejected it. It is not hard to cheat a person out of truth if he does not know what he has. Truth and error are all the same to the ignorant man and so he calls everything truth. Have you heard about the covetous man who constantly hugged his many bags of gold? He never opened them or used the treasure, and thus when a thief stole the gold and left his bags full of pebbles in his room, he was as happy as when he still had the gold.

WHY CHRISTIANS NEED AN ESTABLISHED JUDGMENT IN THE TRUTH

I. PROTECTION FROM THE DAMNING NATURE OF FALSE DOCTRINES

An abscess in the head can be as deadly as one in the stomach. And a corrupt judgment in foundation truths kills as surely as a rotten heart does.

Many people say a person can be saved in any religion if he just follows the light. It does not matter, they say, *what* you believe as long as you believe *something*. But their imagination is making as many roads to heaven as Scripture tells us there are ways to hell. This humanistic rationale may sound good but the end of it does not lead to Christ, who says there is no other way to life but by Him: 'I am the way, the truth, and the life' (*John 14:6*). John declares that anyone who will not hold the one true doctrine of Christ is marked eternally as a lost man. And he who will not take God before he dies, the devil will take as soon as he dies.

No matter how much kindness and logic and religion a man mixes in to corrupt true doctrine, he is an obstinate sinner in God's sight and will receive the same condemnation at Christ's hands as the unrepentant drunkard or murderer. Both stand tied together for hell: 'They which do such things shall not inherit the kingdom of God' (*Gal. 5:21*).

If ignorance in fundamentals is damning, surely error in fundamentals is far more deadly. If a pound of sin is enough to press down to hell, there is no doubt that a ten-pound weight will do it even faster. Error stands farther away from truth than ignorance does and opposes it more vigorously. Error is ignorance with an unseen guillotine.

A man who does not eat enough will die, but the one who swallows poison will lose his life even sooner. The apostle assures us that 'pernicious ways' and 'damnable heresies' bring 'swift destruction' upon those who accept them (*2 Pet. 2:1, 2*). All rivers find their way sooner or later to the sea, but some return with a swift stream and get there before the others. If you want a shorter trip to hell than you could schedule with more conventional sin, then slide into this rushing river of corrupt doctrine and it will not take long for you to get there.

II. PROTECTION FROM THE SUBTLE NATURE OF IMPOSTERS

Because wicked imposters are skillful enough to destroy faith, we must strengthen our judgment in the truths of

Christ. The apostle describes the victims of these sorcerers as people who are 'ever learning' but never coming 'to the knowledge of the truth' (*2 Tim. 3:7*). But to faithful Timothy he says, 'But thou hast fully known my doctrine' (*v. 10*). It is as if he had said, 'I am not worried about you – you are too fully persuaded to be cheated out of the gospel now.'

Seducers, then, wait for unsettled men to stumble into the devil's snare because they do not stand on scriptural ground. 'In vain the net is spread in the sight of any bird' (*Prov. 1:17*). The devil chose to attack Eve instead of Adam because she was the one more likely to be caught; and he has varied his strategy very little since then. He still sneaks over where the hedge is the lowest and the resistance the weakest. Let us look now at three kinds of people who fit into this category.

(a) *'Simple ones'*
Seducers, by pleasing words and convincing speeches, 'deceive the hearts of the simple' (*Rom. 16:18*). These people mean well but lack discernment. They carelessly drink from just anybody's cup and never suspect they are being slowly poisoned.

(b) *'Children'*
'Be no more children, tossed to and fro with every wind of doctrine' (*Eph. 4:14*). Because children assume anything is good if it is sweet, it is not hard to tempt them to eat poison for sugar. Because a child does not have much knowledge of the Word for himself, he is swayed by the slightest suggestion, good or bad. Like Isaac, children bless their opinions by feeling and not by sight and thus fall into the pit of deception because they have not tried their feelings by the truths of God's Word.

(c) *'Unstable'*
False teachers are successful in 'beguiling unstable souls'

(*2 Pet. 2:14*) – those whose understanding is not anchored in the Word. These unstable people are at the mercy of the wind and drift further and further down the stream of fashionable religious phenomena and other current trends, much like dead fish in the tide.

III. UNIVERSAL INFLUENCE OF ESTABLISHED JUDGMENT
   UPON THE WHOLE MAN

Let us examine three vital areas:

(a) *Memory*

The memory is the treasury which stores up and carries images which we have received. The more weight applied to the seal, the deeper the impression made on the wax. And the more emphatic and certain our knowledge of something, the more deeply it sinks into the memory.

(b) *Affections*

The more steady the glass of understanding is, where the light of truth is beamed upon our affections, the sooner they are set on fire: 'Did not our heart burn within us, while he opened to us the scriptures?' the disciples asked on the Emmaus Road (*Luke 24:32*). No doubt they had already heard Christ preach what He was saying now, but they had never been so completely satisfied as when He opened their understanding and Scriptures together.

The sun sends influence and warmth into the earth even when the light does not shed visible beams upon it. But the Sun of righteousness gives His influence only where His light comes to spread truth into our understanding. And as a Christian abides under these wings, a kind of heart-quickening heat is kindled in his heart. While the Holy Spirit is a comforter, He is also a convincer: He comforts us by teaching us.

(c) *Life and behavior*

The eye directs the foot – a man cannot walk safely unless he can see where he is going. Nor can he walk when the earth quakes under his feet. The principles we have in our understanding are the ground our behavior moves upon; if they shift, our actions will stagger too. It is as impossible for a shaking hand to write a straight line as it is for a faltering judgment to exhibit acceptable behavior. The apostle links steadfastness and unmovableness with 'abounding in the work of the Lord' (*1 Cor. 15:58*).

The gospel came to the Thessalonians 'in much assurance' – that is, in evidence of its truth (*1 Thess. 1:5*). And notice how it prevailed in their everyday lives: 'Ye became followers of us, and of the Lord, having received the word in much affliction, with joy of the Holy Ghost' (*v. 6*). They were assured that this doctrine was from God and that assurance carried them through times of affliction as well as rejoicing.

HOW TO ESTABLISH JUDGMENT IN THE TRUTH

I. EMBRACE TRUTH SINCERELY

A disobedient heart and an unsound judgment, like ice and water, are produced mutually by each other. Some men's judgments are fickle because their hearts are so full of guile. A stable mind and a divided heart seldom meet: 'The end of the commandment is charity out of a pure heart, and of a good conscience, and of faith unfeigned' (*1 Tim. 1:5*).

When love receives a truth it is held securely, but lust after worldly interest can cause it to be laid down again. Amnon was soon as sick of Tamar as he had ever been sick for her. And a person can discard precious truths with as much contempt as Amnon showed for Tamar. A wayward heart can easily bribe the judgment to vote on its side. It makes us wonder if such a person were ever in love with these truths in the first place.

II. FOLLOW THE MINISTRY OF THE WORD

One great goal of Scripture is to establish us in truth: 'He gave some, apostles; and some, prophets; and some, evangelists; and some, pastors and teachers; for the perfecting of the saints' (*Eph. 4:11, 12*). Why? 'That we henceforth be no more children, tossed to and fro' (*v. 14*). As you receive the Word, pay attention to the doctrinal part of the sermon as well as to its application. One is necessary to make you a solid Christian, and the other to make you a warm Christian. The Levites 'caused the people to understand the law, . . . and caused them to understand the reading' (*Neh. 8:7, 8*). Planting must go before watering, and teaching should go before exhortation.

III. AVOID CONFINING YOUR JUDGMENT TO ANY PERSON OR GROUP

You must live by your own faith, not someone else's. Look as long and as hard as necessary to see truth with your own eyes. A building propped up by a neighbor's house is too weak to stand very long. So do not let authority from man, but rather evidence from the Word, decide your judgment. Man's conclusions are no stronger than a piece of scrap-wood bracing a building, but truth stands on the eternal foundation of solid rock – God's Word!

Quote Scripture instead of man. Yet in doing this, be careful not to lean so far this way that you lose the proper balance. We must not condemn the judgment of an elder whose wisdom and learning command reverence. Surely God has placed the true path in this matter squarely between defying men and deifying them. Adoration of persons conceives the traitor to truth which makes the crowd cry 'hosanna' to error and 'crucify' to truth. Herod's silver robe dazzled the eyes of spectators while he made an eloquent oration, but when the flatterers shouted, 'It is the voice of a god, and not of a man' he was eaten of worms immediately (*Acts 12:21–23*).

The glittering varnish which some speakers use blinds the judgment of their admirers to the point that they conclude their speech is divine in origin. It is hard, then, to love and esteem man as a man, and to reverence him, and not be in danger of loving his errors also. This is why God would have His children call no one father on earth – to despise none and adore none (*Matt. 23:9*).

IV. BEWARE OF CURIOSITY

The person who listens to every new opinion and covets the newest religious novelties is walking dangerously close to error. The 'itching ears' Paul warns about commonly form a nasty scab of error (*2 Tim. 4:3*). Tamar lost her virginity by being naive – and chastity of the mind is its soundness in the faith. Thus people compromise this soundness if they give themselves to every doctrine which is preached.

We must first be hearers and then disciples. Curiosity concerning many sects and persuasions can make a person skeptical of settling on the truth. Augustine, for example, confessed that he had gone through so many delusions that the errors made him afraid of truth itself. If a person has too many experiences with quacks he will have a hard time trusting the skilled physician.

V. HUMBLY SEEK AN ESTABLISHED JUDGMENT OF GOD

A traveler who is so sure he knows the way that he will not ask directions may be the first one to get lost. Watch out for pride – no matter how confidently it soars now, you will later find it wrecked in the ditch of error. This is the destination God has made for pride, and it must keep His appointment.

Pride can make you a stranger at the throne of grace and

turn humble praying for truth into ambitious arguments. So it is necessary for prideful men to be left to shame so when their understanding does return – if God's mercy allows it – they may 'bless the Most High' the way Nebuchadnezzar did (*Dan. 4:34*).

Guard this judgment deeply in your heart – the God who gives an eye to see truth also gives a hand to hold it. What we have from God we cannot keep without Him. Cherish your closeness with Him or truth will not keep her intimacy with you very long. God is light, but you head for darkness as soon as pride suggests that you turn your back on Him.

VI. DO NOT BE OFFENDED AT DIFFERENCES OF OPINIONS

How can a person know for sure what is truth when there are so many different beliefs in Christianity? Some have stumbled so hard on religious dissension that they have abandoned the truth they once held; and while they are not stranded on the island of atheism they have been driven out into uncertainty, unwilling to anchor their judgments until they see a present resolution of all differences of judgment and opinion to find unity in every aspect of our religion. Surely they are as foolish as the man who refused to eat until all clocks in the city struck twelve at exactly the same time.

VII. KNOW THE VALUE OF TRUTH IN YOUR HEART

Many rare libraries have been destroyed by rude soldiers who failed to realize what a prize the books were. And the destiny of truth, too, depends upon the hands who find it. If it comes to one who draws strength and sweetness from it, truth begins to operate effectually in his heart. But if someone takes it without reaching for its divine comfort and sanctifying power, it is soon dumped in the alley as trash.

And then there are the people who dance around the

candle before they themselves blow it out. When I hear of a man who once held original sin as a truth but later denied it, I fear he got tired and forfeited the effectiveness of the truth before his judgment lost the truth itself. Believers sometimes slide away from cherished old principles of Scripture during unsettled times. Consider the singing of Psalms, for instance. So many have laid down this practice that I must ask if they ever enjoyed precious communion with God in the first place. Have their hearts ever danced up to God with heavenly love as they sang with their lips? How strange to hear a godly person deny this! If you ever met with God at this door of the tabernacle, Christian, did your heart grow cold before you threw away the duty of singing praises to Him?

A FREE AND BOLD PROFESSION OF FAITH

The second way truth is assaulted is by violence; Satan patches the fox's skin of seducers with the lion's skin of persecutors. The bloodiest tragedies in the world have been acted on the stage of the church, and the most inhuman massacres committed on the harmless sheep of Christ. The first man ever murdered was a saint, and he was killed for religion. Luther said that Cain would keep killing Abel until the end of time. The fires of persecution can never quite go out as long as there remains a spark of hatred in wicked hearts on earth, or a devil in hell to fan it into flame.

Many men who could never be torn away from the truth by argument and error have been separated from it by persecution. Therefore the second necessary way of girding truth about the Christian's loins is by courageously professing it. Truth without courage makes a man like a swordfish; he has a sword in the head but no heart to use it. But a person becomes unconquerable when he is empowered with a holy boldness from heaven to draw forth the sword of the Spirit and embrace the naked truth by freely professing it in the face of death. This is to have our 'loins girt about with truth.'

I. MAINTAIN A STEADFAST PROFESSION OF TRUTH

The apostle pressed this instruction upon all Christians when he said: 'Let us hold fast the profession of our faith without wavering' (*Heb. 10:23*). Paul spoke against those who avoided assembling together with saints for fear of persecution, for he believed men who staggered spiritually like this stood next door to apostasy. We must not, then, spread our sails of profession in a calm but fold them up as soon as the wind starts to rise.

Pergamos was commended for her bold profession: 'I know thy works, and where thou dwellest, even where Satan's seat is: and thou holdest fast my name, and hast not denied my faith, even in those days wherein Antipas was my faithful martyr, who was slain among you' (*Rev. 2:13*). It was a season when the deceiver sat in the judge's seat and Christians often drew a sentence of death. Blood was spilled right before their eyes but it did not make them deny the truth of Christ's blood given for them.

Paul delivered a strict charge to Timothy concerning a steadfast profession of truth: 'But thou, O man of God, flee these things; and follow after righteousness, godliness, faith, love, patience, meekness' (*I Tim. 6:11*). While people all around you aim at the world, run after spiritual riches with a chase as hot as theirs.

But what if this business of seeking righteousness cannot be transacted peaceably? Should we close up shop, put our profession on the shelf and postpone holiness until favorable times have come again? Paul's solution is to 'fight the good fight of faith' (*v. 12*). Do not abandon your profession of truth but put your life on the line to keep it.

'I give thee charge in the sight of God, who quickeneth all things, and before Christ Jesus, who before Pontius Pilate witnessed a good confession; that thou keep this commandment' (*vv. 13, 14*). He warned, 'If you hope to see the face of Christ with comfort at the resurrection – who chose to lose His life rather than deny the truth – do not back down from your profession but rather stay put beside it.'

In his *Confessions*, Augustine tells the story of Victorinus, a Roman famous for rhetoric. Late in his life this man received Christ and came to Simplicianus, whispering, 'I am a Christian.' But the pious man wisely protested, 'I will not believe it or count thee so, till I see thee among the Christians at church.' At this, Victorinus laughed and gestured, 'Do these walls make a Christian? Must I openly profess it?' He was fearful, being but a young convert though an old man. Yet time passed and after Victorinus was more confirmed in the faith he seriously considered that if he continued to be ashamed of Christ, Christ would be ashamed of him when He came in the glory of the Father. Again he went to Simplicianus and this time said he was ready to go to church. There he chose to profess his faith openly, saying that he had professed rhetoric for years, so why should he be afraid to own the Word of God?

God requires that Christianity come from both the heart and the mouth: 'With the heart man believeth unto righteousness; and with the mouth confession is made unto salvation' (*Rom. 10:10*). While confession of the mouth without faith in the heart is gross hypocrisy, to imagine faith without profession of the lips is both hypocrisy and cowardice.

II. GOD HAS ENTRUSTED SAINTS WITH HIS TRUTH

Truth is the great treasure which God delivers to His

saints with serious instruction to keep it against all that try to undermine it. Some things we trust God with and some He trusts us with. The most important thing which we put into God's hand to be kept for us is our soul: 'He is able to keep that which I have committed unto him against that day' (*2 Tim. 1:12*). And God trusts us with His truth: 'Earnestly contend for the faith which was once delivered unto the saints' (*Jude 3*). So Paul exhorts Timothy to 'hold fast the form of sound words, . . . that good thing which was committed unto thee' (*2 Tim. 1:13, 14*).

If a man entrusted with keeping the king's crown and jewels is to protect these earthly valuables from being lost or stolen, how much more serious the responsibility of the Christian to protect God's treasure! The Word of truth is the testimony of Himself which God gives to saints, His chosen witnesses whom He calls to live out this truth by a free and holy profession before all men.

III. HOLD YOUR PROFESSION OF TRUTH IN THE FACE OF
    DANGER AND DEATH

We have the truth at a cheap rate now; but how soon the market may rise we do not know. Truth is not always available at the same price. We must buy it at any cost but sell it on no terms.

There has always been, and always will be to the end of the world, a spirit of persecution in wicked hearts. And even as Satan researched Job before he laid his hands on him, persecution is working now in the spirits of the ungodly. Engines of death continually grind out the thoughts of Satan against professing believers of truth. They already know exactly what they will do if power and opportunity are provided for them to carry out their sinister desires.

Satan comes first with a spirit of error and then of persecution; he poisons men's minds with error and then fills their hearts with anger against believers. It is impossible for error to bring any kind of peace; it is a brat of hell that must favor its father. Whatever comes from below can be neither pure nor peaceable. God has let this sulfureous spirit of error remain but He has given us a girdle of truth for protection.

But not everyone who applauds truth will follow it when it leads him to prison. And not everyone who preaches it is willing to suffer for it. Arguments are harmless things – blunt weapons which bring no blood. But when we suffer we are called to fight with the enemies of truth. And this requires more than a sharp tongue and logical brain. Where will disputers be then? They will appear like cowardly soldiers, who, in basic training when no enemy was in sight, seemed to be as brave as decorated heroes. To be on truth's side then meant only recognition and reward, not danger and death. But God has chosen the foolish to confound the wise in this service – the humble Christian, by his faith, patience, and love for truth – to shame men of high standing and no grace.

HOW TO BE GIRDED WITH THE PROFESSION OF TRUTH

The worst that enemies can do is imprisonment or death; but 'love is strong as death' (*Song of Sol. 8:6*). It kills the very heart of death itself. Love does not complain about suffering. Jacob endured the heat of the day and the cold of the night for the love of Rachel. Love is venturous. Jonathan threw away a kingdom and met the anger of an enraged father for David's sake. Love never thinks of itself as a loser as long as it keeps its beloved; it is ready for any danger so it can sacrifice itself for its chosen one.

This kind of love has made saints abandon their worldly possessions, family relations, and even their bodies with joy, not counting it loss to part with them. 'They loved not their lives unto the death' (*Rev. 12:11*). Life itself became their enemy when it came between them and truth.

A man does not love his arm or leg too much to keep it if it hazards the rest of his body; he agrees to have it cut off. Thus David courageously kept his priorities straight when his life was at stake: 'The wicked have waited for me to destroy me: but I will consider thy testimonies' (*Ps. 119:95*). A carnal heart would consider the danger to his business, wife, children, or at least his own life. But David's heart was fixed on a better subject – he focused on God's testimonies and the sweetness pouring in upon his soul as he meditated on them. The more he cleaved to truth, the more his troubles seemed but light afflictions.

It is a mystery to the world why men will risk their lives for what it thinks are only opinions. When our Savior told Pilate that He had come into the world to 'bear witness to the truth,' Pilate asked, 'What is truth?' (*John 18:38*). It is as if he had said, 'Is this any time to be thinking about truth, when your life is in such danger? What is truth anyway, that you should venture so much for it?' The saint full of God's grace might better ask in holy scorn, 'What are the riches and honors and the fading pleasures of this cheating world? What is life itself, that any or all of these should oppose truth?'

Every man goes where his love carries him. If the world has your love, you will spend your life for it; but if truth has your love, you will interpose with your life rather than let it be mangled. Be careful that your love for truth is sincere, though, or it will leave you at the prison door. There are three kinds of imposters whose love is not likely to endure the fiery trial.

IMPOSTERS WHO USE TRUTH

I. THOSE WHO USE TRUTH FOR CARNAL ADVANTAGE

Sometimes truth pays well for her board in the world's own coin, a profitable arrangement which provokes men to invite her in often. These people do not really love truth, only the diamond in her ear. In the days of Henry VIII, many were zealous against abbeys – yet they loved their property more than they hated their idolatry.

Truth finds few people who love her freely, just for herself. And only those few will suffer with truth and for it. When the worldly dowry is gone, the unfaithful are bored with their union with truth. The kitchen fire burns no longer than the fuel with which profit feeds it. If you cannot love naked truth, you will not be willing to go naked for truth. And if you cannot love disgraced truth, you will never agree to be disgraced for its sake.

II. THOSE WHO TALK ABOUT TRUTH BUT DO NOT LIVE IT

Often people will not let truth come anywhere near them. They recommend it but are like one who entertains a suitor and speaks highly of him – but would not think of marrying him. It is one thing to kiss and caress but another really to love. Bucholcerus often said that many kiss Christ but few love Him. True love for Him means the holiest marriage. When a soul gives up itself, because of an inward drawing to Christ as to an husband, to be ruled by His Spirit and ordered by His word of truth, here is a soul that loves Christ and His truth.

The one who refuses to obey truth, however, is so far away from loving it that he becomes afraid of it. And he will persecute truth before he will ever suffer for it. Jerome put it like this: We hate those whom we fear and we want to destroy those whom we hate. For example, Herod feared John and it cost him his life. Fear makes a hard heart imprison truth in his conscience, because if truth had freedom and authority in the soul, it would execute every burning lust that rules there. And the one who imprisons truth in his own heart will never be imprisoned as a witness for truth.

III. THOSE WHO HAVE NO ZEAL AGAINST THE ENEMIES
OF TRUTH

Love is always armed with zeal; and she is ready to draw this dagger against all truth's enemies. Zeal acts like a fire: if it is pent up in the heart of a private Christian and cannot flame forth to punish evil it burns inwardly, grieving and consuming the spirit of the Christian for not rescuing truth from stampeding profanity and error.

It is no joy for a zealous lover to outlive his beloved; he would rather lie down with her in the dusty grave than span a lonely life without her. 'Let us also go, that we may die with him,' Thomas said when Christ told him Lazarus was dead (*John 11:16*). The melancholy of living in evil times prompted Elijah's solemn prayer for death: 'It is enough; now, O Lord, take away my life' (*1 Kings 19:4*). The holy prophet watched as men courted idolaters and killed God's servants. He decided it would be better to leave the world rather than live in the torment of seeing the name, truth, and servants of God trampled by the very people who should have shown the most kindness to them.

But if zeal has any power to vindicate truth's cause, then her enemies will know without a doubt that she 'beareth not the sword in vain' (*Rom. 13:4*). As meek as Moses was, and mute in his own cause, his heart was too inflamed with anger even to pray for his people – as much as he loved them – until he had vented zeal in justice upon the idolaters.

Neutral attitudes, however, can see truth and error scuffling but keep their distance and refuse to get involved in suffering for truth. The pastor who does not have enough love and courage to defend truth in the pulpit will not likely defend her at the burning stake. If the fire of love goes out, or dwindles so that it cannot melt the man into sorrow for the wrongs done to truth, where will the flame be which should enable him to burn to ashes under the hand of bloody men? If he cannot shed tears he will not bleed for truth.

HOW TO HAVE HEARTS INFLAMED WITH LOVE FOR TRUTH

1. MAKE YOUR HEART CONFORM TO TRUTH

Likeness is the ground of love. A carnal heart cannot like truth because it does not resemble truth. How is it possible, then, for an earthly heart to love pure heavenly truth? It is sad when men's understandings clash with their affections, when judgment and will are so unequally yoked. Truth in the conscience scolding lust in the heart! Like a quarreling couple, they may live together for awhile; but the discontent will soon expel truth as Ahasuerus did Vashti, and espouse principles which will not cross his heart in its bent for sin. This has parted many men from truth in these licentious days – they cannot sin in peace and keep sound judgment at the same time.

But if the power of truth has transformed you into its own likeness by the renewing of your mind, and made you bear fruit like itself, you will never separate yourself from it. Before this could happen you would have to part with the new nature which the Spirit of God has formed in you. But now there is a new union between you and truth – or between you and Christ – which can never be broken.

A mighty power goes along with wedlock: two persons who have barely known each other can leave friends and parents to enjoy each other after their affections have been knit by love and their persons made one by marriage. But a mightier power accompanies the mystical marriage between the soul and Christ, the soul and truth. This is the same person who, before conversion, would not have given a penny for Christ or His truth; yet now, knit to Christ by a secret work of the Spirit, he can leave the whole world behind for oneness with Him.

A persecutor once taunted a martyr by asking him if he did not love his wife and children too much to die. 'Yes,' answered the Christian, 'I love them so dearly that I would not part with any of them for all that the Duke of Brunswick – whose subject he was – is worth; but for Christ's sake and His truth, farewell to them all!'

II. LET YOUR HEART BE CONTINUALLY FILLED WITH THE LOVE OF GOD

This will work in you a love for His truth. Love sees what is precious to its beloved and loves it for his sake. For instance, David's love for Jonathan made him inquire about his friend's descendants so he could show them kindness for Jonathan's sake. Love for God makes the soul inquisitive to find out what is dear to God so it can express tenderness to truth and thereby give love to Him.

God has placed a very high price on truth: 'Thou hast magnified thy word above all thy name' (*Ps. 138:2*). Let us look at a few of the ways God values truth.

(a) *God's mercy to give truth*

When God graciously provides His Word to a people He is giving one of the greatest mercies they can receive; He calls them 'the great things' of His 'law' (*Hos. 8:12*). Whatever a people have from God's hand without His truth can no more be compared with that truth than Ishmael's portion (Hagar's bread and water) with Isaac's inheritance. And God, who knows how to prize His own gifts, said of His Word which He showed to Jacob that 'he hath not dealt so with any nation' (*Ps. 147:20*) – that is, not so richly and graciously.

(b) *God's care to preserve His truth*

God has never let truth get lost. In shipwrecks men do not try to save lumber and trivia of little worth but only what is most precious to them. In all the great revolutions of kingdoms and churches, God has preserved His truth. Thousands of saints' lives have been taken away, but the devil despises truth more than all the saints. And this is what still lives!

If truth were not so precious to God He would not allow it to be purchased with the blood of His people – or most important, with the blood of His Son. In that great day when the earth's elements will melt in fire, God's truth will not even be singed: 'The word of the Lord endureth for ever' (*I Pet. 1:25*).

(c) *God's severity to the enemies of truth*

A dreadful curse is pronounced upon anyone who adds to or takes away from truth. One pulls down all the plagues written in the Bible; and the other takes away his part out of the book of life and out of the holy city. It is no wonder that God values truth so highly when we consider what it is – truth is the substance of His thoughts and counsels from everlasting to everlasting. It is the fullest representation that God Himself could give of His own being so we might know and love Him.

Princes used to send their pictures by ambassadors to those they hoped to win and marry. God is such infinite perfection that no hand can draw Him to life but His own; and this is exactly what He has done in His Word – and because of this, saints of every century have joyfully given their hearts to Him.

As we accept or reject truth we accept or despise God. Although men cannot pull God from His throne and ungod Him, they come as close as possible when they attack the truth – they execute God in effigy. Yet God never stops wanting those of us who love Him to cleave to His truth.

III. MEDITATE OFTEN ON THE EXCELLENCY OF TRUTH

The eye is the window where love enters, and a spiritual eye which can see truth in her native beauty cannot help but love her. This was the way David's heart was ravished with the love of the word of truth: 'O how love I thy law! it is my meditation all the day' (*Ps. 119:97*). And he found a great difference between meditating on the truths of God's Word and the best the world could offer: 'I have seen,' he said, 'an end of all perfection' (*v. 96*). In just a few thoughts he could see all the way to the bottom of the world's glory; but when he took up God's truth, his thoughts went on and on in admiration and sweet meditation: 'Thy commandment is exceeding broad' (*v. 96*).

Great ships cannot sail in narrow rivers and shallow waters; and neither can minds full of heavenly knowledge of God find room to move about freely in the world's philosophies. A gracious soul soon runs aground upon these flats; but let it launch out into the meditation of God, His Word, and the mysterious truths of the gospel, and he finds a place of broad waters, an ocean to lose himself in. Let me now direct your meditation to a few lovely properties which you shall find in exploring these truths.

(a) *Truth is pure*

It is not only pure but makes the soul that embraces it pure and holy. 'Sanctify them through thy truth: thy word is truth' (*John 17:17*). It is the pure water which God uses to wash souls clean: 'Then will I sprinkle clean water upon you, and ye shall be clean: from all your filthiness, and from all your idols, will I cleanse you' (*Ezek. 36:25*).

(b) *Truth is sure*

Truth has a firm bottom; we can lay the whole weight of

[43]

our souls upon it and know it will not break. Cleave to truth and it will cleave to you. It will go with you to prison and anywhere else you must go for her sake. 'Not one thing,' said Joshua, 'hath failed of all the good things which the Lord your God spake concerning you; all are come to pass unto you, and not one thing hath failed thereof' (*Josh. 23:14*).

Whatever truth promises, count it as money in your pocket. 'Fourscore years,' Polycarp said, 'I have served God and found Him a good Master.' When men forsake truth to advance themselves they are asking for disappointment. They are flattered away from truth by empty promises and fare no better than Judas after he betrayed his Master into the hands of the Jews.

(c) *Truth is free*

And the man who cleaves to it is free: 'The truth shall make you free' (*John 8:32*). But Christ bluntly told the Jews why they were in bondage: 'Ye are of your father the devil, and the lusts of your father ye will do' (*v. 44*). All sinners are slaves to Satan. The man who has lust living on him like a parasite finds no rest as he serves and provides for it every day. But if all the devil's lusts bolted a single sinner to his dungeon floor, and the truth of Christ opened his heart, you would soon see the foundations of the prison shaken, its doors thrown open, and the chains falling off.

Truth will not be bound. And neither will it stay in a soul that is tied up in sin. Therefore, once truth and the soul agree – Christ and the soul – the person can lift up his head and know that his redemption and delivery from spiritual slavery draw near. The key is already in the lock to let him out. It is impossible for us to know truth as it 'is in Jesus' and remain strangers to the freedom that comes with it (*Eph. 4:21*).

(d) *Truth is victorious*

Truth will prevail over everything. It is the great counsel of God, and although many plots are constantly generating energy against it, this counsel of the Lord stands. Sometimes the enemies of truth take the militia of this lower world into their own hands and truth seems to fall to the ground; and often those who bear witness to its goodness are slain.

But persecutors need not buy marble to record their victories in; dust will be good enough, for they will not last that long. 'Three days and a half' the witnesses may lie dead in the streets, and truth sits by them (*Rev. 11:11*). But after a short time they are up walking again and truth is triumphing along with them.

If persecutors could kill the successors of their victims, their work might not be so temporary; they would not have to fear another man's pulling down what they set up. Yet even then their work would lie open to heaven and could be as easily frustrated as Babel. You might receive news that truth is sick but never that it is dead. It is error that is short-lived. 'A lying tongue is but for a moment,' yet truth's age runs parallel with God's eternity (*Prov. 12:19*).

Truth lives to reign in peace with those who are now willing to suffer for it. Christian, do you not want to be one of those victors who shall ride beside Christ's triumphant chariot into the heavenly city and take a crown with the faithful saints who stood in the militant days when Christ and His truth battled Satan here on earth? With your thoughts, wipe away the tears and blood which now cover the face of suffering truth and present it to your eyes as it will look in glory.

IV. LET YOUR HEART BE FILLED WITH THE FEAR OF GOD'S WRATH AGAINST APOSTASY

When you have accidentally burned your finger you hold

[45]

it next to the fireplace; and the greater fire draws out the pain of the smaller one. Thus if your mind is seared and your heart scorched with the fire of man's wrath, hold them awhile against hell-fire, which God has prepared for the fearful who run from truth's standard.

'Pardon me, O emperor, if I obey not thy command; thou threatenest a prison, but God a hell,' said a defiant martyr who did not fear what man could do to him. And David himself did not fear those who persecuted him without a reason: 'Princes have persecuted me without a cause: but my heart standeth in awe of thy word' (*Ps. 119:161*). Man's fury, even at its zenith, is but a temperate climate compared to the wrath of the living God.

Man's anger has never been able to slow down or stop the love of God and has made saints sing in the fire in spite of their enemies' fuel. But the man under God's wrath is like one shut up in a closed oven – with no crack open to let any of the heat out or any refreshing air in to save him.

2. Truth of Heart or Sincerity as a Girdle for the Will

WHAT IS MEANT BY TRUTH OF HEART
Scripture says, 'Let us draw near with a true heart' (*Heb. 10:22*) – that is, with a sincere heart. *True heart* and *sincere heart* are often joined, one explaining the other: 'Now therefore fear the Lord, and serve him in sincerity and in truth' (*Josh. 24:14*). In the New Testament we read of 'the unleavened bread of sincerity and truth' (*1 Cor. 5:8*).

The opposite of sincerity is hypocrisy, a lie with an attractive cover. An insincere heart is a divided heart. Like a clock whose wheels inside do not coincide with the hands on the face, the inner workings of the heart do not match the behavior of the outer man.

WHY TRUTH OF HEART IS COMPARED TO A GIRDLE

Sincerity, or truth of heart, can be compared to a girdle in the light of the dual purpose of a soldier's belt.

I. TO COVER THE JOINTS OF ARMOUR

Here at the loins the pieces of armour which defend the lower parts of the body are connected to the upper ones. And because it is impossible for these to be perfectly knit together there will be some gaping open between the pieces. Thus a broad girdle is used to cover all the unattractiveness.

Sincerity does the same work for the Christian. The saint's graces are not so uniform, nor his life so perfect, that there are not defects and weaknesses in his warfare. But sincerity covers them all so they cannot expose him to shame or leave him vulnerable to danger.

II. TO PROVIDE STRENGTH

The more closely the belt is drawn to the body the more the loins are strengthened. Thus when God purposed to weaken a people He used this expression: 'I will loose the loins of kings' (*Isa. 45:1*).

Sincerity is the strength of every grace. The more hypocrisy in our graces, the weaker they are. It is sincere faith which is the strong faith, sincere love which is the mighty love. But hypocrisy is to grace as the worm is to the oak – or as rust is to iron – it weakens because it corrupts.

SINCERITY COVERS THE CHRISTIAN'S UN-COMELINESS

I. MORAL TRUTH

This kind of uprightness is like a wildflower which can grow in the waste places of nature. It may demonstrate a measure of truth in its actions, yet it does not have a single fiber of sanctifying, saving grace. For example, God Himself came in as a witness for Abimelech after he had taken Sarah: 'I know that thou didst this in the integrity of thy heart' (*Gen. 20:6*) – that is, he intended no wrong toward Abraham since he did not know Sarah was his wife.

While this moral honesty motivates a man to be kind in his relationships, the Lord's counsel has not changed since He directed it to Samuel: 'Look not on his countenance, . . . for the Lord seeth not as man seeth' (*1 Sam. 16:7*). God's eye looks more deeply than man's and refuses to accept the sacrifices of this uprightness because of its two glaring defects.

(a) *It does not grow from a renewed heart*
False uprightness is like Naaman's leprosy: 'but he was a leper' took away his honor at court and his prowess in battle (*2 Kings 5:1*). And this stains the most noble behavior of the merely moral man in our time: 'but he is Christless.'

A man's morality profits his peers in this world but does not make him acceptable to God in the next. Think of it this way: if God had not left some authority in the conscience to restrain non-Christians within some bounds of honesty, saints would not be able to live in such a world of wild beasts.

Thus these men are led by an overpowering fear from conscience more than by an inward prompting to please God. Abimelech discovered that his honesty had come from God's restraint rather than from any real goodness within himself: 'I also withheld thee from sinning against me: therefore I suffered thee not to touch her' (*Gen. 20:6*).

(b) *It falls short of God's glory*
'Whatsoever ye do, do all to the glory of God' (*1 Cor. 10:31*).

The archer may lose his game by shooting short as well as by shooting wide. The hypocrite shoots wide but the upright moralist shoots short. He usually takes accurate aim regarding the immediate goal of action but always fails to touch the ultimate end.

Thus a servant may be so faithful to his master that he would not cheat him out of a penny's worth of work, but it is all for nothing if God is left out of the story. Scripture commands servants to do 'service, as to the Lord, and not to men' – that is, not *only* to men (*Eph. 6:7*). The master's role is to be respected, but only as it leads to the glory of God. In pleasing his earthly master, the servant cannot sit down at the end of the journey but must go further – as the eye skims through air and clouds to the sun – to God as the ultimate reason for his faithfulness.

No principle can cause a man to aim high enough for God unless that principle has come from God Himself: 'That ye may be sincere . . . Being filled with the fruits of righteousness, which are by Jesus Christ, unto the glory and praise of God' (*Phil. 1:10, 11*). A soul must be planted in Christ, then, before it can be sincere and bear fruits of righteousness to the praise of God. Thus these fruits of righteousness are said to be 'by Jesus Christ.'

What men do by themselves they do for themselves. They eat their own fruit, devouring the praise of what they do. Only the Christian who does everything by Christ does it all for Him. He takes his nourishment from Him, into whom he has been grafted; and this is what makes him fruitful. Therefore he reserves all the lovely fruit for the Husbandman.

II. EVANGELICAL UPRIGHTNESS

Unlike moral truth, evangelical uprightness is a plant which grows only in Christ's garden, enclosed in a soul of grace. Its name distinguishes it from the wild field flower of moral uprightness. And we may also call it 'godly sincerity' or the 'sincerity of God'. 'For our rejoicing is this, the testimony of our conscience, that in simplicity and godly sincerity, not with fleshly wisdom, but by the grace of God, we have had our conversation in the world' (*2 Cor. 1:12*). This evangelical sincerity may appropriately be called the sincerity of God in two respects: because it is of God; and because it aims at God and ends in Him.

(a) *Because it is of God*

Godly sincerity belongs to God, begotten in the heart by His Spirit alone. And because this sincerity is a child of grace it calls none on earth its father.

But not only is this godly sincerity of divine descent; it is a part of the new creature which God's Spirit forms and works only in His chosen ones. It is a covenant grace. 'I will give them one heart, and I will put a new spirit within you' (*Ezek. 11:19*).

(b) *Because it aims at God and ends in God*

The highest aim a person can seek is to please God. And other disappointments and frustrations trouble him no more than it would a merchant speeding home from his voyage loaded with the prize of gold and silver he went for, if he lost a shoestring along the way.

The master's eye directs the servant's hand. Thus if the servant can please his master's mind he is satisfied, regardless of harsh criticism or rejection from those around him. A man like this does not aim at either small goals or great ones, to gain approval of the rich or poor; but his thoughts single out God above all others as the object of his love and fear and joy. Like a wise archer, he directs all his efforts toward this pure goal; and when he has God's approval he knows he has achieved the best. Paul speaks the common sense of all sincere believers concerning the Christian's purpose for serving: 'We labour, that, whether present or absent, we may be accepted of him' (*2 Cor. 5:9*).

The world's true man is one who will not wrong another man. Some boldly remind God that they would not steal a dime from their neighbor; yet these same people are thieves in far greater matters than all the money their neighbor is worth. They steal time from God and consistently conform the Sabbath to their personal plans instead of His. They purpose to sanctify God's name and even pray often for His will but their unholy hearts insist on compromise even though they know His will is sanctification.

But God's true man desires to be first true to the Father and then to man for His sake. For example, when Joseph's brothers feared he might deal with them brutally he freed them from suspicion: 'This do,' he responded, 'and live; for I fear God' (*Gen. 42:18*). He reassured them, 'Do not expect anything from me except what is right. You might think because I am a man of authority you would have no one to intercede for you if I take advantage. But I see One who is above me – infinitely higher than I seem to be above you; and I fear Him.'

One of the Greek words for *sincerity* is an emphatic metaphor picturing something examined by the light of the sun. For example, when you buy cloth you can take it out of the artificial light and hold it up to the sun; if there is the tiniest hole or flaw in the fabric you can see it there. Truly the godly soul looks up to heaven and wants every thought, judgment, affection, and practice to stand before the light which shines through Scripture. (This is the great lamp where God has gathered all light to guide Christians, as the sun in the sky directs our bodies in our earthly walk.) If these agree with the Word and can look on it without being put to shame, then we go on our way and nothing can stop us. But if any one of them shuns the light of the Word – as Adam tried to hide from God – then we are at journey's end.

Things are true or right as they agree with their first principle. When a measure agrees with the legal standard such as the meter or liter, then it is true. Now God's will is standard to our will and the sincere person will rule and measure all his desires by it. Thus David was called a 'man after God's own heart' because he carried the sculpture and image of God's heart within his spirit, as it is engraved on the seal of the Word. Let us now consider what this belt of sincerity covers.

THE UNCOMELINESS WHICH SINCERITY COVERS

I. TEMPORARY EXTERNAL ASSETS

The world honors beauty, heritage, wealth, and intellectual giftedness with more prestige than they are worth. But sincere grace covers them all and re-focuses rightful attention on the person himself. It gains more abundant honor in the sight of God, angels, and men (if they are wise men) than any dishonor and contempt which the lack of external assets can call forth from the world.

(a) *Beauty*

This is a universal idol which the world stares at. But it is wisdom which makes the face lovely. Who would choose an ornate but empty bottle instead of the vessel full of rich wine? If sincere grace does not fill the heart, nature's beauty of the face makes the person worth very little. A beautiful person without true grace is like a pretty weed – it looks best if you see it from a distance. On the other hand, a sincere heart, without the obvious attraction to itself, is like a sweet flower unpainted with such bright colours – it is better to hold than to look at, more pleasant to smell than to see. The nearer you come to a sincere man, the more you sense life radiating from his heart.

(b) *Poor family background*

No matter how unworthy a man's birth may be, real grace brings a glorious coat of arms to it, cleanses the bloodline, and makes the family illustrious. 'Since thou wast precious in my sight, thou hast been honorable, and I have loved thee' (*Isa. 43:4*). Sincerity is like a gleaming mark of honor; and wherever this star shines over a lowly cottage, it tells you a great prince lives inside.

Most importantly, sincerity brings the man into the family of the Most High God; and this new oneness blots out his own tarnished name and lets him carry the very name of God. He is joined to God by faith unfeigned; and who can say the bride belonging to the Prince of Peace is a commoner?

(c) *Poverty*

This word sounds like shame to a proud world. But even if a man is obviously very poor, he has access to a rich mine which will lift him above the world's contempt if a vein of sincere grace runs in his heart. He may have to admit he has no money in the bank but he cannot say he has no treasure; for the man who holds the key to God's treasury is rich beyond compare: 'All things are yours; . . . and ye are Christ's' (*I Cor. 3:21, 23*).

(d) *Mental giftedness*

The tradition of men gives a standing ovation to intellect and loudly applauds the excellency of knowledge. Indeed, mental ability stands more level with man's noblest faculty, reason. Those others (wealth, beauty, high birth) are so far beneath the spiritual nature of reason that they are like those soldiers of Gideon who could not drink water from the stream. A man cannot rejoice in them until he first debases himself far beneath the lofty stature of his reasoning soul. But intellect, abilities and knowledge seem to lift up man's head and stand him at full height. Therefore none are held in such contempt by the 'wise' world as those with lesser mental gifts.

Thus let us discover how sincerity can cover this nakedness of mind. If you grieve because your shallow understanding seems dull and does not measure up to those with sparkling intelligence, be content with your sincere heart. Their pearl is only in the head, and even a toad can wear a jewel; but yours is in the heart. This pearl of grace is your 'pearl of great price' (*Matt. 13:46*).

A sincere heart sets you higher in God's heart than weakness debases you in the world's opinion. And even without the abilities natural men have, you will find your way to heaven; but they, for all their mental achievement, will be tumbled down to hell because they lack sincerity. Just remember that, while your small gifts do not make you incapable of heaven's glory, their unsanctified gifts are sure to make them capable of more of hell's misery. And while you shall get a better head, they shall not get better hearts.

II. SINFUL UNCOMELINESS

This is the worst sort of spiritual unattractiveness because it blackens the soul and spirit, which God intended to be the source of the Christian's loveliness. Whatever stains and deforms the soul must be the most serious hindrance to the beauty of holiness sketched on it by the Holy Spirit's perfecting pen.

The soul-monster of sin has so marred man's sweet countenance that it is no more like the comeliness God created than the fiend of hell's similarity to the holy angel which he had been in heaven. But by His grace Christ has undertaken to heal this wound which sin has given to man's nature. His healing power is at work in His elect, but the cure is not yet so complete that no scars remain; this, then, is the uncomeliness which sincerity covers.

HOW SINCERITY COVERS THE SAINT'S UN-COMELINESS

Pardoning mercy eagerly embraces sincerity. Christ is the One who covers our failures and sins, but He throws His garment of righteousness only over the sincere soul: 'Blessed is he . . . whose sin is covered. Blessed is the man unto whom the Lord imputeth not iniquity.' Everyone likes to believe this, but notice the requirement of receiving this mercy: '. . . in whose spirit there is no guile' (*Ps. 32:1, 2*). Thus Christ's righteousness covers the nakedness of our shameful unrighteousness, but faith is the grace which puts this garment on.

God approves of the sincere man as holy and righteous even though he is not totally free of sin. And just as God does not mistake the saint's sin for sincerity, neither does He unsaint him for it. For instance, Scripture recorded that Job fell into the pit of sin, but God saw sincerity mixed with his transgression and judged him perfect.

Sincerity does not blind God so He cannot see the saint's sin, but makes Him consider it with compassion instead of with anger. This is like a husband who knows his wife is faithful to him so he pities her weaknesses and cherishes her as a good wife. 'In all this,' God said, 'Job sinned not, nor charged God foolishly' (*Job 1:22*). And at the end of the combat God brought Job through with the favorable testimony that His servant had 'spoken of me the thing that is right' (*Job 42:7*). Job himself saw his own earnestness dashed with failures, and this made him confess his sin rather than presume upon God's mercy. But God saw the sincerity.

The Father's mercy for us is much greater than our love

for ourselves, however. The prodigal son – a symbol of the convert – did not dare ask his father for shoes, much less for a ring. His request reached no higher than for lowly servanthood. He never conceived of such a meeting with his father at first sight. And he might have expected him to come after him with a rod or a rope instead of a robe.

Even if the father had met his wayward son with harsh words and whippings before taking him back, this arrangement would have been good news to the prodigal in his starving condition. But even as God has strange punishments for the wicked, He has strange expressions of love and mercy for a sincere son. He delights to outdo the highest expectations and kiss, robe, and feast all at once and on the day of His child's return.

God also demonstrates more mercy to us than our love for each other. We may be ready to condemn a Christian for blatant sin but God claims him as one of His children because of sincerity. Thus we find Asa's failure and perfection verified by God in one breath: 'But the high places were not taken away out of Israel: nevertheless the heart of Asa was perfect all his days' (2 *Chron. 15:17*). And God was the only one who could have cleared this man, for if nothing more than the naked story of his life had been recorded – without God's testimony of approval – his godliness might have been unanimously indicted by a jury of holy men.

Because Elijah could not see anybody else worshiping as zealously as he did, and fearlessly defying idolatry, he moaned to God that apostasy had taken over the whole land. But God overruled Elijah's anxiety: 'I have left me seven thousand in Israel, all the knees which have not bowed unto Baal, and every mouth which hath not kissed him' (*1 Kings 19:18*). God comforted His prophet by saying, 'Calm down, Elijah. Although the number of My people is not very big, there is not such a shortage of saints as you may think. True, their faith is weak and they do not slash the sins of the age the way you do; but your reward is yours. I will not disown My night-disciples who carry their light in a dark lantern because they are so afraid – they have some sincerity, and this has kept them from idols'.

God cautions us to be tender to His lambs, but no one can ever be as gentle as the Father Himself. Scripture lists three ranks of saints – 'fathers,' 'young men,' and 'little children' (*1 John 2:12–14*). The Spirit of God shows His concern by mentioning the young ones first and delivering the sweet promise of mercy to them: 'I write unto you, little children, for your sins are forgiven you for my name's sake' (*v. 12*). In plain terms He says their sins are forgiven. And at the same time He stops the mouth of guilt from discouraging them and opposing the gospel – forgiven for His name's sake, a name far mightier than the name of a person's worst sin.

Sincerity, then, keeps up the soul's credit at the throne of grace, so that no sin or weakness can hinder its welcome with God. Regarding iniquity in the heart, not just having it, keeps God from hearing our prayer (*Ps. 66:18*). This is a temptation which Christians often wrestle with when they let their personal shortcomings turn them away from prevailing prayer – they cower like some poor people who stay away from church because their clothing is not as fine as they would like.

To take care of this problem God has provided the promises – which, in any case, are our only ground for prayer – and has made them to fit the tiniest degree of grace. And as a well-done portrait faces everyone who enters the room, so these promises of the gospel covenant smile upon everyone who sincerely looks to God in Christ.

Scripture does not say, 'If ye have faith like a cedar,' but 'if ye have faith as a grain of mustard seed' (*Matt. 17:20*). Justifying faith is not beneath miracle-working faith in its own sphere. The least sincere faith in Christ removes the mountainous guilt of sin from the soul. Thus every saint is said to have 'like precious faith' (*2 Pet. 1:1*). In Genesis we can barely see Sarah's faith, but in Hebrews 11 God gives it honorable mention, alongside Abraham's stronger faith.

What love is it which brings down the favors of God to a man? It is not, 'Grace be with them that love our Lord Jesus with an angel's love,' but with *sincere* love. Nor 'Blessed are they who are as holy as Melchisedek', holy to such-and-such a degree. But so that no poor saint will lose his portion of the inheritance God promised, 'Blessed are they which do hunger and thirst after righteousness' (*Matt. 5:6*). This takes in all the children of God, even to the least babe who is but one day old in Christ.

In a word, if sincerity could not guarantee our welcome at the throne of grace, God would never accept a single prayer. For there never was nor ever shall be a saint living in the flesh who does not have entire chapters of faults in his life's story and in whom eminent failings may not be found. Elijah, for instance, did great wonders in heaven and in earth by prayer. Yet God's Spirit tells us he was a man like us: 'Elias was a man subject to like passions as we are, and he prayed . . . and he prayed again' (*Jas. 5:17, 18*). Even a weak hand with a sincere heart can turn the key in prayer.

WHY SINCERITY COVERS THE SAINT'S UN-COMELINESS

1. IT FLOWS FROM THE GRACE OF THE GOSPEL COVE-NANT

The gospel covenant relaxes the rigor of the law (which

called for complete obedience) and speaks rather in terms of sincerity and truth of heart. When God entered into the covenant with Abraham He expressed this requirement: 'I am the Almighty God; walk before me, and be thou perfect' – or *sincere (Gen. 17:1)*. It is as if God had instructed: 'Abraham, come and see what I expect of you, and what you can expect of Me. If you set Me before you and sincerely try to please Me, you can promise yourself what an Almighty God can do, protecting you in your obedience and forgiving you when you fall short of perfect obedience. Walk in the truth of your heart before Me, and in Christ I will accept you and your sincere effort as kindly as I would have Adam if he had never sinned.'

'If our heart condemn us not,' John said, 'then we have confidence toward God' (*1 John 3:21*). It is not the presence of sin in us, as the covenant now stands, which conscience can condemn us for. Paul's conscience cleared him – and even afforded cause for holy glorying – while he found sin stirring within himself.

Conscience is set by God to judge for Him in the private court of our own hearts. It is bound up by the same law by which Christ Himself will acquit or condemn at the last day. When we go on trial for our lives, before Christ's bar, the great question will be whether or not we have been sincere. And as He will not condemn the sincere soul, though a thousand sins be brought against it, neither can our hearts condemn us.

But how can God accept such imperfect obedience when He was so strict with Adam that He pronounced one failure as unpardonable? In the covenant God made with mankind in Adam there was no surety to guarantee and stand responsible for man's performance of his part of the covenant, which was absolute obedience. Thus God, to recover His glory and pay Himself for the wrong which man's default would do to Him, stood strictly with Adam.

Yet in the gospel covenant *there is a surety* – Jesus Christ the righteous – who stands responsible to God for all the sins of a Christian's lifetime. And the Lord Christ cancels not only the vast sums of those sins which Christians are charged with before conversion, but also all the dribbling debts which they contract afterward through weakness and carelessness. 'If any man sin, we have an advocate with the Father, Jesus Christ the righteous: And he is the propitiation for our sins' (*1 John 2:1, 2*). So then, without impeaching His justice, God can cross out His saints' debts for which He is paid by Christ. It is mercy to saints but justice to Christ that God should do this. What a precious oneness when mercy and justice kiss each other!

Also, God required complete obedience in the first covenant because man was in a perfect state, full of power and ability to perform it; so God expected to reap no more than what He had planted. But in the gospel covenant God does not infuse the believer with full grace but true grace; and accordingly, He expects not flawless but sincere obedience.

II. IT COVERS FAILURES BECAUSE OF GOD'S GREAT LOVE

It is the nature of love to cover infirmities, even a multitude of them. Esther broke the law by coming into Ahasuerus' presence before she was invited; but love soon created forgiveness in the heart of the king to pardon her of that transgression. He delighted in Esther's beauty in the way God takes pleasure in His children's: 'Such as are upright in their way are his delight' (*Prov. 11:20*).

God accepts the person whose heart is right with His heart. And so, with infinite satisfaction at seeing a ray of His own excellency in His child, He rejoices in him and then takes his hand and lifts him up into the innermost chambers of love.

Only rarely does Scripture speak of an upright man with merely a stark statement of that uprightness; there are usually other circumstances, like costly engravings on tombs, which reveal that no ordinary man lies there. God presented Job as a *nonesuch* when He described his uprightness: 'There is none like him in the earth, a perfect and an upright man' (*Job 1:8*). We also read of the vastness of his estate. God was pleased to point out His servant, but He did not count his earthly affluence worth telling the devil. He did not say, 'Have you considered My servant Job, that there is none so rich?' Instead, He said there was 'none so upright.'

God exalted Caleb to a towering place when He spoke of his uprightness: 'But my servant Caleb, because he had another spirit with him, and hath followed me fully, him will I bring into the land' (*Num. 14:24*). It was as if He had said, 'Here is a man whom I own as My special servant and unusual gem; he carries more worth inside than all the thousands of murmuring Israelites.' How did Caleb come to this honor? God answers, 'He hath followed me fully.'

It was Caleb's sincerity which brought him honor from God. After he had spied out the land of Canaan, he was strongly tempted to give a false report. Ten out of twelve men suited their answers to the discontented majority. And by making a report contrary to theirs, Caleb brought suspicion upon himself and put his life within the reach of a furious crowd. But courage, trusting God, edged out fear and Caleb was faithful to his commission, speaking the exact words which filled his heart. And because he did, the Lord erected a memorial to him that will last as long as Scripture stands.

One final example of God's loving testimony concerning sincerity was uttered by Christ when He saw Nathaniel for the first time. 'Behold,' Jesus said, 'an

Israelite indeed, in whom is no guile' (*John 1:47*). Jesus' heart – like the baby in Elisabeth's womb when Mary greeted her – stirred at the coming of Nathaniel, to bear witness to His own grace in him. Although Nathaniel was wrapped up in the common error of the day – that no prophet could come out of Galilee, much less from an obscure place like Nazareth – Christ saw his honesty and did not give place in His thoughts to Nathaniel's ignorance, but rather showed him divine favor.

INSEPARABLE COMPANIONS OF SINCERITY

1. SINCERITY MAKES THE SOUL WILLING

A perfect heart and a willing mind are joined together. David counseled his son Solomon to 'serve God with a perfect heart and with a willing mind' (*1 Chron. 28:9*). A false heart puts off its work as long as possible and deserves little appreciation for work done under the rod of correction. But the sincere soul is ready for responsibility. Though it may lack skill and strength it will always be eager. Such willingness is like a hawk perched upon a man's hand; as soon as the game is in sight she launches forward and would be in flight immediately, except for the tether holding her back.

'The Levites' were 'more upright in heart to sanctify themselves than the priests' (*2 Chron. 29:34*). Why? They were more willing to work. No sooner had the word come out of the king's mouth concerning reformation than the Levites arose and 'sanctified themselves' (*v. 15*).

Reformation is an icy path which cowards prefer to have well beaten by others before they venture out on it. But sincerity is made of better metal. It is like a true traveler – no weather gets bad enough to stop him after he has determined to make the trip. And the upright man does not stand around looking for loopholes or letting discouragement fester, but takes his orders from God's Word. And once he has them, he will not be turned back by anything short of a counter-command from the same God. His heart is merged with God's will. When the Father says, 'Seek ye my face,' the heart echoes, 'Thy face, Lord, will I seek' (*Ps. 27:8*).

Even when failure is the result of our best effort, willingness speaks success to God. When a father asks his small son to bring him something, an obedient child does not complain that the command is too hard but runs to do it. And even if he uses all his strength but miscarries the simple mission, his willingness stirs up the parent's pity to help him. Thus Christ throws this covering over His disciples' blunders: 'The spirit indeed is willing, but the flesh is weak' (*Matt. 26:41*). Such childlike obedience, like dripping honey, comes without squeezing; and even though there is only a little of it, it tastes sweet to God.

II. SINCERITY MAKES THE SOUL OPEN AND FREE TO GOD
The sincere person does not try to hide his infirmities from God. Even if he could, he would not, for God will uncover what the soul covers. 'If we confess our sins, he is faithful and just to forgive us our sins' (*1 John 1:9*).

Augustus once promised to pay a large sum of money to anyone who could bring him the head of a famous pirate. When this pirate, who had heard of this offer, himself came in and laid his neck at Augustus' feet, he was not only pardoned for his past offenses but rewarded for his confidence in Augustus' mercy. God is like that – though He demonstrates His fiery wrath against sin and unrighteousness, He will not punish the person who comes humbly and freely to give glory to His mercy.

Unlike the sincere soul, the hypocrite hides his sin as Achan concealed the wedge of gold; he broods over his lust as Rachel sat on her father's idols. It is as hard to get a hen off her nest as to persuade a hypocrite to uncover his lusts and openly confess them to God. When the average servant breaks a glass he quickly hides it from his master by throwing away all the pieces where he thinks they will never be found. Just so, a deceived person feels relieved that he handled the problem well and put his sin out of God's sight.

It is not treason itself which bothers the hypocrite, but any public knowledge of his treachery. And although it is as unfeasible to blind the eye of the Almighty as to stop the sun from shining by covering it with our hand, the hypocrite tries to do just that. But God warned against this kind of stupidity: 'Woe unto them that seek deep to hide their counsel from the Lord' (*Isa. 29:15*).

There is a time coming – called the 'month they shall find her' (*Jer. 2:24*) – when God's cry will overtake sin, His terrors ransack the conscience, and reveal what has been so stiffly denied, forcing sinners to face their deceit in shifting the burden of their sin. God never fails to unmask those disguised people who play their game so confidently by rules they invented themselves.

But sincerity steers for a better course. An obedient child does not want to wait until someone else tells his father what he has done wrong; but he goes to him of his own accord and eases his aching heart by a full and free confession. His plain-heartedness makes no excuses but gives full weight to every part and aggravating circumstance of his sin, so much so that if the devil himself should come to glean what is left, he could hardly find a remaining crumb of blackness for making his accusations.

Thus the sincere person confesses his sin in such a flow of sorrow that God, seeing His cherished child in danger of being carried down too far toward despair, comforts instead of scolds.

THE NATURE OF HYPOCRISY AND ITS HATE-FULNESS TO GOD

Just as sincerity covers all defects, hypocrisy uncovers the soul and strips it naked before God despite the richest embroidery of other qualities. This scab grows on even the sweetest perfections and changes the person's complexion in God's eye more drastically than leprosy destroys the fairest face.

It is interesting to see how Scripture portrays the different characters of Asa and Amaziah. The writer says of Asa: 'The high places were not removed: nevertheless Asa's heart was perfect with the Lord all his days' (*1 Kings 15:14*). Like true gold, sincerity allows grains for lightness. Asa's infirmities were not mentioned as flaws to dim his honor but as a wart or mole which an artist might use to accent the beauty of his other features. Thus failures were recorded to give a greater attractiveness to his sincerity, which – in spite of his sins – won a good testimony from God's own mouth.

Yet it is said of Amaziah, 'He did that which was right in the sight of the Lord, but not with a perfect heart' (*2 Chron. 25:2*). His actions were good but his attitude was faulty – and this turned his right into wrong. Thus we see how Asa's uprightness supported him in the midst of many shortcomings, but hypocrisy condemned Amaziah as he did what was right.

Sincerity is the life of all graces and puts life into all our duties, as life keeps the body warm and beautiful. And prayer breathed from a sincere heart is heaven's delight. If sincerity is gone, God must say of prayers what Abraham said of Sarah, whom he had loved dearly while she was alive: 'Bury my dead out of my sight' (*Gen. 23:4*).

'Bring no more vain oblations; incense is an abomination unto me; . . . your appointed feasts my soul hateth:

[65]

they are a trouble unto me; I am weary to bear them' (*Isa.* *1:13, 14*). The thing God loathed which made Him speak so coarsely against His own ordinances was hypocrisy. Hypocrisy makes prayer not prayer but an idol to be broken in pieces; faith not faith but a delusion; repentance not repentance but a loud lie. 'They returned and inquired early after God' (*Ps. 78:34*); but notice how the Holy Spirit interprets this: 'Nevertheless they did flatter him with their mouth, and they lied unto him with their tongues, for their heart was not right with him' (*vv. 36, 37*).

God's wrath came down upon these hypocrites and punished them to the uttermost: 'O Assyrian, the rod of mine anger, and the staff in their hand is mine indignation. I will send him against an hypocritical nation, and against the people of my wrath will I give him a charge, to take the spoil, and to take the prey, and to tread them down like the mire of the streets' (*Isa. 10:5, 6*). We do not need to send a coroner to investigate the cause of death; they were a hypocritical nation and died of hypocrisy.

God would rather see 'the abomination of desolation' standing in His temple causing confusion than the abomination of dissimulation mocking Him to His face as hypocrites worship with their lips and lust with their hearts. Of the two it is more tolerable in God's account to see a Belshazzar, who never claimed to be His servant, carouse with his gods profanely and drink from the sanctuary bowls, than for a people passing for His servants to pollute them in worship by cursed hypocrisy. Woe to the man who dishonors God under the name of honoring Him.

God singles out the hypocrite as the kind of sinner whom He will settle up with hand to hand, and in this life punish in more extreme ways than others. He has arranged for civil authorities to punish thieves and murderers; but God is the only One who can find out secret sins: 'For every one of the house of Israel . . . which separateth himself from me, and setteth up his idols in his heart, . . . I the Lord will answer him by myself. And I will set my face against that man, and will make him a sign and a proverb, and I will cut him off from the midst of my people' (*Ezek. 14:7, 8*). That is, 'My judgments will be so horrible that he will be a shrine of My wrath for others to see and talk about.'

Thus God often pays the hypocrite his wages of sin in this life. Ananias and Sapphira, for instance, died by the hand of God with a lie sticking in their throats. And Judas purchased nothing by his deceitful bargaining but a noose with which to hang himself; in fact, his hypocrisy became his executioner.

But if the hypocrite slips out of this world before his mask falls off and God's anger covers him, it will meet him at the entrance of hell. It will be no comfort then to realize that his friends were confident he was sailing straight to heaven. The reputation which he left with them will not cool the flames in hell for him. All other sinners seem only younger brothers in damnation to the hypocrite, under whom, as the great heir, they receive their portion of God's wrath bequeathed to them by His justice. In the Gospel of Matthew, for example, the master threatens to cut his evil servant apart and 'appoint him his portion with the hypocrites' (*24:51*).

THE OFFENSES OF HYPOCRISY

I. HYPOCRISY VIOLATES THE LIGHT OF NATURE

The same light which shows us there is a God tells us He is to be served in truth, or else all Christianity is vanity. A lie is a sin which blends in with the lifestyle of a heathen; but hypocrisy is the loudest lie of all, because it is told to God Himself. Thus Peter asked Ananias the fatal question: 'Why hath Satan filled thine heart to lie to the Holy Ghost? . . . Thou hast not lied unto men, but unto God' (*Acts 5:3, 4*).

II. HYPOCRISY IS THE SINFULNESS OF OTHER SINS

Hypocrisy is among sins as sincerity is among graces. Sincerity is an ornament which beautifies all other graces. Faith is precious because it is 'unfeigned', and love, because it is 'without dissimulation'. Thus the most hateful of all sins are those committed in hypocrisy.

David, in his description of jeering companions who made him the object of table talk and could not taste their cheer unless they seasoned it with salty remarks quipped against him, calls them 'hypocritical mockers' (*Ps. 35:16*). They cleverly wrapped their idle conversation in language which made some think they were applauding the psalmist. But hypocrisy is rottenness of the heart; and the more of this putrid stuff there is in any sin, the more malignant and deadly it becomes.

David mentioned 'the iniquity of sin': 'I acknowledged my sin unto thee, and mine iniquity have I not hid. I said, I will confess my transgressions unto the Lord; and thou forgavest the iniquity of my sin' (*Ps. 32:5*). This sin was probably his adultery with Bathsheba and the murder of Uriah. And surely the worst part of it all was that there was such hypocrisy in it as David tried to juggle and justify his actions with God and man.

The iniquity of his sin put a deeper color on David's behavior than the innocent blood which he spilled. God Himself, when He described for us the seriousness of David's sin, seems to have done so because of the hypocrisy involved. We see confirmation of this in the testimony He gave of this holy man: 'David did that which was right in the eyes of the Lord, and turned not aside from any thing that he commanded him all the days of his life, save only in the matter of Uriah the Hittite' (*1 Kings 15:5*).

Did not David's walk take other stray steps besides this one? Or did God's Spirit overlook all the other sins he ever committed? No, but these are all drowned here, and hypocrisy was mentioned as the only stain upon his life. Surely this was true because there appeared less sincerity, but more hypocrisy, in this one sin than in all his other sins put together.

Hypocrisy seriously wounded David's sincerity; and while it was not destroyed, it lay helplessly unfruitful for a time, as one lies in a comatose condition. Truly the injury was a complex one since the grace in which the lifeblood of the other graces runs was brutally stabbed. Although God's covenant mercy did not let His child die of this wound, He had good reason to heal David's hurt in such a way that a scar remained to mark for us all the sin which God hates.

The abomination of hypocrisy lies also in the fact that it walks around in spiritual robes and claims a personal relationship with God, a share in Christ and His righteousness, and consolations of the Spirit. These are crimes with a high price on their head. As the wool is coarse or fine, so will the thread and cloth be. The profane person cannot spin a fine thread because he deals only in coarse work. The ignorant man who is a stranger to the ways of God will not have so much wrath poured out upon him as will the hypocrite with his false claims on Christianity.

FALSE WORSHIP AND FALSE CLAIMS

I. THE HYPOCRITE INTRUDES UPON THE HOLY WORSHIP OF GOD

Judas confidently sat down with the rest of the apostles

at the passover and felt as welcome as if he were the holiest guest of them all. The proud Pharisee stood in the temple beside the brokenhearted publican. Yet when men like these pray, they sound to God like wolves howling or dogs barking. David's skillful hand played the harp so peacefully that he soothed Saul's rages. But hypocrites' false playing and false worship make the sweet Spirit of God angry and cause His fury to break out against them.

(a) *The hypocrite mocks God*

But God will not be mocked. Jesus illustrated this doctrine when He cursed the fig tree, whose green leaves invited hungry men to find fruit but sent them away without any. If this tree had lacked the leaves as well as the fruit, it would have escaped Christ's curse.

Every lie mocks the person who hears it, because the liar makes a fool of him by cheating him of the truth. Delilah asked Samson why he had told her lies, as if she had said, 'Why are you trying to make a fool of me?' God's command is that none should appear before Him empty; but this is just what the hypocrite does, and thus mocks God. He may come with a full mouth but he has an empty heart.

As for the formality of religious service, however, the hypocrite often outdoes the sincere Christian. Of all people he may be called a 'master of ceremonies' because he tries to entertain God with his tongue and knee, with only words and outward ceremony. Yet God looks on the heart. If the wine is good a man can drink it from a plain wooden cup. But if a goblet is wonderfully gilded, but has no wine in it, the host mocks his guest by offering it to him.

Christ's charge against Sardis was, 'I have not found thy works perfect before God' (*Rev. 3:2*) – or *full* before Him, as the original text conveys. Sincerity is what fills our duty and all our actions. And the phrase 'before God' implies that this church retained an outward form of devotion and had thus been able to keep an acceptable reputation before men. She had a name to live up to, but her works were not full before God. So He pierced them more deeply than man's probing could do and judged her by what He found inside.

(b) *The hypocrite worships for self-centered reasons*

Selfish motives make the hypocrite's worship even more abominable to God, who will not have His holy ordinances prostituted to serve the hypocrite's lust. Such a person uses worship only as a convenience, a stream to turn his mill and bring about his carnal projects.

When Absalom conceived a plot within his insincere heart and was as big with treason as a serpent with a poisonous egg, he hurried to Hebron to pay an old vow which he had made to God during a time of affliction. Normally we would think a man is becoming honest when he starts to pay delinquent debts. But Absalom saw this errand as nothing more than a means for laying his treason under the warm wing of religion, knowing that a comfortable reputation for being pious would more speedily hatch it.

Have you ever invited guests to an expensive dinner at your house and then watched them throw the main course under your table to the dogs? The hypocrite casts God's holy things to his dogs – some to lust, some to pride, and others to covetousness. How this must grieve the tender heart of God, who invites us to His ordinances, as to a rich feast, where He waits for us to have sweet communion with Him. What horrible sin it is when hypocrites come to God's table for no other reason than to provide for their own lusts! For example, Hamor and his son Shechem persuaded the men of their city to submit to circumcision, arguing that it would make them wealthy: 'If every male among us be circumcised, . . . Shall not their cattle and their substance and every beast of theirs be ours?' (*Gen. 34:22, 23*). Their argument sounded as if they were going to a horse market or a fat livestock show!

Most hypocrites have more ingenuity than to print out their innermost thoughts for the world to read, but consider the words of Queen Mary Tudor. She once said that if someone ripped her apart, the French soil at Calais – which she desired more than any other conquest – would be found in her heart. Thus such low things as vain glory and worldliness will be found engraved in the hearts of all hypocrites as their highest aims in religion.

II. THE HYPOCRITE CLAIMS A RELATIONSHIP WITH GOD
AND CHRIST

Who is faster than the hypocrite to saint himself and to claim the grace and comforts of the Holy Spirit? We see this in the Pharisees, whose ambition was to have a name – not for worldly skills and qualities but for sanctity and holiness. And this is *all* they had: 'Verily I say unto you,' said Christ, 'they have their reward' (*Matt. 6:2*). The crowd thought they were great saints and so applauded their surface holiness that their proverb boasted that 'if but two could be saved, one of the two should be a Pharisee.'

Some profess to know God but in works they deny Him; they boldly brag of their kinship to Christ but their lives are as far as they can be from heaven. Hypocrites are so anxious to pass for saints that they often become great criticizers of the true graces of others to make themselves look better, as Herod burned the Jews' ancient genealogies to defend his own base birth. Who can probe the vulgarity of this high-climbing sin of hypocrisy? It is a sin which offends God intensely, to have such a vile wretch claim kinship to Him. Christ is not 'ashamed to call' the poorest saints 'brethren,' but He despises to have His name seen upon a rotten-hearted hypocrite (*Heb. 2:11*).

Of all sinners the hypocrite does the most harm in this world and therefore will have the most torment in the other world. And yet it is religion which has consistently proved to be the most effective bait of hypocrites, as they seek to snare others into their error and sin while posing as children of God. Ehud, for example, could not have chosen a better key to open the doors into King Eglon's presence than to say he had brought a message from God. This caused such expectation and confidence that Eglon welcomed him. When the two were alone, the king rose to hear the Word of the Lord from the deceiver – but what he received instead was brutal death (*Judg. 3:14-30*).

I confess the hypocrite may act his part so well that he may accidentally do some good. His glistening profession, heavenly speech, and eloquent preaching might bring to the sincere seeker a measure of real comfort. Like an actor at center stage who stirs up passion in the audience by counterfeit tears, the hypocrite, playing his religious role, may temporarily spark the believer's true graces. But that is when the Christian may be in the most serious danger, for he will not readily suspect the person who once helped him spiritually.

It would have been far better had Sisera the Canaanite done without Jael's butter and milk than to be nailed to the tent floor, having been fooled by that woman's seeming hospitality. Thus it is to our advantage not to sample the free gifts and give-away graces of stageplay saints, applauding and drinking ourselves drunk with their admiration. Sometimes a calculated distance from the hypocrite is the safest way to avoid having our heads nailed by errors.

Another injury inflicted by the hypocrite is the scandal brought upon the church when his mask slips. Scripture says of Samson, 'The dead which he slew at his death were more than they which he slew in his life' (*Judg. 16:30*). Truly the hypocrite does more damage when he is discovered than when he seemed to be alive in his profession of faith. The hypocrite then puts a big stick into the hands of the wicked who have been looking for a way to bruise the saints. How fast they can then cause division and smear the face of all believers with the grime they see upon one hypocrite's sleeve!

Accusers of Christianity point out a hypocrite in church and reason that the whole group of believers is just like him. This is as absurd, of course, as to say that no coin is worth anything because we see one brass shilling among the silver. But this language fits the mouth of the ungodly world. And woe to the man's hypocrisy which manufactures these arrows for them to shoot at the saints. It would be better if he had been thrown into the sea with a millstone about his neck than to live and provide occasions for God's enemy to blaspheme.

SEARCH FOR SINCERITY

Because sincerity covers all a Christian's weaknesses, there are several important reasons why we should carefully search our own hearts to see whether sincerity or hypocrisy reigns there.

I. ETERNITY DEPENDS ON YOUR SINCERITY

Your worth and destiny hang on whether or not you have it. This is your making or marring for ever. 'Do good, O Lord, . . . to them that are upright in their hearts. As for such as turn aside unto their crooked ways, the Lord shall lead them forth with the workers of iniquity' (*Ps. 125:4, 5*). The hypocrite will try to crowd in with the godly on that last day and pass for a saint, but God 'shall lead him forth with the workers of iniquity', company which is more his kind.

Paul said, 'I will come to you shortly, . . . and will know, not the speech of them which are puffed up, but the power. For the kingdom of God is not in word, but in power. What will ye? shall I come unto you with a rod, or in love?' (*1 Cor. 4: 19–21*). But it is not Paul but Christ who will shortly come to us; and He will know, not the speech and sophisticated language of people inflated with an empty profession, but the power of God inside His people.

Do you want Christ to come with a rod, to judge you as a hypocrite, or in love with the 'Well done!' for a faithful servant? He will gauge every heart to see what is inside; every man's works will be an open book in the great day of Christ. And because all the hypocrite ever did will be found to be counterfeit, he will be put in irons in hell for trying to cheat both God and man.

II. HYPOCRISY CAN HIDE IN YOUR HEART

Because hypocrisy often rooms next door to sincerity, she passes unnoticed, the soul not expecting to find hell so close to heaven. There are many who perform pious responsibilities and express such outward zeal in their profession that they mistakenly promote themselves to the status of staunch Christians. And while these men insist that all is well, hypocrisy lies at the bottom of their commitment.

But just as hypocrisy is hard to discover, sincerity can be also. This grace often lies low in the heart, hidden by weaknesses like a sweet violet in the valley, covered with thorns and nettles. So then it requires wisdom not to let the weed of hypocrisy stand nor pull up the herb of grace.

III. YOUR SEARCH FOR SINCERITY IS FEASIBLE

The heart of man is like a spool of twisted silk thread, not easily unsnarled; yet with skill and patience it can be untangled and wound up on the right spool, either sincerity or hypocrisy. Satan and his cruel friends worked hard to muddy the stream of Job's spirit by throwing objections like smooth stones into it; yet Job could still see the precious gem of sincerity at the bottom sparkling most brightly.

So be encouraged, my friends. God will help you in your search for sincerity if you go about it with honest desires. A judge will not only sign his warrant to search a suspicious house but, if need be, will command others to assist him. Now you have the Holy Spirit, God's Word, and His ministers to aid you in this work. But remember this – the soul deserves damnation who plays the hypocrite. Like a dishonest constable, he willingly overlooks the sin he searches for and then reports he cannot find it.

THE HYPOCRITE'S FALSE PROFESSION

I. THE HYPOCRITE INSISTS HE CANNOT ENDURE HYPOCRISY

Unless you show proof from holy ground, this is not enough to clear you from being a hypocrite yourself. It is natural for a man to condemn a sin in another person while he harbors the same sin in his own life. How severe was Judah's judgment against Tamar? He was in such a hurry to have her burned that everyone assumed he was speaking as a man of chastity – yet he was the very one who had defiled her (*Gen. 38:24*).

Some men's enthusiasm is kindled against another's sin when it reflects disgrace upon them in the eyes of the world. This is especially true when the wrong is a public one and the person who committed it is a relative. Judah, for instance, was willing for his daughter to be taken out of the way so the blot which she had brought on his family might go with her and remain out of his sight.

Others severely judge faults in order to hide their own flaws, thus enabling them to carry on selfish designs with less suspicion. Absalom, for example, criticized his father's government as a stirrup to help himself into the saddle. And Jehu loved the crown more than he hated Jezebel's whoredoms, even though he swung a keen sword against them. False zeal thus becomes revenge and shoots at the person rather than at his sin; hypocrites can hate the tyrant while admiring his tyranny.

II. THE HYPOCRITE BOASTS OF BEING UNAFRAID

The better way is to test a person's boldness by his sincerity, and not sincerity by boldness. True confidence and a spirit undaunted at death and danger are glorious when the Spirit and Word of Christ stand by to fulfill them. And certainly it is good when a person can give some account of the hope that is in him, as Paul did when he showed people the source of it operating in his life. This was Christian courage, not Roman fearlessness.

But the Christian must pass many rooms before arriving at this place of assurance, which adjoins heaven itself. Faith is the key which lets him enter into all these rooms. First, it opens the door of justification and takes him into peace and reconciliation with God through Jesus Christ: 'Being justified by faith, we have peace with God through our Lord Jesus Christ' (*Rom. 5:1*).

Through justification the seeker passes on to another room – the chamber of God's favor – and is welcomed into His presence: 'By whom also we have access by faith into this grace wherein we stand' (*v. 2*). Not only have we been pardoned from sin and reconciled to God by faith in

Christ, but now we are brought into the royal court under Christ's wing as favorites of the Prince.

We not only enjoy God's grace and favor and communion now, but move on and open the door to a third room – a hope firmly planted in our hearts for heaven's glory later, 'rejoicing in the hope of the glory of God' (*v. 2*).

Finally God brings the Christian to the innermost room which no one can come to until he has passed through all the other ones first: 'And not only so, but we glory in tribulations also' (*v. 3*).

If you have not entered at these doors, you are a thief and a robber; you have taken up confidence which God's hand has not given. If God is bringing you to heaven, He will nonetheless chastise you for this sort of boldness, as He did when Jacob stole his father's blessing. So do not be satisfied with bare boldness and a confidence in times of danger, but find out whether it has a scriptural foundation to stand on. Otherwise the pillars supporting it might be ignorance in your mind and stupidity in your conscience.

If your conscience is dull, your boldness will not last any longer than a drunk man's bravery. When he is wound up and 'wine-sprung', he is sure he can jump over the moon, and ventures out without fear among precipices and pitfalls. But when he is sober he trembles to see what he did in his drunken stupor. Nabal, for one, did not fear anything when he was drunk – but his heart became like a stone at the story Abigail told him in the morning, when the wine was gone out of him (*1 Sam. 25:37*).

III. THE HYPOCRITE REVEALS HIS SECRET DEVOTIONS
The trademark of a hypocrite is that he is a nobody except on stage. He courts the world for applause and will do anything to have it. While it is true that total neglect of closeted devotions marks a person as a hypocrite, the

keeping of such quiet times never demonstrates your sincerity. In this sphere hypocrisy is like the frogs brought on Egypt. No place was free of them, not even the bedrooms; they crept into the most private rooms as well as in the front yard. Even though the place of meditation might be secret, some hypocrites handle the matter in such a way that all the world knows. A hen may retreat to a quiet corner to lay her egg but her cackling tells the whole house exactly where she is and what she is doing.

In all the arts some exceed others in skill: there are apprentices and there are masters. This is just as true in hypocrisy. The gross hypocrite who intends to deceive others lives in a religious environment without doors. But the hypocrite who fights to keep conscience on his side will go to the utmost link of his chain; he will do anything that will not separate him and his beloved lusts. And for insurance, he may even devise a prayer life to protect his sins. It is not the sharpness of the sword which kills, but the force with which it is plunged in. Thus the hypocrite can lay his sword so gently against sin in his own heart that it never feels a thing.

IV. THE HYPOCRITE DECLARES WAR ON SIN

You may not hesitate to display various trophies of your spiritual warfare: 'There was a time when I could not go by the nightclub without being pulled inside by my own lust; but thank God, now I have conquered that sin and I do not even give those places a passing glance.' But the Holy Spirit comes to contest such a victory with several questions.

(a) *How long have you mastered your lust?*

Let me remind you, some lusts do not return as fast as others. The river does not always move in just one manner. Sometimes its level rises and sometimes it falls. And although it does not ever rise when it falls, it has not

[79]

lost its forward motion. Now the tide of lust is sometimes up and sometimes down; the man may seem to run successfully from it, but it can return to him around the bend of the meandering stream of sin.

Who would have thought Pharaoh could be caught in another mad fit after his good mood had agreed to let Moses and his people go? Yet this is what happens when a crisis or temptation comes to our port like an easterly wind and brings in the tide of lust to break upon us. Our souls can be as clear of lust as the bare sands are of water; but in just a few moments we can be covered by deep crashing waves. The longer the banks have held, the better, of course, but even if you never again outwardly fulfilled your lust, would this be enough to clear you of hypocrisy? The question is, *Why* are you trying to stay free of these sins?

(b) *What is your motive?*
The thing which keeps you from the tavern now may be worse than the lust that drew you there in the first place. The money you save by not guzzling colorful cocktails – are you now spending it on finery that only feeds your pride? You have only robbed one lust to sacrifice it to another. Was it God or man, God or your pride, or God or your reputation which motivated you to change? If anything but God prevailed with you, *hypocrite* is the name that fits you more than it did when you were a drunkard. Maybe you have laid down this sin – good! But why? Did you hate it and love God, or does the wrath of God make you too afraid to continue in it?

You have put down evil, but have you taken up good? Only a foolish farmer plows his ground but never plants. It is not the field clear of weeds, but fruitful in grain, which pays your rent and brings gain. So then it is not 'non-drunkenness' or 'non-uncleanness', but rather holiness and pure love and unfeigned faith which prove you sound and bring evidence of Christlikeness for heaven.

CHARACTERISTICS OF SINCERITY

I. A SINCERE HEART IS A NEW HEART

Hypocrisy is called 'the old leaven': 'Purge out therefore the old leaven, that ye may be a new lump' (*1 Cor. 5:7*). Once dough is soured with leaven it will never lose the taste of it. Either the heart must be made new or it will keep its old quality. Although ingenuity and talent may conceal the false heart to make it more pleasant – as flowers and spiced perfumes are arranged around a carcass – both the corrupt heart and the rotten carcass remain unchanged.

'One heart' and a 'new heart' are both covenant mercies: 'I will give them one heart, and I will put a new spirit within you; and I will take the stony heart out of their flesh' (*Ezek. 11:19*). God promises to give one spirit – that is, a sincere spirit toward God and man, contrary to a divided heart, the mark of hypocrisy.

But how does God do this? 'I will take away the heart of stone, and give you a heart of flesh.' In other words, 'I will melt and soften it and mold it all over again, as many pieces of old silver are thrown into the fire to melt and come out as one piece.'

By nature man's heart is a very divided and broken thing, scattered and parcelled out to different lusts and weaknesses. But God throws His chosen vessels of honor into the fire of His Word, where His Spirit melts and transforms them into a holy oneness. At last the heart has been gathered in from all its lusts and looks to God with a single eye in everything it does. If you wonder whether or not you are sincere, consider this: do you have a new heart?

Has God ever cast you into His furnace? Has His Word, like fire, taken a hold on you and refined your impure spirit so the unbelief, pride, and hypocrisy have been made visible and been separated like dross from gold? Only then are you free to sever sin from your soul and confess what a wretched person you have been, even though your spiritual condition appeared attractive in man's eye. Do you grieve to recall the religious pageantry you produced for the community in the name of Christ while you privately entertained lusts inside the locked dressing rooms of your heart? But, even more vital, are you not only sorrowful because of your divided affections but now wholeheartedly determined to fear the name of God?

Do you have just *one design*, to love Christ and be loved of Him? If the mighty power of God's Spirit has renewed your heart and gathered your affections into this one channel, and caused you to run to Him with sweet violence, then you are greatly blessed of the Lord. Mountains and rocks of corruption may surface in your stream to hinder the free course of your soul as it rushes to God; but even with these windings and turnings to block the most direct way to Him, sincerity – like water to the sea – will never turn back until it carries you to Him.

II. A SINCERE HEART IS A SIMPLE HEART

The hypocrite is bred by the serpent, and like him, shrinks up or lengthens himself out to his best advantage, unwilling to expose himself to others. He has good reason, too, because he has the most credibility where he is least known. Hypocrites 'seek deep to hide their counsel from the Lord, and their works are in the dark, and they say, Who seeth us? and who knoweth us?' (*Isa. 29:15*). The hypocrite's pious words and the evil motives of his heart are miles apart.

A sincere heart, however, is like a clear brook; you can see the bottom of this person's intents in his words and measure his heart by his tongue. But whoever made the proverb – 'Speak that I may see you' – was not thinking of the hypocrite, who speaks so you *cannot* see him. For he wraps his deceit in the thickest fog he can find – religious vanity and pious profession.

If you want to find sincerity, look for a plain-dealing heart. Paul and the rest of the faithful messengers of Christ conducted themselves among the Corinthians 'in simplicity and godly sincerity' (*2 Cor. 1:12*). They did not have a secret compartment in which to keep certain facts concealed as the false prophets did. This plainness of heart shows itself in three ways.

(a) *A sincere heart deals plainly with itself*
First, the sincere heart searches itself with determination and power. It will not be put off with excuses like the one Rachel gave Laban as she sat on his idols. And David refused to give up until he had found the disturber of his peace to be in himself. He was not too tender and protective of his reputation to smooth it over, but attacked the thief and indicted his sin by confessing it until God was justified: 'And I said, This is my infirmity: but I will remember the years of the right hand of the most High' (*Ps. 77:10*). David expressed, 'Lord, now I can see the Jonah which caused the storm in my heart and made me restless all this time; it was unbelief that weighed me down and would not let me look up to remember former blessings – and when I forgot them I thought unworthy things of You.'

Are you kin to David in the way you search your soul? Are you serious about it, as if you were looking for a murderer hiding in your house? Are you as aggressive to root out sin as the Papists in Queen Mary's time were to find

[83]

Protestants? Or, when you do this work, do you avoid hunting too hard, trying to overlook what you do not want to find?

Yet David was not satisfied with his own testimony but relied on God to pronounce his soul pure or impure: 'Search me, O God, and know my heart: try me, and know my thoughts: and see if there be any wicked way in me' (*Ps. 139:23, 24*). Even a doctor will not trust his own judgment about his personal health but consults another. Similarly, after sincere Christians have prayed and opened their case to God, they are willing to hear whatever He has to say. These are the Christians who gladly submit themselves to the kind of searching ministry which strips their consciences naked and exposes their hearts. They are like the woman of Samaria who commended the sermon – and the Christ who preached it – because He told her all she had ever done.

On the other hand, a false person does not like to hear out of both ears; he accuses the preacher of trespassing on private property when he steps up close to the conscience, and if he could he would insist that God's minister vacate the premises immediately. John the Baptist, for instance, put his finger on Herod's sore spot; but although the king feared the words he did not love the man and was persuaded to cut off the head that had in it a tongue so bold as to reprove his sin.

Besides self-searching in a diligent way, the sincere heart, when confronted with clear evidence, is ready to pronounce judgment upon itself. It forgets self-pity, lets conscience have free rein, and will not be put off by sentiment. 'I have showed pride and impatience and anger today.' This person is so clothed with fury against sin that he becomes deaf to the cry of the flesh which would bargain for a lighter sentence: 'I have sinned against the

Lord,' David confessed. 'I have sinned greatly' (*2 Sam. 12:13; 24:10*). 'So foolish was I, and ignorant: I was as a beast before thee' (*Ps. 73:22*).

(b) *A true heart is plain with God also*
The hypocrite juggles his prayers and asks for something he does not want God to give anyway and thus is not bothered in the least when the answers do not come. At times Christians pray for greater godliness but corruption does not fade and grace does not grow. This is where your hypocrisy or sincerity will show itself. If you are sincere every minute will be an hour, and every day a year, until you hear some news from heaven. 'Hope deferred' will make 'the heart sick' (*Prov. 13:12*).

'I am a woman of a sorrowful spirit,' Hannah said to Eli (*1 Sam. 1:15*). She had prayed for years but God had not sent the answer. Thus a man may say, 'I have a bitter spirit, because I have prayed for a soft and believing heart but it has never come. Maybe I have not been sincere after all. Why else has my request hung in the clouds for so long?' Such a man is anxious, like a merchant waiting for a rich ship at sea. He cannot sleep on the land until he sees her coming.

But if you pray once and then forget it – as a child scribbles on scrap paper and then wads it up – or if you take denials from God as numbly as a cold suitor when he does not hear from the sweetheart he never really loved, a false heart rules in you. Just hope that God has not decided to answer the secret desire of that heart; for if it happens you will be lost for ever.

Another trait of a false heart is that it stands slothfully still and watches God work, like the man whose cart fell into the ditch. He cried for help but was not willing to put his own shoulder to the wheel. The hypocrite is so eaten up with cowardice and spiritual stagnation that he will not take a second step toward victory. But a sincere soul is conscientious: 'Let us lift up our heart with our hands unto God in the heavens' (*Lam. 3:41*). The hypocrite's tongue wags but the sincere Christian's feet walk and his hands work steadily toward the goal.

(c) *The sincere soul shows its simplicity to men*

'We have had our conversation,' Paul said to the Corinthians, 'in simplicity and godly sincerity, not with fleshly wisdom' (*2 Cor. 1:12*). The Christian will not subject heart to head – conscience to his policy. Because he commits himself to God he does not fear other people; and neither does he risk putting a hole in his conscience to keep his skin whole, but openly trusts God no matter what happens.

The hypocrite, though, shifts his sails and flies whatever colors the world unfurls in front of him. If the coast is clear and no danger is in sight he will appear as religious as anyone else; but no sooner does he discover a problem than he changes his course, concluding that the right road is any one which leads to safety. But 'the highway of the upright is to depart from evil' (*Prov. 16:17*).

III. THE TRUE-HEARTED CHRISTIAN IS UNIFORM

Truth in the heart is an exact copy of the truth in God's Word – they agree as the face in the mirror corresponds to the face of the man who looks into it. Therefore if truth in the Word is harmonious, then truth in the heart, which is nothing but the impression of it, must be also. There is a threefold uniformity in the sincere Christian's obedience. He is uniform as to the object, subject, and several circumstances which accompany his obedience.

(a) *The sincere Christian is uniform as to the object*

The hypocrite may touch the law of God in one point – in some particular command which pleases him – but ignore all the rest; yet a sincere heart stays close to the whole law in desire and action. The upright man's foot is said to stand 'in an even place' – he is sensitive to the will of God in its entirety (*Ps. 26:12*). But Solomon said 'the legs of the lame are not equal' and cannot stand in an even place because one leg is long and the other is short (*Prov. 26:7*).

The Pharisees, for example, pretended to have great zeal for some of the commandments. They fasted and prayed, but prayed for their prey; and when they had fasted all day they ate at the expense of the widow whose house they devoured. It is a sad fast which only leads to a ravenous appetite, to swallow others' property in the name of devotion!

The moralist is punctual in his dealings with man but thievish in his response to God. He would not steal a penny from his neighbor but does not hesitate to cheat God of far greater matters. For instance, he owes God love, fear, and faith; but it does not bother his conscience not to pay anything.

It is the way of Scripture to describe a godly person by one particular grace flowing through his life. Sometimes his character is that 'he feareth an oath' (*Eccles. 9:2*); or he is one who loves the brethren (*1 John 3:14*). This is significant because wherever one characteristic is sincerely performed, the heart opens itself for another. As God has enacted all His commands with the same authority – 'God spoke *all* these words' – so He infuses all graces together and writes the *whole* law in the hearts of His children.

(b) *The sincere Christian is uniform as to the subject*

The whole man, renewed in his spirit, moves one way. All the powers and faculties of his soul join forces and enjoy sweet accord. When understanding discovers a truth, conscience exerts authority on the will and commands it in the name of God to act upon it. And as soon as conscience knocks, the will opens herself and lets it in. Then the affections, like loyal handmaids, see it as a guest, make the will welcome, and express their readiness to wait on it.

But it is not so with the hypocrite. His will and conscience and affections war against one another. When there is light in the understanding the man recognizes truth; but often his conscience is bribed and fails to chastise his will for the neglect of it. Usually conscience will not rouse up the soul to let truth in. But even when conscience forces its way in to plead its cause, it is such an unwelcome guest that it is met with frowns and denials – as a contrary wife makes life miserable when her husband brings home an associate she dislikes. Or even worse, she hides her secret resentment and goes through the motions of entertaining their guest.

(c) *The sincere soul is uniform as to the circumstances of his obedience and holy walk*

He is uniform as to time. This man's religion is not like Sunday clothing to be worn but two or three hours a week. But you can drop in on him and find him clothed in holiness on Monday or Thursday as well as on Sunday. 'Blessed are they that keep judgment, and he that doeth righteousness at all times' (*Ps. 106:3*). You cannot tell anything about the true complexion of a man facing a fireplace; the color may change when the fire dies out. Some people are like flowers; you must be there at the right season to catch sight of their godliness blooming or you will not see it at all.

The sincere Christian may be interrupted in his spiritual course but as soon as the temptation is removed, he returns to the exercise of holiness – all because he has a new nature. The hypocrite, however, fails in the very fiber and frame of his spirit; he does not have the principle of grace to keep him moving.

Again, the sincere Christian is uniform as to place and company. In public or among his closest relatives David's purpose was the same. Of the private sphere he said, 'I will walk within my house with a perfect heart' (*Ps. 101:2*). But also whenever he went out he carried his conscience with him; he did not make it stay behind until he came back, as Abraham required of his servants on the mountain (*Gen. 22:5*).

The Romans had a law that everyone should wear a badge identifying his trade on his hat or coat. The sincere Christian never willingly lays down the badge of his holy profession. When he must be among boisterous or sarcastic sinners he does not expose his beliefs to scorn by casting their pearls before those who would trample them. Some places are so full of profanity and wickedness that sincerity does not have opportunity to speak reproof with safety to the saint. Often a man stays in a situation where he is reluctant to protest sin and, showing foolish disregard for his own soul, he may refuse to leave the place where he is constantly receiving evil instead of good. He would, in such a case, do well to question his sincerity before God.

IV. THE SINCERE CHRISTIAN IS PROGRESSIVE

He never comes to his journey's end until he gets to heaven. This keeps him always leaning into God, thankful for each little favor but not smugly content with great measures of grace. 'When I awake,' said David, 'I shall be satisfied with thy likeness' (*Ps. 17:15*). He had enjoyed many sweet hours of communion at the house of God; and the Holy Spirit had brought him covered dishes of inward comfort from God's banquet table, dishes of which the world knew nothing. Yet David realized he would never have enough until heaven gave him his full portion.

When the Gauls first tasted the wines of Italy, they were

so impressed with their sweetness that they would not just trade for this wine but resolved to conquer the whole land which furnished the grapes! Thus the sincere Christian does not think it is enough to receive samples of grace and comfort from heaven on special occasions, doing long-distance business with God. No, he meditates on taking that holy and blessed place which is the source of these riches and looks forward to drinking the wine of the kingdom *in* the kingdom.

This kind of meditation raises the soul to climb nearer and nearer heaven. The man who aims at the sky shoots higher than he who intends only to hit a tree. Paul said, 'I press toward the mark for the prize of the high calling of God in Christ Jesus' (*Phil. 3:14*). Other people admired the apostle's spiritual achievements and would have been happy with them; yet Paul would have been most unhappy had he never scaled new heights of God's grace. He admitted that he had not apprehended what he was running for. The prize does not appear at mid-way but at the end of the race; and Paul ran toward it with full speed.

Only the hypocrite shortchanges himself in the things of God. He wants just enough knowledge to talk religion among religious people; otherwise he leaves it alone. He chooses enough good works and church attendance to be seen and respected and avoids socially unacceptable sins; but he would never bother to press in for a deeper communion with the holy God. He is like an irresponsible businessman who does not care much about making profits but is content merely to keep his store open and stay out of jail, though engaged in a thousand compromising schemes.

You have seen the inside of a sincere heart; and after examining yourself in the light of these characteristics, your conscience will return one of three reports. Conscience will condemn you as a hypocrite; it will confirm your sincerity; or it will leave you in ignorance and doubt because you dare not accept your sincerity.

INSTRUCTIONS TO THE INSINCERE

Some of you have examined your consciences and found the condemnation of hypocrisy. The evidence is so clear and strong that your conscience cannot reverse its verdict: 'If these are the standards of sincerity, then you must be a hypocrite.' The counsel which I have for you, then, will lead you from bondage into freedom from insincerity.

I. FACE THE DEADLY NATURE OF YOUR HYPOCRISY

There is no hope of cure until you have diagnosed your deplorable disease as hypocrisy. Medicine cannot be swallowed by a sleeping patient; and it is the nature of this illness to make the soul heavy-eyed and numb of conscience through the flattering self-image of hypocrisy. The hypocrite goes through the motions of religious formalities which fume up from his deceived heart like pleasing vapors from the stomach to the head and bind up his spiritual senses into a kind of stupidity. And these fantasy-like dreams entertain him with vain hopes and false joys which vanish as soon as he comes to himself.

The prideful Pharisees, for example – the most notorious hypocrites of their time – were so fast asleep in their carnal confidence that they were not afraid to commend themselves to the holy God: 'God, I thank thee, that I am not as other men are, . . . or even as this publican' (*Luke 18:11*). Thus when Christ dealt with this proud generation His normally gentle voice must have sounded like thunder breaking out of the clouds. And dreadful claps of judgment fell upon them from the mouth of the sweet Savior: 'Woe unto you, scribes and Pharisees, hypocrites!'

(*Luke 11:44*). Yet how many hypocrites were awakened and converted by Jesus' sermon? There were a few, so we could not pronounce the disease incurable; but *very* few, so we would tremble at the thought of it growing inside us.

Peter learned how to handle the hypocrite from his Master. When he spoke to Simon Magus – a man suffering from an advanced stage of the disease – his words were steeped in sharp judgment: 'Thou hast neither part nor lot in this matter: for thy heart is not right in the sight of God' (Acts 8:21). The Father had given Peter an extraordinary spirit to discern that the man's false heart was 'in the gall of bitterness, and in the bond of iniquity' (*v. 23*). And the only thing which made him better than the damned souls in hell was that they were in the fire and he, like a bundle of sticks tied up and ready to be burned, had not yet been thrown in. They were past hope but he still had opportunity to repent.

Another example of this maligning spiritual illness is the church of Laodicea. The Spirit of God sharply rebuked her and mentioned nothing good about the congregation because the leaven of hypocrisy had so puffed up her conceit. Everything which encourages sleep is deadly to a lazy person; and anything soothing is just as damaging to the hypocrite. Some say the surest way to cure lethargy is to turn it into a fever. And the best way to deal with a hypocrite is to jolt him from his false peace and plunge him into genuine misery.

Let this be your starting point, then – see the weight of your sin and let your soul mourn because of it. When the Old Testament priest pronounced a person a leper, the latter was to tear his clothing, go bareheaded, and put a covering on his upper lip – a ceremony used by all mourners – and to cry 'Unclean, unclean' (*Lev. 13:45*). So you too should grieve for this plague of your heart, for you are not fit to come near God or His family the way you are now.

If your body had a disease so nasty that it infected the place where you sat or lay, the food you ate and the cup you drank from, everyone would run from you and leave you alone with sorrow and pain. This is exactly what hypocrisy has done to you spiritually. It is a plague more offensive to God than any contagious disease you could have that causes men to pass by on the other side of the street. It oozes out like a filthy sore through all the bandages of good works you put over it.

But even if you could conceal this hypocrisy and enjoy a religious reputation until death, would it be a consolation to you in hell to know your friends were still commending your memory on earth? Someone put it this way: 'Poor Aristotle! You are praised where you are not, and burned where you are!' Surely it is small comfort to that great heathen philosopher to be admired by scholars who have exalted his reputation from age to age if in fact his intellect, along with his body, lives in the agony of eternal punishment. Is it really worth it, hypocrite, for you to be ranked among saints here on earth just before you are tormented among devils in hell?

II. REALIZE YOU CANNOT CURE YOUR OWN HYPOCRISY

Hypocrisy is like a fistula sore. It seems like a minor eruption on the surface but is one of the hardest wounds to heal because it is hard to find the bottom of it. Your will might promise never to lie or deceive again; but it is an easy thing to be cheated by your intentions: 'He that trusteth in his own heart is a fool' (*Prov. 28:26*).

Many people die because they are reluctant to pay the price of seeing a skilled physician while there is still time. Beware of self-resolution and self-reformation. Only God can cure sin. If you experiment with your own heart instead of seeking the help of heaven you may mend one iniquity but tear open two worse sins.

III. TAKE HYPOCRISY TO CHRIST, THE PHYSICIAN WHOSE SKILL AND FAITHFULNESS CAN MAKE YOU WHOLE

If you must die, die at His door. But for your comfort, remember that no one has ever fallen out of His healing hand; and no case has ever been too hard for Him to handle. He blamed the hypocrites who were ready to trust any charlatan ministering in his own name without God's authority but who would not confess the One who had come in the Father's name. And He who blamed hypocrites for not coming cannot be angry with you if you come. It is His calling.

Christ came to be a physician to sick souls. Pharisees were so settled in their own conceit that the Savior spent His time with those who admitted they needed help. If you cannot do anything but groan under your weight of hypocrisy, and send those groans in prayer to God, your healer will soon come to you. Since His ascension into heaven Jesus has never once laid down His calling, but still practises, granting forgiveness as faithfully as ever.

For example, Christ counseled Laodicea how to be loosed from her deadly disease of hypocrisy: 'I counsel thee to buy of me gold tried in the fire, that thou mayest be rich; and white raiment, that thou mayest be clothed' (*Rev. 3:18*). He warned, 'Laodicea, you are deceiving yourself and others with appearances instead of realities, with counterfeit graces for true ones; your gold is impure and your robes are rotten rags. They do not cover your shame but expose it. Come to Me if you want real treasure.' Although Christ mentioned buying, what He meant was a buyer's spirit, valuing Christ and His grace so highly that, if they could be bought, a person would be willing to spend all the money in his account and even the blood in his veins for it, yet still go home saying it was a bargain. It is the thirsty soul who will be satisfied, but we must be sure our thirst is right and deep.

(a) *Make sure your thirst is right*

It must be a heart-thirst and not merely a conscience-thirst. A very different heat kindles each of these. Hellfire, for instance, may inflame the conscience and make the guilty sinner thirst for Christ's blood to quench the torment kindled in him by God's wrath. But only heaven-fire begets heat in the heart which breaks out in longings for Christ and His Spirit with sweet cooling dews of grace to put out the fires of lust and sin.

(b) *Make sure your thirst is deep*

Doctors describe a thirst which comes from a dryness of the throat and not from any great inward heat of the stomach; such a thirst can be quenched by gargling in the mouth, a drink which is spit out and never swallowed. Truly this is what happens in some people who hear the gospel preached.

Sometimes men's spirits are touched by a spark of the gospel which falls on their emotions and makes them suddenly profess a strong urge for Christ and His grace. Yet because these are only tiny embers of excitement rather than deep desires, their heat is soon gone and the thirst quenched with only a taste of Christ's sweetness. And just when they are almost home, they impulsively spit out that sermon and never enjoy Jesus again.

So look hard to see your own wretched hypocrisy and Christ's fullness of grace to heal it. A man with a parched thirst cannot be satisfied with anything except a full swallow of water, no matter what it costs him. So then you must not be content with anything but Christ and His sanctifying grace – not with profession, gifts, or pardon itself, if it could be separated from grace. No, a sprinkling of grace will not do – you must long for floods of it to purge and free you from the hypocrisy which oppresses you. This frame of spirit will shelter you under the promise – heaven's security – that you shall not lose your longing for Christ.

If the desires of your heart are silver and gold and you collect them with fervor, God may let you roar like Dives in hell, in the center of the flames which your lust kindled, without bringing one drop of water to cool your tongue. But if you want Christ and His sweet grace, if you *must* have them, then surely they are yours: 'Blessed are they which do hunger and thirst after righteousness: for they shall be filled' (*Matt. 5:6*).

INSTRUCTIONS TO THE SINCERE

To those of you whose diligent inquiry has shown sincerity from a pure heart, I counsel you to gird the belt of truth close and walk in the daily practice of uprightness. You are not ever dressed in the morning until this girdle has been put on, for the proverb is true which says, 'Ungirded, unblessed.'

God's promises, like a box of precious ointment, are collected to be broken over the head of the sincere man: 'Do not my words do good to him that walketh uprightly?' (*Mic. 2:7*). But surely it is a dangerous walk when there is no word from God to guide our way. It is a foolish man who dares go on when God's Word lies across his path. Where the Word does not bless, it curses; where it does not promise, it threatens. But God's approval keeps an upright soul safe.

The sincere Christian is like a traveler going about his business from sunrise to sunrise; if harm tries to touch him God Himself will take care of it. The promise is on the saint's side, and by pleading it he may recover his loss at God's expense, for the Father stands bound to keep him protected. With this assurance in mind, let us look at several ways to walk in the exercise of sincerity.

I. WALK IN VIEW OF GOD

What Luther said is most true: all the commandments are wrapped up in the first one. He pointed out that every sin is contempt of God; and so if we break any commandment we have broken the first. 'We think amiss of God before we do amiss against God.' Thus the Father commended a sovereign word to Abraham to preserve his sincerity: 'Walk before me, and be thou perfect' (*Gen. 17:1*).

Uprightness before God kept Moses' girdle close to his loins. He was neither bribed by the treasures of Egypt nor brow-beaten out of his sincerity by the anger of such a powerful ruler, 'for he endured, as seeing him who is invisible' (*Heb. 11:27*). He could see One greater than Pharaoh and this vision showed him the right path.

(a) *Walk in view of God's omniscience*

The Jews covered Christ's face and then flogged Him. And so does the hypocrite. First he argues in his heart that God cannot see, or at least forgets that He can see; and this deception makes him bold to sin against the Most High God. He is like the foolish bird that hides her head among the reeds and convinces herself she is safe from the hunter, as if he could not possibly see her if she did not see him.

Augustine said, 'I may hide Thee from my eye, but not myself from Thine.' Ignorant man, you may hide God by your ignorance and atheism so that you cannot see Him; but you can never hide yourself so well that He cannot find you. 'All things are naked and opened unto the eyes of him with whom we have to do' (*Heb. 4:13*).

Remember God no matter what you are doing, whether you are in your office or closet, in church or on the road.

He sees you as you are and knows your thoughts before you do. Like the scenes of Nebuchadnezzar's dream, your thoughts may fade into vague memories forty or fifty years later. Yet God gathers them all in the light of His countenance, as atoms stay in the beams of the sun.

(b) *Walk in view of God's care for you*

God strengthened Abraham's faith when He told him to be upright: 'I am the Almighty God; walk before me, and be thou perfect' (*Gen. 17:1*). He was saying, 'Act for Me and I will take care of you.' Once we begin to doubt God's protection, though, our sincerity will soon falter. Hypocrisy hides in distrust. The unbelieving Jews, for instance, stored up manna overnight against God's explicit instruction because they did not have faith to trust Him for the next meal. And we do the same thing – first we doubt His care and then we start to lean on our own understanding.

This is the same old weapon Satan has always used to cheat Christians out of sincerity. 'Curse God and die,' he taunted Job through his wife (*Job 2:9*). Her words rang with bitter distrust: 'Why are you still holding the castle of your sincerity for God to live in? You have been besieged long enough with sorrows on every hand. And to this day you have not gotten any news from heaven that God cares anything about you. Why do you not just curse Him and die?'

Jesus Himself faced Satan's identical tactic when he tempted the Son of God to turn stones into bread. We see, then, why it is so important for us to strengthen our faith in the caring heart and hands of God. This is the very reason He has made such abundant provision to shut out all doubt and fear from the hearts of His people. God has placed His promises like safe harbors, so if a storm sweeps the sea or an enemy chases us through the darkest night, we can tie up in one of them and know the comfort of full protection.

'The eyes of the Lord run to and fro throughout the whole earth, to shew himself strong in behalf of them,' or to unite with them 'whose heart is perfect toward him' (*2 Chron. 16:9*). God does not depend on others to keep watch; His own eyes do it. He watches over us in the same way a mother takes care of her own child. Sincere Christians, then, are a people whom the Lord cares for; His eyes are always on us.

No danger or temptation finds the Father napping; but as a faithful watchman is always walking around his camp, so the eyes of God 'run to and fro.' 'He that keepeth Israel shall neither slumber nor sleep' (*Ps. 121:4*). One of these words means the short sleep in the heat of the day and the other, the sound sleep of the night – that is, neither little nor much.

(c) *God's care stretches over the whole earth*

It is an all-encompassing providence which encircles God's people; not one sincere person can be left outside His sovereign care. He has numbered every last one of us and cares alike for each. We mar the beautiful face of God's providence when we imagine it goes out only to favorites or 'the most likely to succeed'.

(d) *God's care powerfully destroys danger for His people*

A sentinel wakes up the city to fight the fury of the oncoming enemy, but God's eyes do more than locate the attack. He saves us from it too. Saints are the only ones who can realistically be a 'happy people,' because we are a 'people saved by the Lord' (*Deut. 33:29*). God not only sees with His eyes but fights with them. The look He gave to the Egyptians turned the sea into a destroyer.

II. ACT UPON LOVE, NOT FEAR

Sincerity and fear cannot agree; one must increase while the other must decrease. 'God hath not given us the spirit

[99]

of fear; but of power, and of love, and of a sound mind' (*2 Tim. 1:7*). The slave who works hard only because he dares not do otherwise is easily persuaded to deny his master; he hates him while he fears him. When subjects fear rather than love their prince they will cut his throat to buy freedom. They welcome anyone to the throne who will let them do as they please.

Thus the person who is pricked with the sword of God's wrath instead of drawn by the cords of His love will quickly and carelessly betray His glory. Israel is an unparalleled example: 'When God slew them, then they sought him: . . . nevertheless they did flatter him with their mouth, and they lied unto him with their tongues. For their heart was not right with him' (*Ps. 78:34, 36, 37*). They feared God but loved their lust.

There must be too much of this cowering fear in the saints' hearts today or else God would not have to use the rod of correction so often. 'Is Israel a servant? is he a home-born slave? why is he spoiled?' (*Jer. 2:14*). It is as if God had asked, 'Why do I have to whip you with such severe blows and heavy judgments?' 'Hast thou not procured this unto thyself, in that thou hast forsaken the Lord thy God, when he led thee by the way?' (*v. 17*).

We have only ourselves to thank for God's dealing with us in such ways. If a child insists on forgetting that he is free-born and nothing but strict discipline works with him, then the father must deal with that child according to his slavish spirit. When God led Israel with a father's love he broke away from Him; and because His people would not be led by love He had to drive them by fear.

Christian, if you act by love you will save God the sorrow of having to whip you in line with His fearful judgment. Love will keep you close to Him and true to Him. The very character of love is that it 'seeketh not her own' (*1 Cor. 13:5*); and what is sincerity, but the Christian's seeking Christ's interests and not his own? Jonathan loved David so dearly that he incurred his father's anger and risked the inheritance of a kingdom rather than be false to his friend. Samson was not able to conceal the secret of his strength from Delilah, whom he loved, even though it meant endangering his life.

Love is the great conqueror of the world. Thus if you are inflamed with love for Christ you will toss all your worldly attractions to the four winds rather than tarnish His honor. Just as Abraham put the sacrificing knife to the ram's throat to save his precious Isaac's life, you will sacrifice all that you have to keep sincerity alive. Love is like fire in that it consumes everything near it. It turns all into fire or ashes. Nothing foreign to the nature of fire can dwell very long with fire's own simple and pure nature. Thus love for Christ will not allow the existence of anything in the heart which is unlike Him.

Abraham loved Hagar and Ishmael in their own place, but when they began to ridicule Sarah and mock Isaac he put them both out. Love for Christ will not let you agree with anything which is against Him but, on the contrary, will take His part against every one of His enemies. And this course of action will keep your sincerity out of danger.

III. MEDITATE ON GOD'S SINCERITY

What more powerful thought can keep us true to God than His faithfulness to us? When you see that your heart is being warped into any insincere practice, consider this: if anything of God is in you, it can unbend that hypocrisy and melt and mold you into the right image again.

When His people sin, God asks what He has done to cause their unkind responses to Him: 'Thus saith the Lord, what iniquity have your fathers found in me, that they are gone far from me?' (*Jer. 2:5*). Just before Moses died he indicted the guilty Israelite nation for their hypocrisy, murmuring, and rebellion against God. And to add greater weight to each charge, his introductory words showed the almighty heart of God which they had rejected. 'I will publish the name of the Lord: ascribe ye greatness unto our God' (*Deut. 32:3*). 'He is the rock, his work is perfect: a God of truth, and without iniquity, just and right is he' (*v. 4*). Now because this one consideration is such a dependable hedge against sin in the heart, let me share some truths which furnish us strength to remain upright before God.

(a) *God acts from sincerity and aims at sincerity*
Love is the principle of God's actions and the good of His people is His goal. He never swerves from these. The fire of love never goes out of His heart, nor their good out of His eye. Every time He frowns with His brow, chides with His lips, or strikes with His hand, even then His heart burns with love and His thoughts meditate peace to His children. 'So will I acknowledge them that are carried away captive of Judah, whom I have sent out of this place into the land of the Chaldeans for their good. For I will set mine eyes upon them for good' (*Jer. 24:5, 6*). This was one of the sharpest judgments God ever brought on His people, yet He designed mercy and projected good into the severest hours of it. When the Israelites cried out that Moses had brought them into the wilderness to kill them, they were more afraid than hurt. God had plans for their good which they could not even imagine; He purposed to humble them so they could at last receive His goodness.

God is so sincere that He gives His own glory as hostage for His children's security. His robes of righteousness are locked up in their salvation and prosperity. He will not, indeed cannot, present Himself in all His magnificence and royalty until His intended thoughts of mercy become realities in the lives of His people. He is pleased to postpone the time of His appearing in all His glory to the world until He has fully accomplished their deliverance so both He and His people may come forth together in their glory on the same day: 'When the Lord shall build up Zion, he shall appear in his glory' (*Ps. 102:16*).

The sun is always glorious, even on the most cloudy day, but this glory is not apparent until it has scattered the clouds which hide its light from the earth. God is glorious even when the world cannot see Him, but the demonstration of His glory appears when the glories of His mercy, truth, and faithfulness break forth in His people's salvation. How ashamed we must feel when we fail to aim at God's glory, for He loves all His children so much that He carries His own glory and our happiness in the same boat – they are shipped together so He cannot ever lose one and save the other.

(b) *God's sincerity appears in the openness of His heart to them*

A friend who is distant and reserved is not easy to understand and thus harder to trust. But the one who carries a window of crystal over his heart, through which his friend can clearly read each thought, is free from the least suspicion of unfaithfulness. This is how openhearted God is toward His saints. 'The secret of the Lord is with them that fear him' (*Ps. 25:14*).

The Holy Spirit is the key which God has given to let us into His very heart and know what His thoughts toward us are, and were before the foundation of the world. This Spirit is the One who knows 'the deep things of God' (*I Cor. 2:10*) and has published in Scripture the substance of those counsels of love which had passed among the Trinity for our salvation. And to ensure that our satisfaction will be complete, God has appointed this same Holy

Spirit to abide in His saints. Every time Christ in heaven presents our desires to Him, He interprets His mind from the Word to us. And this Word answers the heart of God 'as in water face answereth to face' (*Prov. 27:19*).

In a transcendent way God performs the same openness of heart to His people which close friends have with each other. If danger is coming toward them He will not conceal it. David said that God's words warn His servants (*Ps. 19:11*). And surely God does send a messenger to sound the alarm to His saints whether their danger has been caused by enemies or by personal sin.

Hezekiah, for example, stood in danger of inward pride. So God sent a temptation to let him know what was in his heart; he had fallen once and God did not want him to fall again. It is God's way first to tell His people of His displeasure with them and then to correct them soundly for it. But He holds no ill will against them.

Even when the Father must lead His children into affliction He loves them so much that He cannot leave them altogether in the dark concerning His love which will deliver them. To comfort them in prison He opens His heart ahead of time to them, as we read of the Jewish church in Egypt and the gospel church under Antichrist. Before these sufferings came, God had already promised deliverance.

While Jesus was on earth He freely told His disciples about the troubles which would befall them; but He did not hold back the blessed conclusion: He would come again to them. Why? To confirm the persuasion of His sincerity toward them: 'If it were not so, I would have told you' (*John 14:2*). And when God had to conceal truth from His children temporarily it was because they were not able to bear it at that time.

Now Christian, does this glimpse into the faithfulness

and plainness of God's heart make you want to be more open to Him? He pours out His mind to you, so why do you still hide your secrets from Him? The One who shares the most intimate fountains of His love and mercy expects a flow of trust from His people.

(c) *God's sincerity appears in the unmovableness of His love*

As there is no 'shadow of turning' in God's being, so there is no turning away of His love for us. There is no vertical point – His love stands still. Like the sun in Gibeon, it does not go down or decline but continues in its full strength. 'With everlasting kindness will I have mercy on thee, saith the Lord thy Redeemer' (*Isa. 54:8*).

The most flaming affections can quickly cool in the heart of man. His love is like fire in the hearth – it blazes, flickers, and then goes out. But God's love is like fire in the sun. It never fails. In the creature, love is like the waters of a river, rising and falling again; in God, like the waters of the sea, which is always full and knows no ebb or flow. Nothing can destroy or change His love where He has sent it; and neither can it be corrupted or conquered.

(i) *God's love cannot be corrupted.* There have always been people presumptuous enough to bribe God to desert His people. Thus when Balaam tried to win God over to Balak's side he spared no cost. He built altar after altar and heaped sacrifice upon sacrifice, hoping to force a word from God's mouth against His people. Yet the Father stayed true to His children and branded displeasure upon that nation for hiring Balaam and sending him on such a foolish mission. All the while, God continued to persuade them of His steadfast love: 'O my people, remember now what Balak king of Moab consulted, and what Balaam the son of Beor answered him.' Why should they remember this? 'That ye may know the righteousness of the Lord' (*Mic. 6:5*).

This story is mentioned to remind us of God's faithfulness toward His chosen ones. If you want your love for God to be incorruptible, embalm it with the sweet spices of His sincere love for you, which is immortal and cannot see corruption. If you believe God is true to you, how can you ever be false to Him again? It is cruel to return falseness for faithfulness in love.

(ii) *God's love cannot be conquered.* The anger and power of His people's enemies do not even begin to put God's omnipotency to the test, but truly the sins of His people do that. You never hear Him complaining about His enemies' strength, yet His children's sins and unkindnesses break His heart. They make Him suffer in the choice of whether to love them or leave them, whether to vote for their life or their death. Yet whatever such human expressions God chooses to use in Scripture to cause people to resent their unkindness and repent, He is never at a loss about what to do. Love moves His thoughts in favor of His covenant people, even when their attitudes and actions least deserve it.

When the devil found Joshua's soiled garment he thought he had enough evidence to present a dirty case against him before God. But Satan was wrong, for instead of provoking God to wrath, the report moved Him to express compassion – and to declare the coming of His beloved Branch (*Zech. 3:8*). Now meditate on this, Christian. The love of God is so unconquerable that your very worst sins cannot break the knot of that covenant which ties you to Him.

You should try very hard, then, to have the image of your heavenly Father's love more clearly stamped on the face of your love to Him. Nothing can overcome His love to you, so you must not let anything prejudice your love to Him. Speak to your soul this way: 'Let me cleave to God even when He hides His face from me, for He did not cast me off when I turned my back on Him. I will testify to the greatness of His name while everyone else reproaches it. God has kept love burning in His heart to me all the time I was backsliding. Can I again grieve His gentle Spirit and make Him an accomplice to my sin by using His love as fuel for it?'

IV. BEWARE OF PRESUMPTUOUS SINS

These wound a man's uprightness deeply because they are the most inconsistent with it: 'Keep back thy servant also from presumptuous sins; let them not have dominion over me: then shall I be upright' (*Ps. 19:13*). David's single presumptuous sin stands as the only exception to the general testimony which God gave to his uprightness: 'David did that which was right in the eyes of the Lord, and turned not aside from anything that he commanded him all the days of his life, save only in the matter of Uriah the Hittite' (*1 Kings 15:5*). The other sins which David committed were all discounted because they did not cause such a scar on his uprightness as this one sin did.

Just as a single presumptuous sin is inconsistent with uprightness, so habitual uprightness is not consistent with habitual presumption. If one sip of this poison seriously infects the spirit of a gracious person, how deadly must it be to all uprightness if the Christian drinks from it every day? As 'Daniel purposed in his heart, that he would not defile himself with the portion of the king's meat,' we must daily put ourselves under holy bond not to defile ourselves with presumptuous sin (*Dan. 1:8*).

Augustine declared, 'I may err, but I am resolved not to be a heretic. I may have many failings, but by the grace of God, I will labor that I be not a presumptuous sinner.' If you do not want to be a presumptuous sinner, stop making light of sins that seem less serious than others. For example, when David's conscience rebuked him for tearing Saul's skirt he stopped what he was doing and withdrew. David's tender heart reproached him for cutting the garment and thus would not let him cut the king's throat and take his life.

But at another time David's conscience was too dull to warn him of danger and he sent a lustful glance to stay with Bathsheba. Like a dizzy mountain climber about to faint, he was sent tumbling from one jagged sin to another until finally he fell into the deep pit of murder.

When the river is frozen, a man ventures to walk and run where he would not dare set his foot if the ice were melted or broken. And when a godly man's heart is so hardened that he can stand on an infirmity, even a tiny one, and his conscience not crack under him, who knows how far into sin he will go?

V. GET ABOVE THE LOVE AND FEAR OF THE WORLD

A Christian's sincerity is not eclipsed without the intervening of the earth between God and his soul.

(a) *Get above the love of the world*

This is a stubborn root for hypocrisy to grow on. If your heart becomes attached to something in the world, and chooses it above everything else, you will be sick with longing for it and vulnerable to take the first advice Satan offers for getting what you want most. Hunters do not care how they get in – over hedges and ditches and through marshes – just so long as they catch the rabbit.

It is a mystery how a saint, with the precious ointment of Christ poured upon his heart, could still have such a strong scent after the world. It would seem that the sweet perfume which comes from those beds of spices – God's promises – would spoil the Christian's desire for hunting earthly game. The breath from Christ in them should so fill the saint's senses that gross earthly enjoyments would no longer be pleasing to him.

This is true as long as the Christian's spiritual senses are open, but as a head cold stops up the nose from doing its job, so a Christian's negligence obstructs his heavenly graces. And when the saint cannot enjoy Christ's divine savor, the devil takes advantage and immediately sets some worldly attraction before him. Soon the flesh picks up the scent and takes the Christian into a chase which dead-ends in sorrow and shame.

(b) *Get above the fear of the world*

Fear of man brings a snare. A coward will run into any hole, no matter how filthy, to save himself. And when the holiest saints are tempted, they are like all other men. When Peter's reputation seemed to be in a little danger, he did not 'walk uprightly according to the truth of the gospel' (*Gal. 2:14*). Instead he took one step forward and another back again – sometimes he was willing to eat with Gentiles but at other times he was not. Why? Because he feared 'them which were of the circumcision' (*Gal. 2:12*).

VI. KEEP YOUR HEART WITH STRICT SELF-DISCIPLINE

The man who rides a stumbling horse must keep his eye on the path and his hand on the bridle. This is your heart, Christian. It can stumble on the smoothest level ground when you cannot see a problem for miles ahead. Therefore, keep a strict rein on it: 'Keep thy heart with all diligence; for out of it are the issues of life' (*Prov. 4:23*).

Bring your heart into full view every day so it can give an account of itself. The master indirectly encourages his servant to steal if he does not ask him now and then about the money in his pocket. Some men in King Jehoida's day were entrusted with the money for the repair of the temple; and they were not required to account for it because it was known that 'they dealt faithfully' (*2 Kings 12:15*). But it is not best for you to do it this way. Rather, give account of your heart to God and to your conscience every day so Satan's subtle temptations will not embezzle God's investments in you.

God has put many talents into your hands for the repair of your spiritual temple – health, freedom, days of rest and worship, ordinances, fellowship – the work of grace in you. Find out how you are spending each one and you can see how God's kingdom work is moving forward. It is best for you to do this every day because – make no mistake – sooner or later God will have an account of your heart.

COMFORT FOR THE SINCERE CHRISTIAN WHO DOUBTS

You may be genuinely sincere but doubt persuades you otherwise. To you I have a few words of counsel, and I trust God to give His blessing to each one.

1. DO NOT CONCLUDE YOU ARE A HYPOCRITE BECAUSE YOU CANNOT NOW SEE EVIDENCE OF YOUR SINCERITY

The patriarchs had money bundled up in their sacks and traveled all the way to the inn, not knowing what they had until they opened them. There is a treasure of sincerity hidden in many souls, but the time has not come for them to open the sack and know their true riches. Thousands of saints whose voyages were marked by fears about whether or not God's grace was truly in them have crossed the gulf and safely landed in heaven. Faith unfeigned puts a believer into the ark with Christ and shuts the door; but it does not necessarily keep him from getting seasick in the ship.

It is the work of Christ which demonstrates itself in such a way that we can see and own it, whereas the truth of our grace may not so clearly show itself. God has put the Holy Spirit beside the truth of grace to lead the soul into the light and show His children that truth. He alone is the great messenger who is able 'to show unto man his uprightness' (*Job 33:23*).

But even as the eye, which cannot see anything in complete darkness, is still a seeing eye where there is light, so there may be truth of grace where there is not a sense of that truth present. So the person may hunt passionately from one church service to another to get the sincerity he already has, as one who looks frantically throughout the house to find his hat, when all the time it has been on his head.

Mark this down as real truth: 'I may be upright even if I am not able to see it clearly.' Although this insight will not furnish full comfort, it can be support until assurance comes. Even if it will not mend the doubt into a wholeness of faith, it will prop it up until the master workman – the Holy Spirit – comes and with one kind word makes you to stand strong on the promise, the only true foundation of solid comfort.

Please do not be more cruel to yourself than you would to your friend – or even to your enemy. Suppose a person whom you did not love much lay very sick in your house, so sick that if you asked him to tell you if he were alive, his senses and speech were too weak to respond. Would you then nail him up in a coffin and start digging his grave, just because he could not say he was still alive? Surely not! How unreasonable Satan is, to shove you toward the pit of despair, because your grace is not strong enough to speak for itself right now!

II. REALIZE THAT SATAN WANTS TO PUT DOUBT AND
    FEAR INTO YOUR HEART

He is amused when he can distract you with false fears if he finds that you will not be flattered with false hopes. There was a time when you lived in sin and thought yourself better than you really were; but now that you have something of the holy ways of Christ in your spirit, Satan threatens you with apparitions of fear. If he is not calling you a hypocrite, he is questioning the sincerity of your heart.

It is worth the effort to investigate the knocking and see if it is not the same old accuser again, though now at another door. The devil has more temptations than an actor has costumes for the stage. And one of his all-time favorite disguises is that of a lying spirit, to abuse your tender heart with the worst news he can deliver – that you do not really love Jesus Christ and that in your pretending, you are only deceiving yourself.

Thus this foul spirit, like a brazen-faced harlot who abandons her child at the pure man's door, impudently accuses him of guilt which is not his to receive. But she knows that some of her bold charge will stick to the Christian's spirit and force the door open to let in another temptation. And that – the real goal of the devil's plot – is to scare the saint and knock off the wheels of his chariot which used to carry him often into the presence of God in His ordinances. Because he suspects he is not sincere in them any more, he reasons that it is better to stay away from God's people than to join them with a false heart. Did the serpent have any smoother skin or a more fluent tongue when he persuaded Eve to reach out and take the forbidden fruit than he does when he tempts you not to touch or taste of the fruit which God has commanded you to enjoy from His hand?

Yet, Christian, you have reason to bless God when He allows the enemy to stretch his wicked mind thus far, and then allows you to figure out this strategy of questioning your sincerity. Do you not see now who it was who first screamed 'hypocrisy' in your thoughts? Satan could not stand to see you growing so fast in Christlikeness, so he slipped this stumbling block in your path of sincerity which leads to heaven. Keep your eyes on the Author and Finisher of your faith and step right over the devil's entire obstacle course.

You would not bite at the other sins Satan used for bait, so he resorts to troubling your imagination with fears of hypocrisy. It is his last-ditch effort before he must give up on you. Do you think if your heart were really deceitful he would bother you like this? He never sends troops into a territory unless an enemy is there to offend him. Hypocritical prayers do not bother him any more than no prayer at all. And neither is he kind enough to tell hypocrites about the insincerity of their hearts. On the contrary, this is the chain which he has fastened to them; and he takes great care to hide it from them, lest the rattling of it awaken their consciences and make a way for deliverance.

Take comfort, then. Unless conscience brings scriptural proof to condemn your hypocrisy, dismiss the devil's charge as a lie. He will not be the one on the bench when you are tried for your life – and neither will his testimony be worth anything on that day. Why should you let his slander bother you now?

III. LOOK FOR EVIDENCE OF YOUR SINCERITY

This is the 'white stone' with the 'new name' in it, 'which no man knoweth saving he that receiveth it' (*Rev. 2:17*). Paul had this white stone sparkling in his conscience more gloriously than all the precious gems in Aaron's breastplate: 'Our rejoicing is this, the testimony of our conscience, that in simplicity and godly sincerity, . . . we have had our conversation in the world' (*2 Cor. 1:12*).

And Job was not without this evidence either when he appealed to the very thoughts of God while He was ransacking every corner of his heart by His heavy hand – 'Thou knowest that I am not wicked' (*Job 10:7*). He did not say he was without sin – this we hear confessed again and again – but he knew he was not a rotten-hearted hypocrite. The Lord gave way to let him be searched and brought to trial to stop Satan's mouth and to shame him for laying a spiritual felony charge against one of God's elect.

Paul and Job were saints of the highest form, it is true; but the weakest Christian in God's family has the identical witness in him which they had: 'He that believeth on the Son of God hath the witness in himself' (*1 John 5:10*). Christ and the Holy Spirit live in your heart just as they abide in the most holy saint on earth. And you have the same blood of Jesus and the water of the Word to wash you. These will testify for your grace and sincerity as they did for Job's and Paul's. But witnesses in a court of law must wait to give testimony until the judge calls them to the bench. And you can be certain God will call up the right witnesses at the right time. But now let us examine three ways to find the evidence of a true heart.

(a) *Reach up for more grace*

The more a child grows up, the more his complexion clears; and this is true of grace as well. There may be some scaliness on the face of a newborn baby. Although this hides the beauty of the countenance for a time, it will wear off. Thus the spiritual reasoning of a saint ripens as the whole body of grace grows, a maturing process which makes him capable of reflecting on his own actions and judging Satan's objections against his sincerity. If you do not want to survey the whole fluctuating spectrum of sincerity or hypocrisy every day, do not remain a child in grace but grow up to a higher stature in Christ. There you can stand above many of your fears and by the same light that you find growing grace you can see the truth of its presence also.

At daybreak it is hard to know whether daylight or nightlight shines; yet as you see the light growing and unfolding itself, you know it is day. The arms of a child in a portrait will not become stronger by standing there for months and years. Do your love, hope, humility, and godly sorrow grow more and more, and still you question whether you have true grace or not? The fact that you do not recognize your grace becomes as amazing as it was that the Jews did not know who Jesus was, when He had made a blind man see.

(b) *Embrace any call God sends you*

There are a few seasons when God gives opportunities for a man to know his own heart better than he will all the rest of his life. These opportunities are wrapped up in those times when God calls us to deny ourselves for His sake. If we are ready to obey, we will learn much about our hearts because grace in self-denial comes forth with glory like the sun shining on a clear day. As well, God chooses to demonstrate evidence of His grace in a saint who is willing to walk in it anywhere and anytime.

The master commends his servant most tenderly after he has diligently obeyed, no matter how hard the command may have been: 'Well done, thou good and faithful servant' (*Matt. 25:21*). God's call for self-denial might mean giving up business associations, hobbies, or houses or land – or all these and more, even friends and family. Well, friend, do not be sick about the providence standing at your door. If you could see all the way through God's purpose in it, you would invite it in as Abraham welcomed the three angels with whom he feasted so freely in his tent.

God has sent this call for self-denial to let you see your own sincerity and to introduce you to His grace which you have longed to see in yourself for so long. This providence brings you a chariot – like the wagons Joseph sent for old Jacob – to carry you to see the living grace which you had mourned as dead for so long.

Does it excite you to think about getting this assurance, regardless of how God makes you struggle on the way? When the Father told Abraham to sacrifice his son, for instance, he took some painful but straight steps to obey. And God would not let that kind of self-denial go without honoring it: 'Lay not thine hand upon the lad, . . . for now I know that thou fearest God, seeing thou hast not withheld thy son, thine only son from me' (*Gen. 22:12*). Of course God knew this all along but spoke it so Abraham could hear of his sincerity from God's own mouth.

Maybe God is calling you to deny your own education, ambitions, or the friends you value the most, in order to take up a truth or practice and to do so merely because the Word tells you to. If you can do this without being taken under by pride – even though that would be opposite to every shred of human nature and approval – it is an act of deep self-denial. You may be expected to leave everything and everyone familiar to you and walk a path alone; you may find out what it means to love peace so dearly that you must pay anything but sin to purchase it. If your obedience does lead you into this kind of self-denial, you have even more reason to expect God to bring evidence of sincerity to you.

Again, God might want you to deny your own anger and revenge; but He may take an unusual way to test your pride severely. For instance, if He binds your enemy and brings him under your hand, your first impulse might be to invite saints and sinners alike to see what happens when God decides to let His judgment fall on someone who deserves it. No doubt this is the very minute when

temptation will bolster your confidence by whispering –
and using God's name – 'Behold the day of which the Lord
said unto thee, Behold, I will deliver thine enemy into
thine hand, that thou mayest do to him as it shall seem
good unto thee' (*1 Sam. 24:4*).

Now if you can withstand this temptation, and take
revenge upon your revenge by repaying good to your
enemy for his evil, you can escape pride and come out a
humble conqueror. You will consecrate the memorial of
this victory to the praise of God's name and not to your
own. David did not keep Goliath's sword in his home as a
trophy of what he had done, but rather in the tabernacle,
'behind the ephod,' as a memorial of what God had done
by his hand (*1 Sam. 21:9*).

If you can humbly master this self-denial you will be a
graduate student – although always a student – with high
honor in God's grace. David's fame echoes more clearly
for the victory he gained in the obscure cave than for the
triumph over slain enemies in the open field. Through the
bloody battles he won 'a great name, like unto the name of
the great men that are in the earth'; but by the self-denial
of sparing Saul's life he gained a place of honor in
Scripture (*2 Sam. 7:9*).

God sent commendation for David's self-denial in a
more dramatic decoration than a military hero has ever
received – in the mouth of his enemy. Saul could not hold
back God's truth but proclaimed his own shame and
justified David as a holy man: 'Thou art more righteous
than I: for thou hast rewarded me good, whereas I have
rewarded thee evil' (*1 Sam. 24:17*).

(c) *Continue to wait on God in His ordinances*

Even when you come within sight of your sincerity, the
Spirit of God must befriend you or you might sit by the
well like Hagar and never find it. You might search all

over the field and still not discover the treasure hidden there. The only way we can 'know the things that are freely given to us of God' is by God's Spirit (*1 Cor. 2:12*). He lives in God's ordinances as a governor works in his office; and we must go to Him if we want the truth of our graces – evidences for heaven – sealed to our consciences.

Go to God's Spirit and wait. The fact that you are at the right door is comforting in itself. Even if you knock for a long time but do not hear anyone coming, you should not feel ashamed. Eglon's servants waited for a dead man (*Judg. 3:25*), but you are waiting for the living God, who hears from heaven every knock you have ever given on earth. He is a loving God who hears your prayers and sees your tears. And even if He seems like a stranger, as Joseph appeared to his brothers, He is so big with mercy that He will soon fall on your neck and ease His heart by acknowledging and accepting you, and His grace in you.

Lift up your head, then – but remember, you cannot set times for God Almighty. The sun rises at its own hour, no matter what time you decide it should come up. Sometimes God comes to you in an ordinance and His heavenly light radiates into your innermost being while He quickens His Word to you. But have you not spent other nights on your face wrestling with God, wondering why He did not satisfy your soul? When someone brings a candle into the dark room we stir around and look for the thing we have lost and soon find what we had groped for in the darkness for hours. We can gauge more of our spiritual condition in a moment of His revelation than in days or weeks of His withdrawal.

Carefully watch for the seasons when God comes to you; take advantage of them. But even if God chooses to hide the treasure from your sight, comfort yourself. He knows your sincerity is real whether you can see it or not. Say what David said: 'When my spirit was overwhelmed within me, then thou knewest my path' (*Ps. 142:3*). God will sovereignly act for your good – not according to false self-accusations – but according to the testimony which His all-seeing eye gives to your grace.

SINCERITY STRENGTHENS THE CHRISTIAN'S SPIRIT

We have seen why sincerity is compared to the soldier's girdle or belt. Now we proceed to the other use of this girdle, which is *to strengthen his loins and to fasten his armour close to him*. In Scripture, girding implies strength: 'Thou hast girded me with strength unto the battle' (*Ps. 18:39*). He 'weakeneth the strength of the mighty' (*Job 12:21*); in this passage the Hebrew meaning is 'He loosens their girdle.' It is a grace which establishes and strengthens the Christian in his whole walk; on the contrary, hypocrisy weakens and unsettles the heart: 'A double minded man is unstable in all his ways' (*Jas. 1:8*).

A soul has as much of heaven's purity and incorruption as it has sincerity. 'Grace be with all them that love our Lord Jesus Christ in sincerity' (*Eph. 6:24*). So, then, the strength of every grace lies in its measure of sincerity. But not only does sincerity cover all infirmities but strengthens the soul for Christian warfare.

'The integrity of the upright shall guide them: but the perverseness of transgressors shall destroy them' (*Prov. 11:3*). Despite all his clever strategies to save himself the hypocrite eventually sinks into his own instability; but sincerity holds the Christian safe above all dangers.

1. THE PRESERVING STRENGTH OF SINCERITY

Israel's hypocrisy was 'a generation that set not their heart aright'; they had a spirit which 'was not steadfast with God' (*Ps. 78:8*). Stones which are not set right on the foundation cannot stand strong nor long.

We see more of this bitter fruit from the hypocrite's branches in the same Psalm: they 'turned back, and dealt unfaithfully . . . : they were turned aside like a deceitful bow' (*v. 57*). Before a defective bow is bent, you cannot see anything wrong with it. But when you draw the arrow to the head it flies to pieces. This is exactly what happens to a false heart when it is put under stress.

Sincerity, however, keeps the soul pure in the face of temptation. 'He that walketh uprightly walketh surely' (*Prov. 10:9*) – that is, his feet are steady and go over the roughest places with safety; 'but he that perverteth his ways' can choose the most velvet-smooth meadow as his path, but sooner or later will stumble and fall.

We already know that sincerity strengthens and keeps the Christian from the power of temptation. So now let us consider some of the ways hypocrisy leads the soul into temptation.

(a) *Hypocrisy hides in a crowd*
The hypocrite sets his watch by the town clock, not by the sun – the Word. He does what everyone else does; the voice of the people is the voice of his god. Thus you seldom see a hypocrite swimming against the tide of corruption. Light things are carried by the stream, and light spirits by the crowd. But the sincere Christian is a heavy substance and would rather sink to the bottom than surrender to the multitude and float along with them in the flow of sin. Because the hypocrite has no inward guidance, he yields to the tide like a dead fish. But sincerity is a principle of divine life and directs the soul to walk its way without the crowd to lean on – and against the opposition which surely waits up ahead.

Joshua spoke his heart even when ten out of the twelve spies said what the people wanted them to say. And the false prophets' words which massaged Ahab's pride would not fit Micaiah's mouth. He chose to look ridiculous by standing alone rather than agreeing with 'four hundred men' who were unanimously wrong (*1 Kings 22:6–8*).

(b) *Hypocrisy takes the bribe of sin*

No one but Christ – and those who know the truth as it is in Him – can reject the devil's best offer: 'All these things will I give thee' (*Matt. 4:9*). A hypocrite, even at the pinnacle of his professing of true religion, will take advantage of such opportunities though it means being bought and sold by sin, betraying his own soul and God. There is no more difference between a hypocrite and an apostate than between a green apple and a ripe one; wait awhile and you will see him fall rotten-ripe from his profession. Judas, for example, was first a hypocrite in hiding, but soon everyone saw him as an open traitor to Christ.

Fruit will ripen as the seasons get warmer; and some hypocrites go longer than others before they are discovered because they have not yet encountered enough penetrating temptations to draw out their corruption. The fruits of the earth ripen more in a week when the sun is lined up with the Dog-Star than during the whole month before. And when the hypocrite sees an open door to enter in and take the worldly prize, then his inward lust and outward opportunity come together and usher in the day of his fall. The hook is baited and he cannot help nibbling at it.

But sincerity preserves the soul in this hour of temptation. David prayed that God would not gather his 'soul with sinners,' whose 'right hand is full of bribes' (*Ps. 26:9, 10*). 'But as for me,' he purposed, 'I will walk in mine integrity' (*v. 11*). Thus a soul moving in integrity will not take bribes from men or sin itself. David's feet were planted in an 'even place' of righteousness.

(c) *The hypocrite yields to temptation when he can sin without man's control*

Let us examine two specific instances of this truth.

(i) *Hypocrites embrace lust in secret corners.* Notice how the hypocrite behaves when he thinks he is safe from men's sight. Ananias and Sapphira tried to draw the curtain of zeal between their hypocrisy and man's eye by laying some of their money at the apostles' feet. They pocketed the rest without a thought of God's eye and presented themselves to Peter as if they were saints in good standing.

But these two church members did not stand long. Hypocrites depend more on the saving of their credit in this world than the saving of their souls in the next. And when their reputation is insured for the moment, they refuse to venture into thoughts of eternity. To do so would show them to be atheists or unbelievers damned to hell. So they keep a comfortable distance from any kind of decision, not daring to let conscience declare what it thinks of them.

Sincerity preserves a soul from such vain imaginations. Joseph's master was absent but His God was present. 'How then can I do this great wickedness, and sin against God?' (*Gen. 39:9*). Not against his master but *against God*. Sincerity makes men faithful to men for God's sake.

(ii) *Some hypocrites may stand out of the reach of man's justice.* Laban was a great man in his country and oppressed Jacob with a sinister plot because the young man was a poor stranger who was not able to contest the stipulations of his proposal. Even Nero, who played the part of a devil, was at first the Roman hope for a wise and just 'state saint'. If you set the stage of power and greatness for hypocrisy, it will not be long before its mask falls off.

Rehoboam's rebellion against God came when he 'had established the kingdom, and had strengthened himself,' forsaking 'the law of the Lord' (*2 Chron. 12:1*). He concealed his intentions until he had settled himself in his throne. But once he gathered strength and confidence he made his break from God. He was like the deceitful captain who furnished his castle with all kinds of supplies and ammunition first and then declared himself a traitor – only after he thought he could defend his treason. But here is where sincerity makes the difference for the Christian.

Joseph's brothers did something worse than taking his life, as far as they were concerned – they barbarously sold him as a slave into a foreign land. In God's providence these men later fell into Joseph's hands during the zenith of his power in Egypt. Then, when Joseph could have repaid them according to what they had done to him, without fear from authorities, his sincerity exalted him high above all thoughts of revenge. He redeemed their cruelty in his own tears, not in their blood; and he cried for joy to see them, when their only joy had once been to get rid of him.

When the brothers' guilt made them measure Joseph's intentions by their own revengeful hearts, he absorbed all their fear by expressing his deep love for them. He would not even let them darken that day's joy by so much as mentioning their grief for past cruelty. What preserved him in his hour of great temptation? His answer was 'I fear God' (*Gen. 42:18*). It is as if he had said, 'Although you are my prisoners here, I have something which keeps my hands and heart from doing evil to you – I fear God.' This, then, was Joseph's protection – he sincerely feared God.

II. THE RECOVERING STRENGTH OF SINCERITY

Sincerity does not guarantee we will not ever fall but it helps us up again when we do. The hypocrite, however, lies where he falls until he dies. Thus he is said to 'fall into mischief' (*Prov. 24:16*). The sincere man stumbles as any traveler might do, but he gets up and resumes his journey with more caution and speed than before. But the hypocrite plunges as a man from the top of a mast who is engulfed past any hope of recovery in the devouring sea.

We see this principle in King Saul's life. When his false heart discovered itself, he tumbled down the hill and did not stop, but went from one sin to another. In just a few years he had plummeted far from the place where he first left God. Once he had been so ready to worship God that he could not wait for the prophet Samuel to arrive – but later he was so far from seeking God that he went to a witch for counsel. And in the last act of his bloody tragedy, Saul desperately threw his life into the devil's mouth by self-murder.

The reason Saul's sin crushed him to death was that his heart was never right with God in the first place. Samuel hinted at this truth when he told Saul: 'The Lord hath sought him a man after his own heart' (*1 Sam. 13:14*). Of course David himself fell into a sin far worse than Saul's wickedness – for which God rejected that first king – but the difference was that in David's life sincerity was 'the root of the matter' (*Job 19:28*).

There is a double reason for the recovering strength of sincerity. One stems from the nature of sincerity itself and the other proceeds from God's promise which settles into the sincere Christian's soul.

(a) *The restoring nature of sincerity itself*

Sincerity is to the soul as the soul is to the body, a spark of divine life kindled in man's heart by the Spirit of God. It is the seed of God remaining in the saint. A tiny seed planted in the womb of the earth is made alive by the influence of heaven upon it and lifts its head fresh and green in the spring, in spite of many cold nips it has had throughout the winter. And sincerity, after temptations and defeats, raises the Christian above hard, dirty barriers when God is looking over it with beams of His awakening grace.

The hypocrite is a Christian by outward appearance only, not by a new nature. A puppet looks like a man in his outward shape but is moved by the joints and hinges the workman fastens to it; and it is not furnished with a soul of its own. When an image like this is worn by time or broken by violence, it cannot do anything to renew itself but crumbles away in pieces, until at last it comes to nothing. Thus the hypocrite's profession is wasted because he is without vital truth to withstand the ruin coming upon him.

(b) *The restoring nature of God's promises*
'The law of the Lord is perfect, converting the soul' – or *restoring* it (*Ps. 19:7*). But the sincere Christian is the only rightful heir of God's Word, that Word which can bring back the soul to life. The Father has carefully laid out many sweet promises to assure His children of His help through dangers and temptations. 'Whoso walketh uprightly shall be saved . . .'. Yet notice how the opposite is true: 'But he that is perverse in his ways shall fall at once' – that is, suddenly and irrevocably (*Prov. 28:18*). 'God will not cast away a perfect man, neither will he help the evil doers' (*Job 8:20*). So then the hypocrite is not only destitute of a promise for help but also lies under a curse from God.

No matter how hard he tries to build his house, the hypocrite leans on his finished effort to find that 'it shall not stand'. With all his might he tries to hold it together but 'it shall not endure' (*Job 8:15*). 'A little that a righteous man hath is better than the riches of many wicked' (*Ps. 37:16*). And God published the reason for all to understand: 'For the arms of the wicked shall be broken: but the Lord upholdeth the righteous' (*v. 17*).

A little true grace mixed with much corruption in the sincere Christian is better than the hypocrite's riches – all the faith, zeal, and devotion he brags about. The sincere man has the blessing of the promise to restore him when his spiritual condition starts to decay; but the curse of God will destroy the hypocrite in all his pomp and glory. His doom can only grow 'worse and worse' (*2 Tim. 3:13*).

The ordinances which work effectually to heal the sincere person through the blessing of God's promises will curse and ruin the hypocrite. The Word which opens the eyes of one puts out the sight of the other, as in the case of the hypocritical Jews. The Word was sent to make them blind. It melts and breaks a sincere soul, as in Josiah; but truth only hardens a deceitful heart.

Before a sermon, hypocrites talk a very spiritual language: 'Whatever God says we will do.' But when the sermon is finished they are farther from obeying Him than ever. The hypocrite hears, prays, and fasts, but all to his detriment. Every ordinance is a wide door to let Satan in more fully to possess him, as Judas found in the last supper.

III. THE COMFORTING STRENGTH OF SINCERITY

Sincerity lifts the Christian's head above the water and makes him float on the waves of trouble with a holy presence and courageous spirit. 'Unto the upright there ariseth light in the darkness' (*Ps. 112:4*), not only light when the night is past, but light *in* the darkness also. The affliction which eats out the hypocrite's heart becomes vigorous nourishment to the sincere man's grace and comfort.

The hypocrite's joy, like strings of a musical instrument, cracks in wet weather; but sincerity keeps the soul in tune through all seasons. Unstable people let circumstances control how they feel – cheerful in sunshine but depressed in rain. And this is the way of the unsound heart. A few trying situations weaken his spirit and destroy him as a cold winter kills feeble bodies. Afflictions, however, help the Christian grow by uniting him even more closely with Christ. Trouble sends him straight to the arms of the Lord, as the bee flies to her hive in a storm. He is glad who has such a comfortable pillow as the lap of Jesus.

Sincerity keeps the Christian's mouth open to receive the sweet consolations which drop from the Word and the Spirit. In fact, God directs every one of His promises here. But hypocrisy is like a man with a badly inflamed throat, he burns inside but cannot swallow anything to quench the fire which sin has kindled in his soul. When God offers precious promises the hypocrite's conscience tells him, 'These cannot be for you; you are not right with God. Surely you can understand that God's Word comes to sincere men; but what are you?'

How different is this hypocrite, then, from Dives in the recesses of hell's misery? This tormented man burns and cannot get a drop of anything to cool his tongue. When the hypocrite is burning in affliction he is offered not a drop but a river, a fountain full of water – even the blood of Christ – but he cannot drink it. His mouth is locked shut by this time and no key can open it. His hypocrisy crouches like a watchdog at his door and will not let comfort come near him. And which is worse, a person who has no bread or he who has it but cannot eat?

No one is more cunning and clever than the hypocrite. In his prosperity he expertly wards off reproofs and avoids the counsel of Scripture. And in affliction, when the conscience is awake, he disputes against any encouragement from the Word. Now that he is God's prisoner, no comfort can come near him. If God speaks terror, who can speak peace? 'Give them sorrow of heart, thy curse unto them' (*Lam. 3:65*).

The Hebrew word for sorrow pictures a shield that covers over; according to one commentator it denotes the disease which doctors say restricts the heart as with a lid, blocking out all relief. This is the hypocrite's sorrow in affliction, once conscience revives and God fills him with an amazing awareness of his sin. But now let me explore some particular kinds of affliction and show what comfort sincerity offers in each one.

(a) *Sincerity supports the soul under reproach from men*
These are not just petty trials; they are known among the saints' martyrdoms as 'cruel mockings' worthy of being recorded in the sufferings of Christ (*Heb. 11:36*). The matchless greatness of Jesus' spirit appeared not only in His enduring the cross but in 'despising the shame' which the foul tongues of His bloody enemies unmercifully loaded upon Him (*Heb. 12:2*). Man's ambitious mind cannot put up with shame; applause is the idol he reaches out for and pays unbelievably high prices to have.

Diogenes once stood naked holding a heap of snow and drew gawking spectators to admire his patience – until someone asked him whether he would do the same thing if no one were watching. The hypocrite feeds on credit; he lives on what the breath of men's praise gives him. When that fails, his heart aches with disappointment; but when acceptance turns to scorn he dies because he does not have the approval of God while being reproached by man.

Sincerity, however, supports the soul against the wind of man's vain breath because he has conscience and God

Himself as his character witnesses at the trials brought against him. A good conscience and God's Spirit work together to make a Christian rejoice in time of reproach. It does not matter then if the hail of man's accusation batters the doors and roof. The Christian is secure inside.

David is a prime example of the security which sincerity affords. 'By this I know that thou favorest me, because mine enemy doth not triumph over me' (*Ps. 41:11*). He had fallen into great sin and the hand of God was chastening him when his enemies decided to charge him with hypocrisy. 'An evil disease, say they, cleaveth fast unto him' (*v. 8*). Could he have been any lower, with his trusted friend turning against him and God letting him suffer in the wake of his wrong? Yet even in all this, David's spirit did not fail; God gave him such inward comfort that he wiped off his enemies' scorn as fast as they threw it at him. Their reproaches fell like the snow which melts as fast as it falls.

How did David get this holy greatness of spirit? 'As for me, thou upholdest me in mine integrity, and settest me before thy face for ever' (*v. 12*). It is as if he had said, 'Lord, You do not treat me the way my enemies do; if there were only one sinful sore in my life, they would light on it like flies. But You overlook my stumbling feet and pardon my sin. You see my uprightness and hold it up amidst all my many infirmities. You set me before Your face and communicate love and favor to me even when sin is mingled with my obedience.' God's mercy merged with sincerity to make the psalm end in praise: 'Blessed be the Lord God of Israel from everlasting, and to everlasting' (*v. 13*).

Christians, we live in bitterly critical times. Anyone who is so preoccupied with protecting his own name that he will not tolerate suffering for Christ or bear the muck thrown by reviling tongues must find a path to travel by himself to heaven. But while sincerity does not guarantee the luxuries of first-class, problem-free travel, it will not let the dirt on your coat soak into your soul, either, to dampen your joy and chill your inward comfort. Reproaches from without can be endured and triumphantly worn as a crown if they do not have to wrestle with a reproaching conscience within.

Sincerity will do more than comfort you from the persecution of slander. Not only will it quench the flames spat in your face by tongues set on fire by hell, but it will sustain you in the face of physical persecution also, if God allows that. Sincerity makes you fearful to sin. You would not dare reach out and touch one of the coals; but sincerity will make you bold to burn, and joyfully hug the flames of martyrdom. *Foxe's Book of Martyrs*, for instance, mentions an Italian servant of Christ who overheard officials quarreling over who would buy wood to burn him at the stake. And in an ultimate demonstration of grace and peacemaking, he offered to pay the bill himself!

(b) *Sincerity strengthens the soul during affliction from God*

The Father lets His righteous children walk through many different kinds of afflictions. Let us see how He delivers us out of them all.

(i) *Sincerity is a comforting companion.* Above all else the hypocrite dreads falling into God's hands; and he is justified in this fear, for God's wrath is a serious matter. Like a murderer whose sentence of execution is plainly written in the law, he gives himself up for dead once he is locked inside the prison. Job's wife railed at her husband for blessing God when he was being battered severely by the Lord's hand: 'Dost thou still retain thine integrity?' She saw nothing but brutal blows from heaven and resented Job's trust. He called her a foolish woman but leveled no anger toward God (*Job 2:9, 10*).

Sincerity enables the Christian *to think and speak well of God*. A deceitful man's countenance droops and his heart enlarges with venom against God. He dares not let it come out of his mouth but it festers in his deepest thoughts. Because the wretched man does not love God, he has no place in his soul to reflect on God's goodness. He fumes and frets and forgets the abundant blessings God has brought in the past and gives in to resentment because of his present problems. And he would much rather curse God than take the blame himself.

But the sincere Christian cherishes such sweet thoughts of God that his meditations unite him with peace and he would not consider speaking unworthily of God's glory or goodness. We see this in David: 'I was dumb, I opened not my mouth; because thou didst it' (*Ps. 39:9*). Both his spirit and body were afflicted at the same time; he was sad and sick, yet he remembered where the affliction came from. 'This is from You, Lord, and I love You dearly; so I can take it without fear. After all, You might have thrown me into a bed of flames instead of a bed of sickness; so let me accept my correction thankfully.' Thus he fielded the blow without sending words of resentment or anger back upon God.

Sincerity enables the soul *to expect good from God*. It would break a heart of stone to read the sad cries which David's soul made when he was in anguish of flesh and agony of spirit. Yet even in this storm he cast out his anchor until it took hold of God: 'In thee, O Lord, do I hope: thou wilt hear, O Lord my God' (*Ps. 38:15*). His expectation of good from God absorbed the bitterness coming from his pain: 'I am poor and needy; yet the Lord thinketh upon me' (*Ps. 40:17*). His condition was pitiful but his comfort was even stronger: 'God has not thrown me away. I am in His mind day and night, and His thoughts are at work to do me good.'

Job proved his sincerity by the confidence he expressed in God from the deepest conflict of affliction: 'Though he slay me, yet will I trust in him: but I will maintain mine own ways before him. He also shall be my salvation: for an hypocrite shall not come before him' (*Job 13:15, 16*). He affirmed, 'If I were not sincere I could not believe and appeal to God while He kills me.'

The hypocrite, though, dares not entrust himself to God's hands when his neck is on the block and God's knife is at his throat. If it were possible he would never come in His sight again, for his conscience chides that God knows him too well to intend any good. Thus when God begins to afflict, he senses the smell of hell-fire in his soul. Although his afflictions are a cloud no bigger than a man's hand, they will surely spread until the shades of everlasting night overtake and encompass him in hell's utter darkness.

(ii) *Sincerity comforts the Christian when visible success evades his life's work.* It is a heart-aching trial for the minister who spends his strength for twenty years preaching the gospel to a mocking, ignorant and profane congregation with no more life in them than the pews they sleep in. It costs the mother no small pain to bring forth a living child; but what about the anguish of one who labors to deliver one born dead? This is the travail of a minister with dead-hearted people. But then God has always called on His most eminent servants for the hardest work.

Sincerity lightens afflictions and supplies what the Christian needs to bear them. For example, Paul realized he could not take everyone who had ever heard him preach to heaven with him. To many men, the gospel was a 'savor of death unto death' (*2 Cor. 2:16*). The sweet perfume of the gospel proved a deadly scent to hasten and heighten their damnation. The tender physician hurts to see his patients die under his hands – yet he thanks God who makes him 'triumph in Christ' (*2 Cor. 2:14*). But how can the minister rejoice when souls are dropping into hell from under his pulpit? He does not triumph because they perish, but that he is not guilty of their blood; not that they are damned, but that he sincerely invested all God gave him for their salvation. 'For we are not as many, which corrupt the word of God: but as of sincerity, but as of God, in the sight of God speak we in Christ' (*v. 17*).

If Paul had dropped some wild gourd of error into his doctrine, or mingled some ingredient of his own in with what Christ the great Physician had ordered, he would have had no reason to rejoice. But he preached a pure gospel with a sincere heart, so he could first triumph in the Savior who made him faithful. He knew that he would meet the unbelievers again at the last day and witness against them to their face and vote with Christ for their eternal destruction.

I can hear all the faithful ministers of Christ giving an account to Him in the language of Jeremiah's prayer: 'Neither have I desired the woeful day; thou knowest' (*Jer. 17:16*). 'We warned those wretched men because the life of their souls was precious to us. We would have sacrificed our own temporal lives to save their souls for eternity; but nothing we could say or do would make them change their minds. They went to eternal punishment over all the prayers, tears, and pleading of Your Word, which stood between them and hell.' Sincere ministers of Christ can lift up their heads with joy, then; but it will make the tormented rebels hang their heads in shame to look at Christ – although now they stare at preachers with defiant resentment for invading their stubborn 'right to

[133]

THE CHRISTIAN IN COMPLETE ARMOUR

decide for themselves.'

So, when you do not see the seed which you sowed in godly examples, holy instructions, and seasonable corrections coming up, be comforted. David walked in his 'house with a perfect heart' (*Ps. 101:2*). But there were failures too: one child was incestuous, another guilty of washing his hands in his brother's blood, and another greedy for his father's crown. Yet in the turmoil of his family relations, David rested peacefully on his deathbed: 'Although my house be not so with God; yet he hath made with me an everlasting covenant, ordered in all things, and sure' (*2 Sam. 23:5*). He had sincerely done his best, and here was the evidence of his inclusion in God's covenant, which was all his desire and salvation.

In a word, when the flood of God's wrath comes rolling in upon a nation like irresistible waves through the wide breaches made by sin, and righteous men stand in the gap and beg for the life of the nation, God will not answer their cries. But even then, sincerity will be a sweet support if we must share in nationwide adversity.

Even when the righteous are men beloved of God like Noah and Daniel, sometimes God still denies bail for a people under the arrest of His judgment. Jeremiah, for instance, boldly testified against the sins of the times and interceded in earnest prayer for the people; but he could not convert them by preaching or divert God's wrath by praying. Finally the Jews asked him not to prophesy against them any more and God commanded him to stop praying for the nation.

Judgment hovered like an eagle closing in on her prey. And the only thing that eased Jeremiah's heart, swollen with grief for Israel's sins, was his memory of sincerity to God and man: 'Remember that I stood before thee to speak good for them, and to turn away thy wrath from

[134]

them' (*Jer. 18:20*). It is as if he had said, 'Lord, I cannot make this rebellious generation repent of their sins, and I cannot seem to prevail with You to reverse Your decree of punishment; but I have been faithful in my place both to You and to them.'

On the contrary, horror and a terrified spirit is the portion of hypocrites in seasons of judgment. Pashur, for example, was a bitter enemy of Jeremiah and of the prophet's message from God. He put in long efforts to soothe the king with vain hope of golden days just ahead. And all this against the Word of the Lord at the mouth of Jeremiah! When the storm began to fall in torrents of judgment, Jeremiah tore away all such imaginary shelter by telling Pashur he would carry a personal brand of God's anger, besides sharing in the common calamity of the people (*Jer. 20*).

(iii) *Sincerity strengthens the Christian deprived of the chance to serve God*. If a servant of Christ could choose any affliction, he would select everything else before he would endure the pain of being a broken instrument, unserviceable to God. A devoted servant values his life by the opportunities he has to glorify God.

When God had promoted Joseph and honored him in a strange land he did not think carnally about his personal accomplishments, but interpreted the whole series of events as being sent from God's hand. Even when he stood next to the king in rank and power, he saw his place as an occasion to serve God in the preservation of His church, contained at that time in his father's family. 'God sent me before you to preserve you a posterity in the earth, and to save your lives by a great deliverance' (*Gen. 45:7*).

It is a sad affliction, then, when opportunities for service are taken away and the saint is laid aside. But comfort comes in remembering when he faithfully stewarded his time and talents for God. He counts it a deep sorrow that God is no longer using him the way He once did, yet he is not sorry that God's work can go on without him. Though he dies, God lives to take care of His own work. The snapping of one string – or all of them – cannot muffle the music of God's providence. He can freely perform His pleasure without using any creature for His instrument.

In a word, it makes the Christian's heart ache to be taken from any work wherein he might glorify God. Yet he has this unique truth which no thief of time can break through and steal: when the saint sincerely wants to serve Christ with all his heart in some work, *God counts it done*. David's desire to build the temple, for example, was as much finished in God's sight as if he had been able to complete it himself.

At the last day many with giving hearts will be rewarded as the greatest benefactors though they had no clothing to give or bread to share with the poor of the earth. 'Then shall the King say unto them on his right hand, Come, ye blessed of my Father, inherit the kingdom prepared for you from the foundation of the world: for I was an hungred and ye gave me meat, . . .' (*Matt. 25:34, 35*). He did not say, 'you who were wealthy,' but 'you who shared your souls with the hungry.'

Hear this, precious ones made sincere by God, and take comfort. You may have a low standing in the world, and your material goods valued next to nothing; your job may seem unimportant and not prestigious in any way. But do you desire to walk in the truth of your heart and be accepted by the Father in every moment of your life? Sincerity is a bird which sings as sweet a note in your breast as if you were the most famous monarch in the world.

The love and favor of God, devotion to Christ, and the precious promises which in Him are 'yea' and 'amen' – these bring comfort and refreshing to both the greatest saint and the lowliest one in God's family. It will not be how much we have done for Christ, but how much we have done for Him *sincerely*: 'Well done, thou good and faithful servant' (*Matt. 25:21*). Not, 'Well done, for you have done great things and ruled kingdoms; you have been a famous preacher in your time.' But, 'You have been faithful, even in the most obscure corner of the world.'

When Hezekiah was on his sick-bed he did not tell God how many major spiritual projects he had completed – although no one had done more – but only reminded Him of the sincerity in his heart: 'Remember now, O Lord, I beseech thee, how I have walked before thee in truth and with a perfect heart, and have done that which is good in thy sight' (*Isa. 38:3*).

IV. SINCERITY'S STRENGTH AGAINST TEMPTATION

Do you have power to repel temptation when the only weapon you have left for defense is God's command forbidding the sin, or maybe some arrow taken out of the quiver of the gospel, such as Jesus' love for you, or your love to Him?

Maybe the temptation has been so skillfully woven into your convenience that you can sin and save your reputation too. Since the back door is open you can enter secretly; no one will ever find out, and to outward appearance you have sacrificed none of your Christian commitment. But just then God stands up and His Spirit tells you it is against His glory and inconsistent with your profession of love. Now what will you do? Can you inform Satan that sin is no match for you until you can reconcile sinning against God and loving Him at the same time? If

[137]

you were a hypocrite you could no more resist available sin than dust defies the wind.

The false heart quickly gives in to the conqueror – but the sincere Christian takes heart even when he loses ground. Uprightness makes the soul rebound higher in holy purposes against sin by those same falls into sin. 'Once I have spoken' – he means sinfully – 'but I will not answer: yea, twice; but I will proceed no further' (*Job 40:5*). David, for example, begged God for time to recover his spiritual strength before death. He did not want to leave the battlefield in defeat. He earnestly desired to live long enough to recover his losses to sin by repenting and gaining new victory over it. Only then could he welcome death. He was like the mortally wounded captain who asked someone to hold him up long enough to see the retreat of the enemy.

Try to deal impartially with your soul now. What effect do your falls and shortcomings have on you? If they wear off the cutting edge from your conscience so it cannot sharply reprove for sin, if they bribe your emotions to compromise – then your heart is not right with God. But if you meditate revenge on the sin which overpowered you, then sincerity is in you.

V. THE IMPORTANCE OF STRIVING FOR SINCERITY

Without sincerity we cannot withstand temptation or get up again once we have fallen. David knew he needed more of this grace when he said, 'Create in me a clean heart, O God; and renew a right spirit within me' (*Ps. 51:10*). How foolish it is to build a house with flaming beams! Yet it is true – what the hypocrite builds must come to nothing. There is a fire unquenched – the power of unwounded hypocrisy – which will consume his profession.

VI. THE BLESSING OF SINCERITY

Crowns and royal jewels cannot be compared with

sincerity in value because truth in you will make a heart after God's own likeness. Nothing can make you more like Him in the simplicity and purity of His nature. When Haman was asked what should be done to that man whom the king delighted to honor, he assumed the king referred to himself and flew as high as ambition would take him. He chose to be clothed with the king's own royal apparel! When God gives you sincerity He clothes your soul with His own robes. 'I put on righteousness, and it clothed me: my judgment was as a robe and a diadem' (*Job 29:14*). This robe of righteousness makes you a greater conqueror than Alexander, who overcame a world of men. But you have defeated a world of lust and devils.

Have you ever looked at a frog and felt thankful God created you a man instead of such an ugly creature? How much more grateful should you be that He has changed you from the hypocrite you once were by nature into an upright Christian? Lactantius asked, 'If a man would choose death rather than have the face and shape of a beast – though he might keep the soul of man – how much more miserable is it for the shape of a man to carry the heart of a beast?' The hypocrite is in the worst shape of all, for he carries a beastly heart in the disguise of a saint.

VII. SINCERITY'S ASSURANCE AGAINST THE FEAR OF APOSTASY

As we have noted before, sincerity shall not always keep you from stumbling or doubting – but your blood covenant with Christ will preserve you from final apostasy. Because the supply of grace in your hand is small, it is easy to question your security. 'Can these weak legs really bring me to my journey's end? Can these few pennies – the little grace in my heart – possibly pay all the charges to heaven, the many temptations and expensive trials of faith?'

Actually the answer is 'No'. The loaf in your breadbox is not enough to feed you the rest of your life. But you have a covenant! Has not God taught you to pray for your 'daily bread'? If you diligently follow His calling every day, His blessing supplies everything you need.

And you have a Provider of spiritual 'daily bread' as well. You have a precious Brother, a Husband who purposely has gone to heaven, where there is plenty of grace, so He can sustain your soul in this demanding world of stress and pressure. All power is in His hands: He goes to the Supply and sends whatever you need. Can you ever starve, then, when He who has fullness of grace has undertaken to provide for you?

The two coins which the Samaritan left were not enough to pay for the board and recovery of the wounded traveller: so he gave his word that he would pay whatever was required when he came again. Christ does not just give a little grace from His hand, but 'more grace' (*Jas. 4:6*), as much as necessary to take us to heaven with Him. 'The Lord will give grace and glory: no good thing will he withhold from them that walk uprightly' (*Ps. 84:11*).

VIII. WARNING AGAINST GLORYING IN SINCERITY

It is true – sincerity empowers you to resist temptation and will lift you out of sin; but who empowers sincerity? Where does the root grow which feeds your grace? Not in your own ground but in heaven. It is God alone who holds you and your sincerity in His life; and He who gave it will keep it. The Lord is your strength; let Him be your song. What can the axe do, even a sharp one, without the workman? Shall the axe brag that it has cut down something? Or the chisel boast that it has carved? Is it not the skill and art of the workman? When you resist temptation there is only one truth you can speak: 'If the Lord had not been on my side I would have fallen.'

Even though the Psalm promises to give grace and glory to the upright, God will not give the glory of His grace to uprightness. For instance, David asserted his uprightness and told how he was preserved by it: 'I was also upright before him, and have kept myself from mine iniquity' (*2 Sam. 22: 24*). He declared how God had testified to his uprightness by rewarding him for it: 'Therefore the Lord hath recompensed me according to my righteousness; according to my cleanness in his eyesight' (*v. 25*). But to avoid the applause of his own goodness he quickly limits his expression: 'God is my strength and power: and he maketh my way perfect' (*v. 33*). It is as if David corrected his hearers' imaginations: 'Do not misunderstand; I cannot take any credit for my victories or uprightness. God did it all; He is my strength and power. He found me like a crooked man on a crooked path, but He has made me and my way perfect and straight.'

IX. INSTRUCTION TO FEAR HYPOCRISY, NOT AFFLICTION
Believe this, friends – affliction is a harmless thing to the sincere person. It cannot grow big enough to separate him from comfort and joy. Even in the hardest affliction the Christian who is full of grace can spare tears for himself and spend them on the hypocrite headed for hell. He takes a more comforting view of his afflictions than his onlookers do. Once a holy man who was dying asked a servant standing near his bed why she was crying. 'Do not be afraid,' he reassured her. 'My heavenly Father will not do me any hurt.'

Affliction is not pleasant to our flesh, but after we find out what precious comforts God sends His prisoners, we sing a new song. At first the bird fights against the bars of the cage and flutters to register her dislike of restraint, but later sings a sweeter song than she did when she could fly anywhere she pleased.

Do not be so thoughtful about affliction, then; but do be careful to guard against hypocrisy. If the bed of affliction proves hard and uneasy to you, trust God. What a horrible conversation it would be in your dying hour to cry, 'Lord, Lord, have mercy on me', and to hear God's answer: 'I never knew you.' It is not the voice of the sincere saint, but that of the hypocrite, which screams from his bed of sorrow.

What will you do if you fall into the hands of God, with whom your profession has juggled and attempted to manipulate to your own advantage? He has known all the time that you never really loved Him. If Joseph's announcement – 'I am Joseph your brother, whom you sold into Egypt' – so humbled his family that they could not stay in his presence because of their guilt, what will it be like to hear God's voice in that final hour? 'I am God whom you have mocked, abused, and sold for the enjoyment of your lusts. Why do you come to Me now? I have nothing for you but a hell to torment you through all eternity.'

7: Sixth Consideration: The Christian's Breastplate

And having on the breastplate of righteousness (Eph. 6:14).

T HE second piece of armour commended to all Christ's soldiers is a breastplate, and the metal it is made of is righteousness – '*and having on the breastplate of righteousness.*'

THE MEANING OF RIGHTEOUSNESS

I. LEGAL RIGHTEOUSNESS

Three things make up the law-righteousness which God required of man under the old covenant, the covenant of works: 'Moses describeth the righteousness which is of the law, That the man which doeth those things shall live by them' (*Rom. 10:5*). But now let us study this legal righteousness further.

(a) *Perfect obedience to God's law*

This obedience had to be perfect extensively, regarding the object; and intensively, regarding the subject. A man had to keep the whole law with his whole heart, for the least flaw denied it all.

(b) *Obedience personally performed by the righteous man*

In His covenant God had nothing except man's single bond for performance – there was no surety or guarantor engaged in it with him. So in case of default it was necessary for God to exact the debt personally on every man.

(c) *Perpetual obedience*

If the law were broken, even by one wrong thought, the

covenant had no room for repentance. And regardless of the person's faultless life afterward, it was still impossible for him to make up for his disobedience.

How desperate we would be right now if we could not be in Christ's army until we had this type of breastplate! Adam's righteousness was merged with his being; his heart and the law were in unity, as face answers face in a mirror. It was as natural for him to be righteous as it is now for his posterity to be unrighteous. In creation God engraved His own image of righteousness and holiness upon man. His design was so perfect that He did not change or add anything but saw that all was 'very good' (*Gen. 1:31*). And as the crowning masterpiece of His creativity, God 'made man upright' and 'in his own image' (*Eccles. 7:29; Gen. 1:27*).

But because Adam sinned and defiled our nature, now our nature defiles us. This is why Adam's breastplate – righteousness, I mean – could never fit any mere man. Even if God would save all the world for one such righteous man – as once He offered to spare Sodom for ten – that person could not be found.

Scripture divides the entire earth into 'Jews and Gentiles,' and the apostle is not afraid to strip away all religious veneer – they are 'all under sin' (*Rom. 3:9*). Even the holiest saint who ever lived cannot stand as a righteous man in that court. 'Enter not into judgment with thy servant,' said David, 'for in thy sight shall no man living be justified' (*Ps. 143:2*). Man can never approach life and contentment by law-righteousness again – God drove nails into the wood of that door and made a better way.

II. EVANGELICAL RIGHTEOUSNESS

This righteousness is twofold – imputed and imparted. *Imputed* righteousness is what Christ works *for* the believer, the justification which lets him stand righteous before God. This is called 'the righteousness of God' (*Rom. 3:21*). By way of distinction, *imparted* righteousness is what Christ works *in* the believer.

(a) *Imparted righteousness is performed by and in Christ*
Although this righteousness is not inherent in God's children, we receive the benefit of it by faith, as if we had effected it ourselves. This is why Jesus is called 'the Lord our righteousness' (*Jer. 33:16*).

(b) *God ordained imputed righteousness to be the basis for our justification and to be also the ground of acceptance of imparted righteousness*
This righteousness belongs to the fourth piece of armour, 'the shield of faith' and is called 'righteousness of the faith' because it is applied by faith to the soul (*Rom. 4:11*). The righteousness therefore which is compared to the breastplate here is the righteousness of sanctification *imparted* by Christ into the spirit of a believer. This gift is a supernatural principle of new life planted in the heart of every child of God by the powerful operation of the Holy Spirit. It is the only way Christians can seek God's approval and man's and is the only way we can perform what His Word requires of us. We shall now study this work of God's Spirit in more detail.

(i) *The efficient workman, the Holy Spirit.* If God's Spirit is not at the root, no 'fruit of the Spirit' – holiness – can be found on the branches (*Gal. 5:22*). 'Sensual' and 'having not the Spirit' are inseparably coupled (*Jude 19*). When man fell he lost both God's love to him and his likeness to God.

Christ restores both losses to God's children – the first, by His righteousness imputed to them; and the second, by His Spirit re-imparting the image of God, which consists of 'righteousness and true holiness' (*Eph. 4:24*). No one but a man can impart his own nature and beget a child like

[145]

himself; and no one except the Spirit of God can produce a likeness of God by making man a partaker of the divine nature.

(ii) *The work produced – a supernatural principle of new life.*

A principle of life. Although the Christian is passive in this production he is active afterward, co-working with the Spirit in all expressions of holiness, not as a lifeless instrument in the hand of a musician but as a living child in his Father's hand. The child is then 'led by the Spirit of God' toward a sweet and powerful disposition inclining toward holiness (*Rom. 8:14*).

A principle of new life. The work of the Holy Spirit is not to revive or recover what is failing but to work life in a soul that is absolutely dead: 'You hath he quickened, who were dead in trespasses and sins' (*Eph. 2:1*). The devil comes as an orator to persuade by argument when he tempts; but God's Spirit comes as a creator when He converts. Satan draws out and kindles the trash he finds raked up in the heart; but the Holy Spirit puts something into the soul which was not ever there – what Scripture calls the 'seed' of God (*1 John 3:9*). This is Christ 'formed in you,' the 'new creature,' and the 'law' put by God in the inner man, which Paul calls 'the law of the Spirit of life in Christ Jesus' (*Gal. 4:19; Gal. 6:15; Jer. 31:33; Rom. 8:2*).

A supernatural principle. By this we distinguish it from Adam's righteousness and holiness, which was as co-natural to him as sin is to us now. If he had stood and not fallen, righteousness would have been passed on to us as naturally as his sin now is, multiplied to all generations. Holiness was as normal to Adam's soul as health was to his body, for both resulted from pure principles conceived and delivered from the heart of God.

(iii) *The soil in which the Spirit plants holiness.* 'Because ye are sons, God hath sent forth the Spirit of his Son into your hearts' (*Gal. 4:6*). There is not one child in all God's family who is unlike his Father – 'as is the heavenly, such are they also that are heavenly' (*1 Cor. 15:48*). And no other people on earth except the Lord's children have this mark of true holiness. As Paul concludes, we 'have not the Spirit of Christ' if we are 'in the flesh' – in an unholy lifestyle – and we cannot be His if we 'have not the Spirit' to sanctify us (*Rom. 8:9*).

In a broader sense, however, there is a sanctification which may be found in those who are not God's children. Scripture says that the children of believers are 'holy' who are not all children of God (*1 Cor. 7:14*). And there are many who pretend to be sanctified when they are not; but that work which Scripture calls holiness and righteousness is a sculpture which the Spirit engraves exclusively upon God's children. And He will not sanctify any except those whom Christ prays that His Father will 'sanctify'; these are His own peculiar chosen ones given to Him by God (*John 17:17*).

(iv) *The spiritual energy of this principle.* The heart, which is the principle of natural life in a body, always pumps blood from the moment it is infused with life. Thus 'in Christ Jesus' the 'new creature' is not stillborn; true holiness is not a dull habit which sleeps to avoid confronting sin and doing good (*Gal. 6:15*). The woman healed by Christ got up 'and ministered unto them' (*Matt. 8:15*).

No sooner does the Spirit plant this principle of new life in man's heart than he rises up to wait on God and to serve Him with all his might. The seed which the sanctifying Spirit puts in the soul is not lost or dead in the soil but quickly proves its life by the fruit it bears.

(v) *The imperfect nature of this principle.* Evangelical

[147]

holiness makes the Christian *willing* but does not auto-matically guarantee that he will be *able* to obey fully. Mary demanded, 'Tell me where thou hast laid him' (*John 20:15*), implying she wanted to carry the body of Jesus with her, on her shoulders – a desire she was not physically able to perform. Her affections were much stronger than her back.

The principle of holiness in a saint, then, makes him try to lift a duty which he can barely move; he can do little more than desire with all his heart to see it done. Paul sketches his own character from the sincerity of his will and efforts, not from the perfection of his works: 'Pray for us: for we trust we have a good conscience, in all things willing to live honestly' (*Heb. 13:18*). He was so willing to follow God into holiness that he did not hesitate to claim 'a good conscience,' although he could not accomplish everything he wanted to do.

(vi) *Uniformity of the principle.* True holiness will not divide what God joins: 'God spake all these words' (*Exod. 20:1*). There God gave together the four commandments concerning Himself and the six concerning man. And a truly sanctified heart does not want to skip over or blot out one word God has written but desires to be a doer of the whole will of God.

(vii) *Order of performance.* 'To God and man' – first to God and then to man; this is the sequence of a sanctified life. Paul said the Macedonians first gave 'their own selves to the Lord, and unto us by the will of God' (*2 Cor. 8:5*). A sanctified person first obeys God and then, out of obedience to His will, serves his fellow man.

(viii) *The rule of righteousness.* In Christianity we cannot write a right line without a rule, or with a false one. And every standard except the Word is a false rule – 'to the law and to the testimony: if they speak not according to this word, it is because there is no light in them' (*Isa. 8:20*). Whatever the Word of God requires is the rule of God's Spirit; apocryphal holiness – doubtful, marginal, or extraneous – is not true holiness at all.

WHY RIGHTEOUSNESS IS COMPARED TO A BREASTPLATE

I. THE BREASTPLATE PRESERVES THE PRINCIPAL PART OF THE BODY

A stab wound is more deadly where the vital organs of man are close together than in other parts farther from the fountain of life. A person may survive an injury in the arm or leg but a wound in the heart is a certain herald of death. Thus righteousness and holiness preserve the main part of the Christian – his soul and conscience. Damage to a saint's property or any other worldly investment does not touch or hazard his life any more than shaving a beard or trimming fingernails.

A spiritual dagger – sin which hunts 'for the precious life' – is the lethal weapon Satan uses to stab the conscience (*Prov. 6:26*). This is the 'dart' which pierces the young man 'through his liver,' who runs to lust 'as a bird hasteth to the snare, and knoweth not that it is for his life' (*Prov. 7:23*). Righteousness and holiness are God's protection to defend the believer's conscience from all wounds inflicted by sin.

II. THE BREASTPLATE MAKES THE SAINT BOLD

There is not much difference between an army cowering in fear and an army killed. A dead soldier will do as much good as a dead-hearted one paralyzed with anxiety; his heart is attacked and murdered while he is still alive. A naked breast exposes the unarmed soldier's trembling heart; but one having his breast well defended by a plate of proof will more fearlessly venture out to the front lines.

Thus righteousness, by defending the conscience, fills the creature with courage in the face of danger and death; whereas guilt – nakedness of the soul – locks the stoutest sinner into the stocks of fear. 'The wicked flee when no man pursueth: but the righteous are bold as a lion' (*Prov. 28:1*).

Just as sheep are scared by the clatter of their own feet as they run, so the sinner is overwhelmed by the roaring din of his guilt. As soon as Adam saw he was naked, he became as afraid of God's voice as if he had never known Him before. We cannot recover our courage until we recover our holiness. 'If our heart condemn us not, then we have confidence toward God' (*1 John 3:21*).

CONNECTION OF THE BREASTPLATE AND THE GIRDLE

The linking word *and* securely buckles this piece of armour to the girdle and makes us notice how lovingly truth and holiness have been joined, like sister-curtains of the tabernacle. And it is abominable for anyone to unclasp anything God has so united. Remember – *truth and holiness must go together*.

I. TRUTH OF DOCTRINE

An orthodox judgment coming from an unholy heart and an ungodly life is as ugly as a man's head would be on a beast's shoulders. The wretch who knows truth but practises evil is worse than the man who is ignorant. If you are a slave to the devil it does not matter where the chain fastens you to him, the head or the foot. He holds you just as surely by the foot – in your actions – as he would by the head – in your blasphemy.

Christian, your wickedness is greater because it is committed in the face of truth. Many men are betrayed into unholiness by mistakes of faulty judgment; but your judgment lights another path for you, unless you intend to heap up more sin by fathering your unholiness on truth itself.

Sinners miss their way to heaven in the dark, or are misled by erroneous judgment, which, if corrected, might bring them back to the path of holiness. But you sin in the broad daylight of truth and boldly head for hell at high noon. This makes you favor the devil himself, who knows truth from error as well as any angel does – but he refuses to be ruled by it.

If a soloist sang to a sweet melody with her voice but with her hand played a different tune, the dissonant chords would offend the hearer more than if she had sung what she played. Thus, to sing to truth with our judgment but play wickedness with our hearts and hands is more abhorrent to God than the harmony of poor judgment and an unholy life.

Hanun, for example, would not have enraged David so much if he had charged against him with twenty thousand men as he did by abusing his ambassadors in such a base way. The open hostility which sinners express by their lives does not provoke God so much as the vile dishonor they give to His truth, which He sent to make them free. When God sees men scorn His truth by imprisoning it from having any command over their lives, this sight kindles the fire of His wrath into a consuming flame. It is a dangerous choice to walk contrary to the light of God's truth.

II. TRUTH OF HEART

Truth and holiness must stay linked with each other. Men only pretend to be sincere if their lives are not holy. *God does not recognize any unholy sincerity*; the terms clash and war against each other. Sincerity teaches the soul to point to the only worthy end of all its actions: the glory of God.

It is not enough to turn and face this goal; we must walk in the right way to it. We will never arrive if we walk out of the path His Word has set before us.

Holiness and righteousness is the sincere man's path, mapped out by God Himself as the causeway on which he is to travel, both to glorify God and to be glorified by Him. Anyone who tries to take a short cut is opening himself up to pain and defeat. If he finds a new way of glorifying God, which God has not charted, then he must find a new heaven which God has not prepared!

Hell is full of good intentions – plenty of people are there who 'meant well' on earth, but their lives failed to demonstrate their 'basic honesty.' Who would believe the man's argument that his well was full of sweet, pure water when all he had in his bucket was sour, muddy water? You say you have an upright heart and moral thoughts, when everything coming out of your life is evil? Surely you do not believe that yourself!

1. Why Every Christian Should Keep on his Breastplate

We have surveyed the ground and drawn the plans; now it is time to lay the bottom stone of our foundation and build one main structure of truth concerning the breastplate of righteousness. And it is this: *The person who intends to be a Christian must keep the power of holiness and righteousness in his life and conduct.* He must have 'the breastplate of righteousness' and have it on also.

The righteous man has a work of grace and holiness in his heart just as a living man has the principle of life within him. But this man maintains the power of holiness by exerting it vigorously in his daily walk, just as the heart empowers each part of the human body to do its strenuous work. Jerome described the life of the early Christians this way: 'The blood of Christ was yet warm in their veins.'

They were serious about keeping their breastplate of righteousness on and drew it close so it could not be loosened by negligence or broken by presumptuous sin.

In the early days of Christianity a saint's character was distinguished from that of a worldly man by his consistently holy walk. Zacharias and Elisabeth, for instance, 'were both righteous before God, walking in all the commandments and ordinances of the Lord blameless' (*Luke 1:6*). Paul's everyday exercise was 'to have always a conscience void of offense toward God, and toward men' (*Acts 24:16*). And we who follow the same holy profession must bind ourselves to pure behavior so we will walk in holiness and righteousness as they did.

I. GOD WANTS HIS CHILDREN TO BE HOLY

This should be enough in itself to make every Christian agree to the desire of God's heart. A man deserves to have his name blotted out of Christ's roll-call if he does not stay ready to march or even run forward at the Master's signal. David, who 'served his own generation by the will of God,' made it the priority of his life to carry out God's desires (*Acts 13:36*). And every heart touched with the same magnet of God's love will want to do this.

All the personal ambitions of a sincere saint are swallowed up in this, that he may do the will of God in his generation. This is all his prayer – 'Not my will, but thine, be done' (*Luke 22:42*). His sole purpose is to find and do the 'good, and acceptable, and perfect, will of God' (*Rom. 12:2*). Now I want to show you how I know it is God's will for all His children to be holy. It runs like a silver thread through all His other designs.

(a) *In His decrees*

Why did God choose some men and leave others to sink in torment and misery? The apostle tells us 'He hath chosen us in him before the foundation of the world, that we

[153]

should be *holy*' (*Eph. 1:4*). Not because God foresaw that we of ourselves would ever be holy, but because He resolved He would make us holy. It was as if a highly skilled carpenter saw a forest of trees growing on his own ground – all alike, not one better than another – and he marked a certain number and set them apart in his mind, determining to make of them some wonderfully crafted objects.

Thus God chose some out of all mankind and set them apart to carve His own image of righteousness and holiness upon them. This is workmanship of such high quality that when He has finished it, and will show it to men and angels, it will outshine the universe itself.

(b) *In sending His Son into the world*

Glorious angels who behold the face of God continually are ready to fly immediately wherever He assigns them. But God had such an important work to be done that He would not trust His servants, but rather His only Son, to accomplish it. And note the motive, the bottom of His heart in this great undertaking: He 'gave himself for us, that he might redeem us from all iniquity, and purify unto himself a peculiar people, zealous of good works' (*Tit. 2:14*).

If man had kept the righteousness which God originally created in him, Christ's pain would have been spared, for it was man's lost holiness He came to recover. Neither God's glory nor man's happiness could be attained until this holiness was restored. As God is glorious in the holiness of His own nature and works, so He is glorified by the holiness of His people's hearts.

When man's carnal nature bows to the influence of sin, can he give God glory and defy Him at the same time? If Christ's purpose had been merely to forgive man but not to restore his holiness, He would have been sin's minister, and man would have unrestrained freedom to dishonor God.

Man's happiness rests in his likeness to God and his enjoyment of Him. But he must be like God before God can take pleasure in him. Further, God must take full contentment in man before He lets him enjoy Him – so then Christ undertakes the miracle of making His people holy: 'Be ye holy; for I am holy' (*1 Pet. 1:16*).

The apostle Paul was quite justified in bringing a heavy charge against all unholy persons in that 'they are the enemies of the cross of Christ' (*Phil. 3:18*). Christ came to destroy the works of the devil, but the careless walker goes about trying to destroy the work of Christ. The Lord Jesus has laid down His heart's blood to redeem souls out of the hand of sin and Satan so they can freely serve God without fear, in holiness. Yet the loose Christian – if indeed he can be called a Christian – denies the Lord that bought him and gravitates to his old bondage from which Christ ransomed him with a precious price.

(c) *In the regenerating work of the Spirit*

Because it is God's will to make His people righteous, He promises: 'A new heart also will I give you, and a new spirit will I put within you' (*Ezek. 36:26*). An old heart would serve well enough to accomplish the devil's drudgery. But because God has a higher place for His people, His mighty Spirit lifts their head out of sin's dungeon and brings them into His personal courts of service. Thus He throws away their jail-clothes and beautifies them with the graces of His Spirit. This is regeneration.

When God ordered the temple to be built with such precise care and costly materials, He declared it for holy use. But that structure was not nearly so glorious as the spiritual temple of a regenerate heart, which is the

[155]

'workmanship' of God Himself (*Eph. 2:10*). And why has He been such a compassionate Artisan? We read that His saints are 'created in Christ Jesus unto good works, which God hath before ordained that we should walk in them' (*v. 10*).

God's exalted purpose for man, then, underscores the unrighteousness of a saint and hands down a more serious verdict upon his sin than upon the sin of others because it has been committed against such a mighty work of His Spirit. A sin in the temple was more grave than that same sin committed by a Jew in his house, because the temple was a consecrated place. Because the saint is a consecrated person, then, his unholy acts profane God's temple. The sin of a natural man is theft because he robs God of the glory due to him; but the sin of a saint is sacrilege because he robs God of the sacredness which his profession of faith has vowed to Him.

Surely it is better not to repent at all than to repent of our repentance. Scripture says it is better for us not to vow and dedicate ourselves to Him than later to scheme so we can sidestep that promise (*Eccles. 5:5*). To do this, the person must tell the world a baneful lie – that he has found some weakness or iniquity in God which changed his mind about following Him.

In a word, the Holy Spirit has consecrated the saint to God and also endues him with new life from God: 'You hath he quickened, who were dead in trespasses and sins' (*Eph. 2:1*). When God breathed a rational soul into man, he purposed that he should live up to His principles of holiness and righteousness and not follow the ways of life of carnal men. God clearly spoke His mind – 'As ye have therefore received Christ Jesus the Lord, so walk ye in him' (*Col. 2:6*).

The apostle Paul blames the Corinthians for living

below their calling, like men of the world, in corrupt passions. 'Are ye not carnal, and walk as men?' (*1 Cor. 3:3*). Some sin against the light of God in their consciences; that is the worst they can do. But when you act in an unholy manner, Christian, you are sinning against the very life of God in your heart.

The more unnatural a sin is, the more horrible it is. For example, it is not natural for a mother to kill the child in her womb. Yet by your unholy walk you are killing the babe of grace in your soul. Herod has been branded a bloody criminal because he would have butchered Christ when He was a newborn on earth; so can you continually attempt the murder of Christ newly formed in your heart and expect to escape God's anger?

(d) *In God's Word and ordinances*

The Word of God is both seed to beget and food to nourish holiness in the Christian's heart; every part of it contributes abundantly to this design.

(i) *The preceptive part.* This portion of God's Word affords a perfect rule of holiness for saints to walk by, one which is not changeable and vague, as men's laws are. Those laws are often made to fit crooked minds, as tailors alter garments to fit the crooked bodies they are designed for. The commands of God are suited to His holy nature, not to the unholy hearts of men.

(ii) *The promises.* God has made these as encouragements to draw us along the way of holiness. But the promises are so cautiously laid out that an unholy heart cannot claim any of them. God has set a flaming sword – conscience – inside the sinner to keep him from tasting the fruit from this tree of life. And if a profane person is so bold as to touch the treasure locked up in the promises he cannot keep it very long; sooner or later God makes him throw it down as Judas did his thirty pieces of silver. His

[157]

conscience will let him know he is not the rightful owner of it. False comforts from the promises, like riches, 'make themselves wings' and 'fly away' from the unholy man, just when he thinks they are his (*Prov. 23:5*).

(iii) *The threatenings*. The admonishing and warning part of Scripture rushes like a devouring river on either side of the narrow path of holiness and righteousness, ready to swallow up every soul who does not walk in it. 'For the wrath of God is revealed from heaven against all ungodliness and unrighteousness of men' (*Rom. 1:18*).

(iv) *Examples*. God's goodness did not leave us without examples in the way we should walk. God's promises are confirmed by holy men and women who have beaten the path of holiness for us and 'through faith and patience' have obtained these promises in heaven. What unspeakable comfort to us who are climbing the hill after them! But God has also added examples of unholy men who have damned their own souls to hell. Their carcasses have been washed up on the shore of the Word, exposed to our view in reading so we will not be engulfed in the sins which drowned them in hell. 'These things were our examples, to the intent we should not lust after evil things, as they also lusted' (*1 Cor. 10:6*).

Just as a doctor may prepare the same medication several ways to make it more effective and to refresh his patient, so the Lord gives His Word in the ordinances of sacraments, prayer, hearing, or meditation. His Word is the subject matter of them all and His purpose remains the same in them all – to bring about holiness in His children. The ordinances of God, then, are veins and arteries by which Christ conveys His lifeblood of holiness into every member of His mystical body. The church is the garden, Christ the fountain, and every ordinance is a pipe from Him to water the beds, making them more abundant in the fruits of righteousness.

(v) *In all His providences*. 'All things work together for good to them that love God' (*Rom. 8:28*). As God uses all seasons of the year for the harvest – the ice and cold of winter as well as the heat of summer – so He uses both good and bad, pleasing and unpleasing providences, for promoting holiness. Winter providences kill the weeds of lust and summer providences ripen the fruits of righteousness.

Even when God afflicts it is for our good, to make us partakers of His holiness. Bernard has compared afflictions to a sharp, scratching burr called a teasel, which was used to make cloth more pure and fine. And God loves purity in His children so much that He will rub as hard as He has to in order to get out the dirt ingrained in our natures; He would rather see a hole than a spot in His child's garment.

But sometimes God's sovereign direction is more gentle, and when He lets His people sit under the sunny bank of comfort, sheltered from the cold gusts of affliction, it is to draw forth the sap of grace and hasten their growth in holiness. Paul understood this when he urged the Roman saints 'by the mercies of God' to present their bodies 'a living sacrifice, holy, acceptable unto God' (*Rom. 12:1*). He implied that God expects a reasonable return on the mercies, mercies which have all come from Him.

When the farmer lays his compost on the ground, he intends to receive it again at harvest in a fuller crop; and so does God, by His mercies. Thus He firmly indicted Israel for her unthankfulness: 'She did not know that I gave her corn, and wine, and oil, and multiplied her silver and gold, which they prepared for Baal' (*Hos. 2:8*). God was angry because Israel embraced adultery at His expense.

Surely the Father would not have His children to taste any unclean thing. The nourishment God wants for Himself and His children is made up of the pleasant fruits of holiness and righteousness which Christ comes into His garden to feed on: 'I am come into my garden, my sister, my spouse: I have gathered my myrrh with my spice; I have eaten my honeycomb with my honey; I have drunk my wine with my milk' (*Song of Sol. 5:1*).

II. SATAN WANTS GOD'S PEOPLE TO BE UNHOLY

The devil's design is so strong against the saint's holiness that he always has a *no* for God's *yes*. The devil delights to lodge in man. Even when he dwelled in the serpent, it was to deceive Eve. If he could choose his address it would always be *man*, because only he is capable of sin and unrighteousness.

Just as Satan prefers to live in men, he would rather possess their souls than their bodies. Nothing but the best room in the house will serve him as the place to vomit blasphemies and spit out his malice toward God, since the soul is the proper seat for holiness or sin.

In all the ways Satan plagued Job, he never chose to make a forcible entry and possess his body. Not that pity influenced his decision; he was holding out for higher stakes, hoping to possess Job's soul. It would have been a thousand times more satisfying if Job himself had blasphemed God (rather than the devil, having possessed Job's body, belching out curses through him). That would have been Job's sin, not Satan's.

Your holiness is what the devil wants to steal from you. He calls no gain victory until he makes a Christian lose his righteousness. And he will allow a man to have anything, or be anything, rather than be truly and powerfully holy. It is not your riches and worldly pleasures he covets; it is your holiness. For all we know, Job might have enjoyed his herds and children and servants without any disturbance from hell, if Satan had not seen him to be a godly man – 'one that feared God, and eschewed evil' (*Job 1:1*).

But when Job's righteousness ignited Satan's wicked spirit, his anger spread like a torch. He tried to strip Job of his breastplate of righteousness by butchering his family, destroying his estate, and scoring his body with boils. He tortured Job the way thieves torment their victims to make them confess and give up their treasures. If Job at any moment had thrown Satan his purse – his integrity – and let him take his conscience captive, Satan would have unbound him immediately, not minding if he regained property and children and servants.

Wolves tear the fleece so they can devour the flesh of the sheep and suck his blood. And the lifeblood of holiness is what this hellish murderer hungers to drain from the Christian's heart. It is not a form of godliness, or counterfeit displays of righteousness, but the *power* which Satan slanders. It is not the name but the new nature itself which brings this lion out of his den.

The devil can live peaceably and confidently as a quiet neighbor to the man who is satisfied with an empty name of profession. Satan knew, for example, that Judas' profession of faith did not put him one step out of his way to hell; the subtle deceiver can usher a person to damnation even through ordinances of Christian worship. Because the covetous heart which Judas carried with him to hear Christ's sermons tied him to the devil, Satan allowed plenty of freedom for the traitor to keep his reputation awhile. He did not care how long the disciples thought he was a believer – Satan knew his personal slave.

In a word, superstitious holiness does not bother Satan. How can it, when he is its father? Through the ages it has been his purpose to undermine genuine holiness in the hearts of men, but the church has discovered the wicked conspiracy Satan has plotted against Christ and Christ's people. His counterfeit has been to the power of holiness what the ivy is to the oak. The lewd embraces of this hollow holiness round about religion have smothered the heart of scriptural holiness wherever it has prevailed.

Not even religious affluence bothers the devil; he is a sworn enemy of holiness in its naked simplicity as it is founded on Scripture and nurtured by the Holy Spirit.

Simple holiness, then, is the flag which the soul hangs out to declare open defiance of Satan and friendship with God, even as the devil strives to shoot it down. And here is the ground of that quarrel, which will never end as long as Satan is an unclean spirit and the saint a holy child of God: 'All that will live godly in Christ Jesus shall suffer persecution' (*2 Tim. 3:12*).

Persecutors often try to disguise their malice under the pretense of good works; but the Spirit of God looks through their hypocritical mufflers and knows the instructions they have from hell. God's Spirit tells us that godliness is the target at which Satan levels his arrows. Of course there are more kinds of godliness in the world than one, but Satan opposes only the true one: 'all that will live godly *in Christ Jesus*.'

Christian blood is sweet to Satan but the blood of the Christian's godliness is far sweeter. He prefers to sever the saint from his godliness rather than butcher him for it. Yet so he will not be too conspicuous, he often plays at small game and expresses his cruelty upon saints' bodies; but this happens only when he cannot capture their souls: 'They were sawn asunder, were tempted, were slain' (*Heb. 11:37*). What the persecutors wanted more than anything else was to entice them into sin and apostasy; thus they tempted Christians severely before they killed them. The devil considers it a complete triumph if he can strip away the saint's armour and bribe him away from steadfastness in his holy profession.

The devil would rather see Christians defiled with sin and unrighteousness than defiled in blood and pain, for he has learned that persecution only trims the church, which soon comes right back up all the thicker; it is unrighteousness which ruins it. Persecutors, then, only plow God's field for Him and all the time He is sowing it with the saints' blood.

THE EXCELLENCY OF THE POWER OF HOLINESS

I. IT APPEARS ONLY IN MAN

Inferior creatures have a certain goodness proper to them, but only intellectual beings are capable of inward holiness. And if we give up our crown of holiness we become worse than beasts themselves; indeed, it is righteousness which makes one man differ from another in God's eye.

All men stand on level ground before God until holiness is added. Earthly kings have the power and prerogative to assess the just value of every coin – how much every penny is worth. Surely, then, the sovereign God has even more right to say, 'The righteous is more excellent than his neighbor;' or 'The tongue of the just is as choice silver,' and 'The heart of the wicked is little worth' (*Prov. 12:26; 10:20*).

II. IT FURNISHES EVIDENCE FOR HEAVEN

'Follow peace . . ., and holiness without which no man shall see the Lord' (*Heb. 12:14*). Before Enoch was translated to heaven he walked the earth with God as a holy man; and this is why God wanted him in heaven with Him, for heaven is a city where righteousness dwells. Can we actually expect to get there when we do not care about keeping our behavior holy or about exercising righteous acts of godliness? Certainly what God has written about holiness will stand; He shall never blot out or revise His Word for anybody. So we must either renounce our hope of going to heaven or resolve to walk in the only path that will lead us there. It is vain breath which does not set the sails of our affections and the movement of our feet in the direction of our desired destination.

III. IT EMPOWERS US FOR COMMUNION WITH GOD

Communion with God is so wonderful that many pretend to have it when they do not even know what it is. It is like the man who brags about knowing the king but never has seen his face nor met him. God's Spirit calls it a lie when a man says he knows the Lord but entertains unrighteousness too: 'If we say that we have fellowship with him, and walk in darkness, we lie' (*1 John 1:6*). Communion is rooted in union, and union in likeness. 'Can two walk together, except they be agreed?' (*Amos 3:3*). There is a big difference between communion with God and familiarity with ordinances. A man may live with ordinances every day but still be a stranger to God. Not everyone who walks around in the palace talks with the prince.

Ordinances are a kind of exchange where holy saints trade with God by His Spirit for heavenly treasures, an enriched filling of grace and comfort. But because an unholy heart has nothing to trade with God, the Father will not communicate His pure grace to him. Even the holy person under the power of a temptation is unfit to have communion with God until he overcomes the sin.

Solomon explained it like this: 'A righteous man falling down before the wicked is as a troubled fountain, and a corrupt spring' (*Prov. 25:26*). How much more true when a saint falls before the wicked one and yields to temptation, his spirit clouded with impurity! If we know better than to drink from a troubled spring, though wholesome in itself, but wait until it settles and becomes clear again, how can we expect God to taste communion with a godly person before his stream runs clear with repentance for sin?

IV. IT PROVIDES PEACE

I do not say that peace is founded on our holiness or righteousness, but it is supported and attended by these. 'There is no peace, saith the Lord, unto the wicked' (*Isa. 48:22*). We could as easily force the sea to stay always still as we could make the unholy heart quiet. Wars inside a man's heart are started by his own lusts and make him feel torn in two. These break the peace and keep the man in continual tempest. Yet if the spirit of holiness comes and Christ's 'sceptre of righteousness' takes sweet control over the life, this storm is calmed more and more.

The unholy ways of unrighteous men, however, walk around in their thoughts as John's ghost troubled Herod. While both asleep and awake they have the terrors and scent of hell-fire all about them. This restlessness makes men discontented in every situation – they cannot enjoy the sweetest pleasures nor bear the bitter taste of afflictions. Of course there are ways to deaden the conscience and bind up the feelings of an unholy heart temporarily; but the strength of this opium soon wears off and the horror returns with an even more severe attack.

Let me share an example. A notorious drunkard shook off the warnings which Christians had tried to fasten on to his conscience, as easily as Paul dropped the viper from his hand. Instead of surrendering to God he forged ahead into more sin, fortifying his mind with the presumptuous hope of God's mercy in Christ. After a few years, though, the man got sick; and when his companions visited, he was so cheerful and confident in God's mercy that his false hopes motivated them to indulge in lusts even more. Yet just before death came the old sinner's guilty conscience was fully awakened, and the poor man roasted in the scorching flames of his former ungodly practices. And as he died he screamed in despair: 'I had prepared a plaster, and thought everything was all right; but now it will not stick any longer!' His condemned conscience tore his hope away as fast as his trembling hands could put it on.

This is true, my friends. The blood of Christ Himself will not cleave to an unrepentant soul which holds any sin in his heart. God will pluck up men from the altar who run *to* it, but not *from* their unrighteousness. Then He will slay them in sight of the sanctuary which they had so boldly trusted in.

You know the message of Solomon to Adonijah: 'If he will shew himself a worthy man, there shall not a hair of him fall . . . ; but if wickedness shall be found in him, he shall die' (*1 Kings 1:52*). It is futile for a man to think he can hide under Christ's wing from the cry of his accusing conscience if wickedness is taking sanctuary in him. God never intended to secure us *in* unrighteousness but to save us *from* it.

V. IT HAS A STRONG INFLUENCE ON OTHERS

When this power of holiness works in the lives of Christians it mightily affects the spirits of men. It stops the mouths of the ungodly who are ready to reproach religion and to throw the dirt of a saint's sin in the face of every profession of faith they hear. It is said that frogs stop croaking when light is brought near them. And the light of a holy life serves as a padlock on profane lips and forces the sinner to acknowledge God in the saint: 'Let your light so shine before men, that they may see your good works, and glorify your Father which is in heaven' (*Matt. 5:16*). Not only does the power of holiness shut their mouths, but it

[166]

opens their hearts to embrace Christ and His grace.

One reason so many souls came into the gospel net in early times was that the divinity of the gospel doctrine was evident in the holiness of Christians' lives. Justin Martyr, for instance, writing of his own conversion, said: 'The holiness which shined in Christians' lives and the patience that triumphed over their enemies' cruelty at their deaths made me conclude the doctrine of the gospel was truth.' And even Julian, as far from the kingdom as he was, reported that Christianity was growing because Christians were a people who 'did good to all and hurt to none.'

Yet in these times when scandal spatters the robes of righteousness in the Christian religion, it is harder to get those outside to come under the net of the gospel. There are some animals which, when they as much as breathe on the grass, will by that keep others from feeding in that pasture for some time. And, sadly, until the bad reputation of pride, dissension, error, and carelessness has worn off, there is not much hope of crowds of converts flowing into Christianity.

The minister cannot preach day and night – he may spend two or three hours a week in the pulpit holding the mirror of the gospel before the faces of his congregation; but the lives of Christians preach all week long. If they were holy they would serve as a repetition of the minister's sermon to families in the world and would keep the gospel sound continually ringing in their ears.

Nobody enjoys talking to a person who has bad breath, and that is the way we often think of the person who speaks to us in reproof. Thus Christians need a sweet-scented life when they must reprove and give counsel. Reproofs are good strong medicine but it is hard for a person not to vomit them up in the face of him who gives them. Now nothing is more effective to keep a reproof

THE CHRISTIAN IN COMPLETE ARMOUR

from being spit out than the holiness of the one who reproves. 'Let the righteous smite me,' said David. 'It shall be a kindness: and let him reprove me; it shall be an excellent oil, which shall not break my head' (*Ps. 141:5*). Reproof can be more easily received from such a hand because of the authority that accompanies holiness.

No one but a hardened sinner will fight back at the righteous man who has given reproof softly, like oil gently rubbed into an infection, with compassion and love to the hurting person. Thus it is easy to see how influential the power of holiness would be in the life of the wicked man. And it is no less effective upon Christian brothers and sisters.

When a Christian sees holiness sparkle in the life of another believer, the grace within him springs up as the baby in Elisabeth leaped at the sound of Mary's voice. Truly, one holy man is enough to put life into a whole society; but on the contrary, the looseness of a single professing Christian endangers the entire group of people who know him. Therefore God has given us a strict charge: 'Follow peace with all men, and holiness . . . , looking diligently lest any man fail of the grace of God; lest any root of bitterness springing up trouble you, and thereby many be defiled' (*Heb. 12:14–15*).

A scab on the wolf's back is not dangerous to the sheep because they cannot easily be lured to spend time with him. But if the sore spreads into the flock, among Christians who feed, pray, hear, talk, and walk in fellowship together, then there is a great fear and danger it might spread. Thus a careless Christian helps the devil with more efficiency than whole troops who never profess to believe. In fact, Satan had a whole fistful of sins and errors that he did not know what to do with until he found a way to hire unholy professors of the faith as his brokers to recommend and dispense them to others.

In a word, then, the man who will not keep up the power of holiness in his life, in some measure, makes himself useless to Christ. Do you want to pray for others? A heathen could tell an evil man to hold his peace and not let the gods know he was aboard the ship when a storm swept in. Is it comfort you want to speak to a grieving person? Or counsel to a friend? They will think you are only joking until your commendation of holiness is joined by holiness in your own life; that is to say, until you commend it to yourself.

VI. HOLINESS AND RIGHTEOUSNESS ARE THE PILLARS
OF NATIONS

Righteous men are the only ones who keep a nation's roof from falling in on its people's head. The presence of 'ten righteous men' could have prevented the fire and brimstone which consumed Sodom and entombed her people in their own ashes. Indeed, that judgment was delayed and the destroying angel's hands tied as long as the righteous man Lot was among them: 'Haste thee, escape thither; for I cannot do anything till thou be come thither' (*Gen. 19:22*).

God records other examples of unrighteousness and righteousness turning the tide of history. Rehoboam and his kingdom were strengthened for three years, and might have been for twenty more, if his unrighteousness had not pulled it down upon himself and his people; for this downfall is dated from the very day he walked away from God (*2 Chron. 11, 12*).

On the other hand, when Josiah came to the crown he found Judah crumbling to pieces; yet because his heart was turned to God, and prepared to walk before Him, God accepted Josiah's plea for a people under arrest and at the prison door. Their safety was linked to the ruler's life, for

soon after Josiah died the nation tumbled into ruin again
(*2 Kings 23:25–27*).

When Martin Luther foresaw the black cloud of God's
judgment coming toward Germany he told friends that he
would do his best to keep it from falling in his lifetime; and
he believed that it would not. But he concluded, 'When I
am gone, let them that come after me look to it.'

The power of holiness has deteriorated among us,
compared to what it was a generation ago! Christianity
runs unclean and full of dregs, murky and unholy among
professing believers in Christ. And we know God will not
put up with it much longer. If Egypt knows a drought is
coming by the low ebbing of the Nile, surely we can see
judgment hovering by the fall of the power of godliness.

We hear many people mourning for what they have lost
– some for the lives of friends in war, others for their
wealth and possessions. But the group who must claim
first place among mourners are church-goers who have
lost their first love. Thorough decay has set in because
they have forfeited their compassion for Christ, His truth,
worship, fellow servants, and their holy walk before God
and man.

We are a people redeemed from countless dangers and
deaths. It is a poor time for a rescued man to start stealing
and cheating again, as soon as the rope is cut from his
neck. Surely it added to Noah's sin to be drunk almost as
soon as he had safely landed on shore, after he had seen the
whole earth sinking before his eyes. Here was the one
righteous man God had left to plant His world again with a
godly seed.

The earth has hardly yet drunk in the rivers of blood
which have been shed in our land, and the towns are still
digging out of the debris which the miseries of war piled
on them. The sounds of grieving widows and orphans,

whom the sword bereaved, are not yet stilled by their own deaths. Once we were terrified to see this nation – like a candle lighted at both ends – burning every day with the flames coming nearer and nearer us. Yet now the people who claim Christ's name are forgetful and are still turning away from God to prefer pride and lust.

What right do we have to celebrate our peace, when the result of our deliverance is that we presume to commit worse abominations? This is like one whose malaria has gone but its after-effects leave him in poorer health than the disease itself did. Surely our God laments to look at the exchange: to have war, pestilence, and famine removed, and to be left swollen up with selfishness, error, and defiant, godless behavior.

Again, we are a people who have made more pretensions to righteousness and holiness than our forefathers ever did. Or what did all the prayers to God and petitions to man mean? We put ourselves under a covenant for personal reformation and then another for national reformation. These intentions echoed such a loud report in foreign nations that our neighbor churches wondered how these glorious beginnings might ripen. But now, after putting forth leaves and thereby telling God and man to expect fruit from us, our barren condition brings us nearer to a curse than ever before for disappointing the just expectations of both.

Nothing can save the life of a nation, or lengthen peace through mercy to it, except the recovery of the much decayed power of holiness. This surge of righteousness would be as a spring of new blood to a dying body, reviving it and bringing many more happy days, more than it has ever seen before. Yet we are degenerating from bad to worse, and wasting in lingering death. Each day our breath gets shorter and shallower. If the sword should be drawn among us, would we really have enough strength to survive?

2. How the Christian Expresses the Power of Holiness

IN THE CONTEST WITH SIN

I. AVOID THE APPEARANCE OF SIN

Walking in holiness means refusing to commit sin and shunning the appearance of evil at the same time. The dove flies away from the hawk, but she will not so much as smell a single feather that falls from its body either. Scripture commands us to hate 'even the garment spotted by the flesh' (*Jude 23*). A clean (and sane) person would not think of washing his hands in sewage – only the deranged would do that. But neither does this man come close enough to the conduit to get a tiny spot of filth on him as he eats his meal. The Christian, then, should keep his name as pure as his conscience.

Bernard's three questions are worth asking when we are in doubt whether or not to do something. First, *is it lawful?* May I do it and not sin? Second, *is it becoming to a Christian?* The behavior which commoners practice – is it fit for the prince? Nehemiah knew his kinship to God made him a special person: 'Should such a man as I flee?' (*6:11*). Finally, *is it expedient?* May I do it without offending my weaker brother?

Although a man could run his horse at full speed without harming himself, he might do irreparable damage if he raced through a town with children in the streets. There are some things you could do if there were no weak Christians in your path whose tender consciences might be run over and badly bruised.

Unfortunately the Christian way appears too narrow for many professing people nowadays; they must have more room for their broad-mindedness, or else leave their alleged faith behind altogether. *Freedom is the Diana of our generation.* For example, we are seeing widespread accept-ance of ungodly appearance – elaborate, worldly hair styles, gaudy and sensual fashions, painted faces, naked breasts. There was a time when solid Christians censured immodest personal appearance and apparel, but now the jury finds these questionable practices to be 'not guilty.' Many are so attached to the way of the world that they think it is wrong to draw the line on Christ's side of Christian liberty.

Some people who call themselves Christians are so far from holy living that they virtually have contests to see who can come the closest to the pit of sin without falling in. Yet Paul's warning was straightforward and strong: 'Abstain from all appearance of evil' (*1 Thess. 5:22*). The person who saunters out into the appearance of evil in the name of 'freedom in the Spirit' may find himself commit-ting gross sin under some appearance of good.

II. COMBAT SIN FOR GOD'S REASONS

Some people resist sin for such shallow motives that God hardly notices their victory. When we have fasted and prayed He asks, 'Did ye at all fast unto me, even to me?' (*Zech. 7:5*). When we are unselfish and kind to others, though, a 'cup of cold water' given 'in the name of a disciple' is more valuable in God's sight than a cup of gold for selfish purposes (*Matt. 10:42*).

God wants it to be His love which constrains us to renounce sin. Princes prefix documents with their coat of arms and royal names before sending them out; and God sets His glorious name before His commandments too – 'God spake all these words' (*Exod. 20:1*). God would have His children to sanctify His name in everything they do.

Just as the Father commands His family to turn away

[173]

from evil, it is for His sake that He wants us to mourn over those sins we do commit. Sometimes grief can be so selfish that a man is satisfied to snatch his soul from eternal damnation even if this somehow defamed the glory of God. But a gracious soul's mourning runs in another channel: 'Against thee, thee only, have I sinned' (*Ps. 51:4*).

There is a vast difference between a man who works for another person and one who is his own boss. The independent person assumes all his losses himself, but the servant who trades with his master's stock must put every loss on that account. Christian, you are a servant. All you have is not really yours, but God's. And when you fall into sin, your sorrow must be for the way you have wronged *Him*: 'I have dishonored my God and wasted the talents He has given me; I have wounded His name and grieved His Spirit.'

III. MORTIFY SIN

A hidden wound may be covered but not healed; it is possible for physicians to drive disease deeper into the body if they do not drive out the cause of it. If that happens, corruption, like unslaked lime, is left inside the person to burst into flames, though now it may lie quietly like gunpowder in a barrel.

Historians say that the opening up of a chest of clothes – which had not been aired and cleared from infection in the house – was the cause of a great plague in Venice, though the clothing had lain there for many years without causing any danger. Thus some men walk a long time in the unblameable role of saints before they stumble into abominations like the opening of that apparently harmless chest – all because they have never mortified sin. Nothing less than death to the roots of sin can satisfy the life of a holy Christian – and his God.

Hear the words of the apostle Paul, who walked in the power of holiness: 'I die daily' (*1 Cor. 15:31*). Sin is like the beast which almost died of its wounds but as time passed, was strangely healed and active again. Thus many Christians who do not keep a constant, tight rein over latent corruption have been thrown from the saddle and dragged precariously into temptation. Because they are unable to fight off the fury of lust, when it gains the upper hand they are broken and crushed from a tragic fall into sin.

So if you want to grow in the power of holiness, Christian, never give up your work of mortifying sin, even when temptations are out of sight. A person who has allergies takes medication not only when he has an attack but continually, to prevent sickness. So then the saint should endeavor to keep his soul spiritually healthy every day, regardless of what his feelings tell him. Finally, avoid the practice of some who take in healthful nourishment one day but swallow enough swill the next to seriously retard their growth in holiness.

IV. GROW IN THE GRACE CONTRARY TO THE SIN

Just as each poison has an antidote, every sin has its opposite grace. And the Christian who wants to walk in the power of holiness must not only work to avoid sin but to possess this contrary grace. In Scripture we read of a house which stood empty because the Holy Spirit did not come in after the evil spirit had been driven out. A merely negative Christian, then, will leave the sin he once walked in but still will not move toward holiness. This is to lose heaven with short-shooting. God will not ask us where we were *not*, but where we *were*! It is not enough that we did not swear and take God's name in vain. God will ask, 'But did you sanctify My name?' It will not be enough that we did not persecute Christ; instead, God will want to know, 'Did you receive Him?' Maybe we did not hate His saints –

[175]

yet did we demonstrate love for them? 'It is true you never drank yourself into a drunken stupor, but were you filled with the Holy Spirit?'

A competent physician both gets rid of disease and supplies strength. And the true Christian will not be satisfied with the bare laying aside of wrong choices but will keep trying to exercise himself in the corresponding graces. For example, are you frustrated and impatient because of affliction? It is not enough for you to silence your quarrel with God; do not stop until you bring your heart to rely on Him. David did more than chastise his soul for being disquieted; he commanded it to trust in God and then to praise Him.

Are you holding a secret grudge against a brother? God wants you to quench that spark of hell; but also He expects you to kindle a heavenly fire of love that will cause you to pray fervently for him. When you have an envious or unkind thought – and who is so holy that he does not have such vermin crawling around at times? – go to the throne of grace and strongly protest against your sins and earnestly ask for the increase of good.

V. FIGHT SIN IN THE LIVES OF OTHERS

A loyal citizen is one who not only works to live quietly under his government, but is also ready to serve that authority against those who refuse to obey it. True holiness, like true love, begins at home – but it is not confined behind its own doors. It takes action against sin wherever it might show itself.

A person who is so neutral that he does not care how much his companions slander God might well question his own attitude toward sin. David asked, 'Do I not hate them, O Lord, that hate thee? and am I not grieved with those that rise up against thee? I hate them with perfect hatred: I count them mine enemies' (Ps. 139:21, 22).

Right after that he asks God to ransack his heart: 'Search me, O God, and know my heart: try me, and know my thoughts: and see if there be any wicked way in me' (*vv. 23, 24*). David's prayer is a model of sincerity. It is as if he had said, 'Lord, this is as far as my line can measure; but if it is possible that sin could be hiding in a place beyond my reach, please find it out for me and "lead me in the way everlasting" ' (*v. 24*).

VI. DENY SELF-GLORY

Every Christian who earnestly fights sin must be careful to deny all temptation to glory in his triumph over it. The very excellency of gospel holiness consists in self-denial: 'Though I were perfect,' said Job, 'yet would I not know my soul' – that is, 'I would not be conceited and proud of my innocence' (*Job 9:21*).

When a man's talent merits attention and his pride rises to the occasion we say, 'He has done a good job, but he knows it.' He reflects too much on himself and enjoys his own face too often in the mirror of achievement. The higher mountain climbers ascend, the more they stoop with their bodies to stay safe; and Christ's Spirit teaches saints the same principle. The higher we climb to overcome sin, the more we must bow in self-denial.

Scripture instructs us to keep ourselves in the love of God and to wait, 'looking for the mercy of our Lord Jesus Christ unto eternal life' (*Jude 21*). We are to 'sow in righteousness' and 'reap in mercy' (*Hos. 10:12*) – that is, Christians sow on earth to reap in heaven. The seed is righteousness; and when this sowing has been done, we are not to expect reward from the hand of our holiness but from God's mercy.

IN WORSHIP

The same light which shows us there is a God shows us He

[177]

must be worshiped in holiness. Under the law, God was particular about every facet of worship. The tabernacle, for example, had to be made of the best materials; the workmen were gifted with rare talent; only the most excellent sacrifices were acceptable; and the persons who ministered to the Lord had to be holy in a peculiar way. God is wonderful in His worship!

I. BE CONSISTENT IN ALL ORDINANCES

God hates partiality, especially in ordinances of worship, all of which have their origins in Him. And surely we must not reject anything God chooses as a blessing to His children. He communicates Himself with amazing variety to keep our hearts encouraged. The spouse looks for her Beloved in secret at home but does not find him; so she goes to the public places and meets him whom her 'soul loveth' (*Song of Sol. 3:4*).

No doubt Daniel had been to the throne of grace often, but God reserved the fulness of His love, and the opening of some mysteries to him, when he added fasting to his prayers. Only then did God send a messenger from heaven to let Daniel know His mind and heart.

The Holy Spirit sometimes gives more blessing in some duties than He does in others, to fill the Christian with extraordinary refreshment. Sometimes the baby takes milk from one breast and then from the other. While David was *meditating*, a heavenly heat kindled in his heart until at last the fire caught and spread. The eunuch was *reading* the Word when God sent Philip to join his chariot. Christ revealed Himself to the apostles as they were *breaking bread*. And He joined the two disciples on the road to Emmaus as they were *having fellowship* with each other. Cornelius was *praying* in his house when a vision from heaven directed him in the way he should walk.

Be careful, then, Christian, not to neglect any one privilege of worship – it might be the door where Jesus stands waiting to enter your soul! The Spirit is free. Do not bind Him to one duty only; but wait on Him in every one of them. It is not wisdom to let any water run past your mill which might be useful to send your soul moving toward heaven.

Maybe you do not receive as much enlightenment as you want when you seek God in public services. Let me ask you this – what kind of communion do you have with Him in secret? Here is a hole wide enough to lose everything you get in public, if you do not repair it. Samuel would not sit down to the feast with Jesse and his sons until David – the youngest of the family – was brought in to join them. If you want God's presence in any of the ordinances you must bring back the one you sent away; it might be the least important in your way of thinking but the one God has chosen to crown with His most special blessing to your soul.

II. SEEK GOD'S GOALS

God has two purposes in worship. First, He intends for us to honor Him as sovereign Lord. And second, worship is the way He communicates His presence and blessings to His children.

(a) *Homage to our sovereign Lord*

If there were no worship, how could we declare that it is in Him that we live and move and have our being? One of the first things God taught Adam and his children was divine worship. And the holy person makes it the most important thing in his life to sanctify God's name and give Him glory. A subject may offer a present to his prince in such a ridiculous fashion that the ruler may be more scorned than honored; the soldiers bowed their knees to Jesus but their hearts mocked the holy God.

[179]

Our behavior betrays what we think of God. For instance, the man who performs spiritual duties with a holy awe upon his spirit, who comes to them filled with faith and fear, joy and trembling, he it is who declares plainly that he believes God to be a great and good God, glorious and majestic. But the person whose worship is careless and slovenly tells God to His face what crude and meager thoughts he has about Him.

Errors in worship happen because the person does not know the God he worships. Whatever is engraved on the seal will be printed on the wax. And a man's thoughts of God are reproduced in the religious services he performs. Abel proved to be holy while Cain showed himself to be wicked. The difference was that Abel aimed at the end which God held up for His worship, the sanctifying of His name.

(i) *Abel brought God his best.* Abel did not bring just any convenient animal from his flock, but offered the 'firstlings.' Nor did he give God the lean and keep the fat for himself; he gave God the best of the best. Cain, on the other hand, 'brought of the fruit of the ground an offering unto the Lord,' but Scripture does not record that it was the first fruit or even the best fruit (*Gen. 4:3*).

(ii) *Abel gave God his heart.* Abel did not hope God would be satisfied with a choice animal or two, though. Along with these he gave Him his heart. 'By faith Abel offered unto God a more excellent sacrifice than Cain' (*Heb. 11:4*). The inward worship of Abel's soul was what God took up with approval from him. And as a result, Abel obtained the precious testimony from God's own mouth that he was a righteous man.

Cain, on the other hand, thought it would be plenty – if not too much – to give God a little fruit of the ground. If he had considered who God was, and what His purpose was in requiring an offering of him, he could not possibly have reasoned that a handful or two of corn was in itself what God prized, except insofar as it be a sign of spiritual worship, which he expects to accompany outward ceremony.

Christians! Remember when you get ready to honor God that He will be worshiped as Himself. 'Cursed be the deceiver, which hath in his flock a male, and voweth, and sacrificeth unto the Lord a corrupt thing: for I am a great King, saith the Lord of hosts, and my name is dreadful among the heathen' (*Mal. 1:14*).

David was deeply conscientious about the temple he purposed in his heart to build because the palace was not for man, 'but for the Lord'; thus he prepared with all his might for the house of his God (*1 Chron. 29:1*). And we must approach worship with the same seriousness and humility: 'I am not ministering to man, but to the Lord God Almighty.'

(b) *Communication of God's blessings*

The psalmist spoke of Mount Zion, the place of God's worship where the temple stood: 'There the Lord commanded the blessing, even life for evermore' – grace and comfort which swelled into eternal life and streamed out from God to man. The saints of the church have always drawn their water out of these wells: 'Your heart shall live that seek God' (*Ps. 69:32*).

But the souls who will not seek God at Mount Zion must die. The farmer cannot expect a crop where he has not plowed or sowed; the merchant will not get rich if he never opens his doors to let customers in. And it is just as illogical for a person to expect the benefits of grace when he refuses to converse with the ways of God.

God does great things for those who commune with Him. The power of holiness appears when a person makes it his priority to seek and find God through worship. The diligent student who goes to the university gives up riches and fun so he can give himself to learning. And the holy Christian is stirred up by the Spirit of God to go from one aspect of worship to another, as a bee flies from flower to flower, to store up more grace.

The holy man does not seek God for an admirable reputation among Christians or for some sort of excitement. Instead, he is like the merchant who sails from port to port, not for sightseeing but for taking in costly pearls as he discovers them. And a Christian should be even more ashamed than the trader who returns home from his search empty, with no treasure.

Are you watching others grow rich in grace through their part in God's ordinances while you come away as a beggar? God sees a precious hunger in those who value Christ and His grace as the strongest need in their lives. 'Ho, every one that thirsteth, come ye to the waters, and he that hath no money; come ye, buy, and eat; yea, come, buy wine and milk without money and without price' (*Isa. 55:1*).

The Spirit of God alludes here to a custom in maritime towns – when a ship came in to port, her traders went about the village crying out the arrival of their goods: 'All who want certain commodities, let them come to the waterside, where they can be bought for a price.' Thus Christ calls everyone who sees his need of Him and of His graces to come to the ordinances, where these gifts can be had freely.

IN EMPLOYMENT

Holiness must be written upon the Christian's vocation as well as upon his religious services. The construction superintendent who observes the building code is as exact in framing the kitchen as he is the parlor; so by the law of Christianity we must be as precise in our worldly business as in the duties of worship. 'Be ye holy in *all* manner of conversation' (*1 Pet. 1:15*). We must not leave our religion, as some people leave their Bibles, on the pew at church.

Man's most complex ability – the power to reason – guides even his simplest actions, such as eating and drinking and sleeping. Similarly in a Christian, grace – the highest principle – is to steer him in *all* his behavior. The Christian is not to buy and sell as a mere natural man but as a Christian man.

Christianity is not like that statesman's robe which was thrown down when the man went to play: 'There, lord treasurer – you stay over there for a while.' No, wherever the Christian is, whatever he is doing, he must keep his holiness on. He must not do anything in which he cannot show he is a Christian. Now the power of holiness shines forth in our respective callings in several ways. And take the whole spectrum together and you will see 'the beauty of holiness' appear in the symmetry of all the parts (*Ps. 96:9*).

I. DILIGENCE

When God calls us to be Christians, He calls us out of the world but not out of work. It is true, when He called Elisha he left his plow; and the apostles put down their nets, but not because they were saints. These men were called to an office in the church. Some in our day are ready to send their preachers back to the plow; yet surely the pastor has his hands full, providing more for souls during the week than the layman provides for bodies.

But I am speaking to the private Christian. It is impossible for you to be holy if you are not diligent in a particular calling. The law of man labels a person a vagrant if he does not have a place to live; and God's Word counts the man disorderly who will not work at a job and act for God's glory through it. 'We hear that there are some which walk among you disorderly, working not at all' (*2 Thess. 3:11*).

God does want His people profitable, like sheep which do good to the ground they feed on. Everyone should be better for knowing a Christian. For instance, when Onesimus was converted, he became 'profitable' to Paul and to Philemon also – to Paul as a Christian and to Philemon as a servant (*Philem. 11*). Grace made a diligent servant out of a runaway. An idle believer is a useless believer; and while the man who will not work does no one any good, he hurts himself the most.

II. CONSCIENCE

Many men need no spur to drive them to diligence. Is it their conscience, because God commands it? No – if that were true they would pray as hard as they work; they would go when God says go and stop when He says stop. If conscience were the key that opened their shop on Monday, it would close it on Sunday.

Some people are like hawks flying so low after the world's prey that they will not accept God's most precious gifts. Although conscience in God's name calls to them – 'Come apart for awhile and wait on God for one day in your closet' – they still chase the world with a greedy diligence. It is plain to see what sends them on this trip – not conscience, but their own lusts.

If you want to walk in the power of holiness, though, you must be diligent in your work because of Christ in you. The same thing which makes you 'fervent in prayer' must make you 'not slothful in business' (*Rom. 12:11*). Your attitude will be an humble determination to please the Father: 'This is the place God has put me. I am His servant in my shop, and I must serve Him as I would have my children serve me – and even more so, for they are not mine as much as I am His.'

III. SUCCESS

The worldly person who does not go to his business every morning by way of a prayer closet rarely returns home in the evening to give thanks to God. He begins the day without God and it would be unusual for him to end it with Him. The spider that spins her web out of her own body dwells in it when she is through; and the person who operates his enterprises by his own ingenuity entitles himself to recognition as a 'self-made man.' Thus it is easier for such a person to worship his own wisdom than to worship God.

Once a man overheard his neighbor thanking God for the rich stand of corn in his field and reacted to this praise: 'Thank *God*? Why I would rather thank my manure-cart!' It was the speech of a sewer-spirit, more filthy than the load on his cart. If you want to be a Christian you must acknowledge God in all your ways and not lean unto your own understanding (*Prov. 3:6*). This selfless attitude will lead you to crown God with praise when success crowns your work.

Jacob worked as long and hard as any other business-man for his wealth; yet the foundation of his diligence was in prayer and in the expectation of blessing from heaven. He attributed his valuable holdings to the truth and mercy of God, who promised to provide for him when he was still a poor pilgrim on his way to Padan-aram (*Gen. 28:2–4*).

IV. CONTENTMENT

Necessity was the heathen's schoolmaster to teach contentment; but faith is the Christian's. Faith is what teaches the saint to enjoy the supplies of providence with sweet complacency as the will of God concerning him.

This is godliness that triumphs – when the Christian can carve contentment out of God's providence, no matter what dish it sets before him. If he gathers little, he is satisfied with his small meal. And if he gathers much, he has no more than his grace can digest and turn into good nourishment. Either way, there is nothing left over to gorge his pride.

Paul knew how 'to abound and to suffer need' (*Phil. 4:12*). If you take away contentment from godliness, you take away one of the loveliest gems she wears over her heart. 'Godliness with contentment is great gain,' not godliness with impressive worldly possessions (*1 Tim. 6:6*).

v. PRIORITY

The world operates with such an encroaching nature that it is hard for us to be friends with it and not be captured and held in bondage. When Abraham showed Hagar more respect than usual she began to overstep her place with Sarah. And our worldly vocation will nudge out heavenly appointments if we do not keep a strict hand over them. With this in mind, let us examine two important ways to protect the power of holiness.

(a) *The Christian does not let his vocation steal his time for communion with God*

We can watch Satan's plot unfold in everyday action. Have you noticed that it is almost impossible to think about serving God or God's people without some excuse pressing itself on to the scene to put you off? Solomon stated the devil's tactic of manipulation like this: 'He that observeth the wind shall not sow; and he that regardeth the clouds shall not reap' (*Eccles. 11:4*). As long as a man listens to the worldly distractions of the flesh he will never find time to pray, meditate, nor commune with God.

It is sad when the master must ask the slave what to do,

or when the Christian must take his orders from the world, asking its permission to wait on God. Holiness in its power – like Samson in his strength – can sever the excuses that would separate him from God as easily as God's man snapped the cords of flax which restrained him. Holiness frees the saint to make his way into the presence of God even through the pressing crowd of worldly encumbrances.

David said, 'In my trouble I have prepared for the house of the Lord an hundred thousand talents of gold, and a thousand thousand talents of silver' (*1 Chron. 22:14*). Surely there must have been dozens of worthy causes – including military expenses of his reign – which demanded David's money; but as Rome showed her confidence by sending aid to Spain when Hannibal was at her gates, so David displayed his trust in God by planning to build His temple in a season of national distress.

That person is a Christian indeed who lays aside a good portion of time every day, even in the middle of a stressful schedule, to have communion with his Father. Of whomever he must request an extension for a debt, this man will never be so bold with God as to try and serve Him in half measures. One devout man made it his practice to excuse himself from guests when it was time for his communion with God, telling his company that a Friend was waiting to talk with him.

(b) *The Christian does not let his schedule drain his affections for God*

The husband deals with different groups of people all day and devotes his energy and intelligence to each one; yet no-one on his agenda makes him love his wife and children any less. When he goes home at night he takes his love to them as whole and vibrant as it was when he left. It is a relief, in fact, to be away from the pressures of business and at home alone with his family once again. This is a sweet frame of spirit – but a hard one to keep.

Can you really say, after you have spent an entire day in the profits and losses of the business world, that you bring God your whole heart, when you return to His presence to wait on Him? It is not easy to hold on to the world all day and then shake it off at night, to enjoy privacy with God. The world treats the Christian as a little child treats his mother; if he cannot keep her from leaving, he will cry to go with her. And if the world cannot prevent us from going into service for God it will whine to be taken along with us.

IN BEHAVIOR TOWARD OTHERS

I. THE POWER OF HOLINESS WITHIN THE FAMILY

It does not do any good to talk about holiness if we do not have the practical testimony of godliness within the family God has set us in. It is sad when the people who know us best cannot see holiness in our lives. Few people are shameless enough to walk out into the street naked; if they have anything to cover themselves with, it will certainly be put on before they go outside. But what kind of person are you inside your own home? A negligent husband spends money freely in public but fails to provide for his family. Can the man, then, be a good Christian if he spreads his spiritual strength all over the country but allows little or nothing of God to flow from him to his family?

Some well-known men who enjoy a dynamic reputation in Christendom fall short of unbelievers who take care of their children and wives in kind, practical ways. What sort of Christian can the man be when he acts like a tyrant and so embitters his wife's spirit that she covers 'the altar of the Lord with tears, with weeping, and with crying out' (*Mal. 2:13*)? Many wives who are far from having a work of true grace in their hearts are obedient to their husbands; but is it possible for a Christian wife to walk in holiness if she jars the whole house with her subtle selfishness and explosive temper? The authority of a natural conscience restrains servants from railing out with angry language against their masters. Is not grace able to keep pace with nature?

David knew how close this Christian responsibility was to the heart of godliness when he purposed, 'I will walk within my house with a perfect heart' (*Ps. 101:2*). But let me mention four specific facets of this power of holiness as it appears in family relations.

(a) *Choosing our authorities*

Sometimes we have no choice about our relationships – a child cannot select his own father or the parent his son. But when God does allow us freedom to choose, He expects a wise choice every time.

(i) *Select spiritual masters.* Be careful to show your holiness in the authority you put yourself under. First, find out if the air inside the doors is as healthful for your soul as it is for your body outside. Will you voluntarily submit to ungodly men? It is hard enough to serve two masters, even when both have similar personalities; but it is impossible to serve a holy God and an ungodly man and please them both.

If you are already under the roof of wicked authorities, though, do not forget your responsibility to them even if they forget about God altogether. Your faithfulness might cause them to seek God for your sake as Nebuchadnezzar did for Daniel's. Besides, sinners would undoubtedly take the ways of God more seriously if there were more beauty upon Christians' lives to invite them into the kingdom.

We are more likely to choose a book if the print is attractive and clear and to ignore one with dull or tiny lettering. How often do employers throw away all thoughts of Christianity because their Christian employees turn in performances of pride and carelessness? The natural conclusion inevitably follows: 'Is *this* what comes of your belief? Well, God keep me from such a religion!' Christian, your blameless behavior is the best way for ungodly or carnal employers to see the ways of God. But let me add a practical suggestion – maybe you are doing everything you can to bring God's truth into that place but the soil is so hard and cold that there is no visible hope of planting for Him there. Then it is high time to think about transplanting yourself; for if the field is too bad for you to sow Christianity in, it cannot be very good for you to grow in either.

(ii) *Select spiritual servants.* When you hire an employee, choose for God as well as for yourself. How can he fit in with your plans if he does not fit in with God's? Of course you want his work to be successful. But on what ground can you anchor that hope if the hand that does your labor insists on sinning as he performs it? 'A high look, and a proud heart, and the plowing of the wicked, is sin' (*Prov. 21:4*).

A godly servant, however, is a great blessing. He can work hard and then seek God to work for your good also: 'O Lord God of my master Abraham, I pray thee, send me good speed this day, and show kindness unto my master' (*Gen. 24:12*). Surely this prayer helped Abraham as much as the servant's good judgment did.

If you were to plant an orchard you would find the best-quality fruit trees instead of wasting your acres cultivating thistles. There is far more loss in a graceless person in your employ than a fruitless tree in the orchard. While David was at Saul's court, for example, he saw the disadvantage of having ungodly servants. No doubt his recognition of evil in a disordered house made him determine to have the highest standards when God would make him head of that royal family: 'He that worketh deceit shall not dwell within my house: he that telleth lies shall not tarry in my sight' (*Ps. 101:7*).

(iii) *Select a godly mate*. There is no one area wherein Christians, even those recorded in Scripture, have betrayed their weakness more often than in choosing ungodly husbands or wives. 'The sons of God saw the daughters of men that they were fair' (*Gen. 6:2*). You would think the sons of God would have looked for grace in the heart rather than for beauty in the face; but even they are quite capable of being turned aside by a pretty outward appearance without first looking into the person's spirit.

Remember, though, that God did not leave the mistakes of His chosen ones on record to be followed but to be shunned. Only a simple-minded man swallows every experience of Scripture's saints. It is true that wicked men break their necks over the sins of saints – but do you want to stumble over them and break your legs?

Do not look around and point to a godly woman, one whom you think God is using, and assume it was all right for her to marry into a heathen family and lie with a profane man. Instead, look all the way up to God's standard if you want to keep the power of holiness. It is as clear as a sunbeam written in the Word: 'Be ye not unequally yoked together with unbelievers: for what fellowship hath righteousness with unrighteousness?' (*2 Cor. 6:14*). Even when God gives the widow permission to marry again, He adds this crucial condition: 'To whom she will; only in the Lord' (*1 Cor. 7:39*).

Anyone without faith is 'without God in the world' (*Eph. 2:12*). Because the Lord's family is in the church, you marry out of the Lord when you marry out of His kindred. Or, 'in the Lord' might be taken to mean 'with God's blessing.' We all agree that parental consent is important, but what about your heavenly Father? Will He ever give His consent for you to give yourself to an earthworm?

Through the ages, holy men have paid a precious price for ungodly unions. What a horrible plague Delilah was to Samson! And neither did Michal help David. It would have been better if he had married the poorest girl in all Israel – with nothing more than the clothes on her back – rather than such an arrogant companion who mocked him for celebrating God's faithfulness.

(b) *Interceding for our family*

A Christian cannot pass God's grace on to his child or join his wife to his own holiness; but he must do all he can to draw them to the Father. God commanded that Abraham's entire household be circumcised so they could be moved that much closer to the desire of His heart for them. Grace turns love for our family into a spiritual channel and makes us pray for – and work for – their eternal good.

What sets the Christian's love above the world's love? Do not the heathen lay up an inheritance for their children? And do they not take care of their employees as well as others do? Our love must go further. Augustine complained when his friends highly commended his father's diligence to educate him: 'But my father did not train me up for God. His project was that I might be eloquent, an orator, not a Christian.'

My brothers – if God is worth everything to you, is He not worth your family's knowing Him too? One house holds you now; do you not want one heaven to hold you together for eternity? Can you think, without trembling, what grief you would feel if those who dwell together in your family should be broken up by death, with some of your children going to heaven and the rest of them going to hell?

By the law of Lycurgus, the father who failed to provide education for his child when he was young had to forfeit his right to the help due him from his child in his old age. I will not comment on the righteousness of that law but I will say this – those who do not teach their children the rightful relationship to God lose the reverence and honor which should be paid them by their children.

(c) *Freeing ourselves from snares*

Some families are like renegades in that they do nothing but lead each other into temptation by drawing out one another's corruption from year to year. What can we call homes like this, except so many hells above ground?

Satan is always ready to take advantage of family passions to cause mischief, provoking even godly members to defile each other. For instance, Abraham's fear laid the snare for Sarah, who was easily persuaded to lie on behalf of the husband she loved so dearly (*Gen. 12:13*). And Rebekah's vehement affection for Jacob, coupled with his reverence of her, changed him from a plain man to a subtle schemer, to deceive his father and brother. At first it was too big a sin for him to swallow – 'I shall seem to him as a deceiver; and I shall bring a curse upon me, and not a blessing' (*Gen. 27:12*). Yet the skillful coercion of his mother made the bulky sin go down into the innermost being of Jacob's life, although he had strained hard against it at first. And remember, these were godly persons who faltered and fell.

Be careful not to cause your family to sin. It would be a heartbreaking thing to watch your child suffer and bleed from a wound you had given him. But even an affliction like this would be better than an infection of sin and guilt which you had caused.

Next, let me remind you to be just as careful to protect yourself from receiving infection from your family as of breathing it on them. You have a strong love for your wife, and that is good. But do not let it make the apple of temptation more desirable, when her hand holds it out to you. You love yourself and God too little if you sin for her sake. Even if you wives are submissive to your husbands, obey 'in the Lord': do not turn the tables and put the seventh commandment before the first one. Obey God before you obey your husband. You might need to question your soul in this process: 'Is it possible for me to keep God's command in obeying my husband's wishes?'

In business we first pay the biggest debts which are already due. Are you more deeply indebted to God or to your mate? Travel as far as you can with your relatives in God's company, but no farther – because you do not want to leave holiness and righteousness behind. No one – family or otherwise – can ever repay you in the loss of those treasures.

(d) *Taking instruction from godly relatives*

A holy father, a gracious husband or wife – even a godly maid or gardener – the good from their holiness is like precious ointment which betrays itself wherever it lingers. Christian, if there is a holy person in your family, see what you can learn from watching how he behaves under affliction, how he worships and receives God's mercies, and how he directs his daily life.

Elisha asked the widow to bring all the vessels she could find or borrow to hold what would flow from the pot of oil in her house. Those who are poor in grace must take advantage of the holy oil of grace which drops from the lips and lives of their godly relatives. Set your memory, conscience, heart, and affections to receive all the expressions of holiness that pour from them.

Let your memory keep the instructions, reproofs, and comforts drawn out of the Word by these saints; and then let your conscience apply them to your soul until they distil into affections and you become more and more in love with the holiness of Christ yourself. It is sad to see what an evil heart does with the gifts and graces of his family – it envies and maligns the saints. And instead of gaining good, the person himself becomes worse. For instance, when Joseph told his prophetic dream to his brothers, their envy – which had been smoldering in their hearts – caught fire and flamed into unnatural cruelty against 'the dreamer.' That was all the use they made of the prophecy.

Thus, Christian, this is what you can do with the righteous breathings of the Spirit in the saints you live with. Note the passages of their holy living as you would those of an excellent book which you have borrowed. Our friends and relatives have only been loaned to us for awhile, and whether we learn from them or ignore them, God will call them back before very long.

One of God's ministers, Reverend Bolton, gathered his children around his deathbed to give them one last word of wisdom: 'I charge you, my children, not to meet me at the great day before Christ's tribunal in a Christless, graceless condition.' We can be sure God keeps an exact account of all the means He gives us for our salvation; and the lives of His holy servants are not the least of these. You have noticed that He has been particular in Scripture to record exactly how long His faithful saints lived on earth. And surely one reason for this is that He reckons with those who lived with them – for every year and even each day and hour they had with the prophets: godly fathers, mothers, brothers, sisters, and so on.

II. THE POWER OF HOLINESS IN THE NEIGHBORHOOD

God has not commissioned your power of holiness to be confined behind bolted doors, but to walk out into the streets and visit your neighbors. Your behavior and conversation with those about you must be holy and righteous. In Scripture, 'righteousness' and 'living righteously' often imply the whole responsibility of the Christian to those around him. These terms are distinguished from 'piety,' which has God for its immediate object; and from 'sobriety' or temperance, which immediately respects ourselves. But see them all together, where 'the grace of God that bringeth salvation' teaches us to 'live soberly, righteously, and godly, in this present world' (*Tit. 2:11, 12*). If one of these graces is stabbed, they all die – and the life of holiness trickles out through the open wound.

It is true that there is a moral righteousness which leaves us short of true holiness; but there is no true holiness which leaves us short of moral righteousness. It is also a fact that no Christian can be bad, unless he is a hypocrite. You must either renounce your baptism or curse all thoughts of unrighteousness. Actually, you might escape better if you let the world know you claim no kinship with Christ before you practice sin.

Some people wonder whether Aristides, Socrates, Cato, and a few other heathens famous for their moral righteousness are in heaven or hell. But has there ever been any real doubt what would become of the unrighteous Christian in the other world? Hell opens wider for him than for anyone else. 'Know ye not,' said Paul, 'that the unrighteous shall not inherit the kingdom of God?' (*1 Cor. 6:9*). He may as well have said, 'Surely you do not think there is any room for such cattle as these in heaven!' What crevice of hope is left, then, for their salvation, these men whose unrighteousness has a thousand times more wickedness and rebellion in it than anyone else's?

For their unrighteousness heathens will be indicted and be condemned as rebels to the law of God. But the unrighteous 'Christian' will also be found guilty by the gospel. Surely the heaviest charge is the one the gospel brings against those whose unrighteousness, while professing to believe, has made them the 'enemies of the cross of Christ' (*Phil. 3:18*). If a person hunted for the ultimate expression of contempt against Christ's cross, Satan himself could not help him express it more fully than to clothe himself in a gaudy profession of faith and then roll around in the kennel of sordid, vulgar acts of unrighteousness. It makes the profane world blaspheme the name of Christ and abhor every profession of Him, when they see any of this filth in the behavior of one who has taken the name of *saint*.

One minute the tongue is earnestly praying to God and the next it is lying to man. Eyes read through the sacred Scriptures only moments before they steal away on lust's secret errand. Sometimes the hands which were devoutly stretched upward to heaven are the same ones that rob a neighbor's pocket. How can your legs carry you to worship God on the Sabbath and then take you into the business world on Monday to cheat your associates?

In a word, do you really think you can persuade heaven to waive your unrighteous acts toward man just because you exercise outward semblances of zeal to God? Will your vocal, artificial love for the Father excuse the malice in your heart against your neighbor? Does devotion to God displace your obligation to pay what you owe to man? God forbid that you should deceive yourself this way! But in case you do, Peter's counsel to Simon Magus is my advice to you: 'Repent of this thy wickedness, and pray God, if perhaps the thought of thine heart may be forgiven thee' (*Acts 8:22*).

In the name of God, I charge everyone who wears Christ's armour to take this piece of righteousness to the conscience if you do not want to bring the vengeance of God upon yourself for those blasphemies belched out by the world because of hypocrisy. Further, the power of holiness regarding our neighbor will be preserved when the Christian takes heed of the following:

(a) *Holiness must be uniform*

Our holiness must be lived out every day and be equally distributed among all the responsibilities we have toward our neighbors. Righteousness runs, like blood in the veins, through every one of the laws in the second tablet of God's Ten Commandments. The fifth commandment calls for obedience to parents natural, civil, and spiritual; the sixth deals with preserving our neighbor's life; the seventh stresses purity; the eighth concerns property; the ninth protects a good name; and the tenth teaches the keeping of our desires within due bounds.

Health in the body is preserved by keeping the passages of life open, for the blood and other vital fluids to move freely from one part to another. If any obstruction blocks them from flowing, the whole body will soon be in danger. So then the spirit and life of holiness is preserved by the Christian's diligence to keep the heart free and ready to perform each of the various responsibilities he owes his neighbor, as he moves through the several paths in every commandment.

(b) *Holiness must be evangelical*

Outward obedience to the law is a road where Jews, Christians, and heathens may be found walking along together. How can we distinguish the Christian from these others, when heathens and Jews also are obedient children, loyal citizens, and loving neighbors?

The motive and goal make all the difference. It is common for men to wrong Christ and yet treat their neighbors with respect and fairness; they choose right behavior but not because love for Christ has constrained them. And without this love you may be an honest, moral heathen but you can never be a Christian.

Suppose a man trusts his employee to pay a certain creditor a sum of money. The person does this, not out of respect to the command or love for his boss but out of fear of being called a thief. As far as the creditor is concerned he has done his job but that is all – his attitude has wronged his employer. Men scorn Jesus like this every day; they are exact and righteous in their transactions with their neighbors and associates, but insulting to Him. Love carries out righteousness because it wants to please God's holy Son.

Christ called evangelical love to our neighbor 'a new commandment' (*John 13:34*). This love to our brother takes fire from God's love to us. It is impossible to perform any commandment unless we first love Christ and then do it for His sake. 'If ye love me, keep my commandments' (*John 14:15*).

Just as God set His name before His Ten Commandments, for the same reason Christ set His name before the Christian's obedience to those Ten Commandments. That is, we are to keep them because they are Christ's word and law, and so that we may illustrate our love to Him who has redeemed us from the curse and brought us out of a far worse kind of bondage than Egypt was for Israel.

3. Guidance for the Christian who Desires Holiness

HOW TO MAINTAIN HOLINESS

I. LAY A GOOD FOUNDATION

There is only one foundation for you to build the beautiful structure of righteousness on – a heart changed by the power of God's sanctifying Spirit in you. You must *be* holy before you can live a holy life. If a ship has not been constructed right it will never sail properly; and if your heart has not been molded again by the Spirit's workmanship and fashioned according to the law of the 'new creature,' you will never have a holy walk (*2 Cor. 5:17*). It is grace in the vessel of the heart which feeds profession in the lamp – holiness in the life! This thorough change of heart needs to be examined through two questions:

(a) *What do you think about sin?*

There was a time when sin looked as good to you as it did to Adam when Eve offered him the forbidden fruit. And unless you change your mind it will always seem pleasant. Circumstances might keep you from expressing that secret longing for sin, but inwardly your heart will be continually hankering after it. When two lovers are kept apart by their friends one will eventually break loose and escape to the other, as long as their affection stays strong. Thus lust will lure you back again and again unless you are convicted to hate it as much as you once loved it.

(b) *Are you content to live in Christ?*

There is no reason to fear degeneration after Christ has tied you to His service by the heartstrings of love. The devil finds it easy to separate a person from kingdom work when the person never really liked doing it anyway. A student learns more in a week when he is pleased with the sweet taste of learning then he will in a month when he attends class merely to please his teacher. A man is diligent about the thing that satisfies him. If a person's heart is turned to his garden, for instance, it will become a beautiful place. Out of his excitement he spends hours of hard work growing rare, delicate flowers that please him.

The soul that really loves Christ, then, delights in holiness and spends all his strength on it. If only this man can be more holy, he does not mind if he is behind in every other race.

II. KEEP YOUR EYE ON THE RIGHT RULE

Every calling has its own rule, peculiar to itself, to go by; and we must study to get insight into it. Men vary their methods and means in earthly professions; and even in the same trade there always seems to be an exception or appendage to the rule. But no calling affords a more sure and perfect standard than the Christian's. The saint has one standing rule, the Word of God, which is able to perfect him.

If you want to excel in the power of holiness you must study the Bible. The doctor consults with his Galen, the attorney with his Littleton, and the philosopher with his Aristotle – the masters of those arts. How much more, then, should the Christian consult the Word to settle questions and provide answers! My brother, you probably feel pulled in several directions at once – business dictates one thing, friends recommend something else, common sense reasons in still a different vein, and pleasure beckons beyond them all. That is when you need to consider seriously the question Jehoshaphat asked: 'Is there not here a prophet of the Lord besides, that we might inquire of him?' (*I Kings 22:7*). Does God not open my understanding of His Word and show a place in it where I can run and be sure to find truth?

Now there are three ways for men to miss God's direction, each one a precarious bypass to the power of holiness. Some walk by *no* rule; others by a *false* rule; and still others by the true rule, but only *partially*. The first is the rebellious harlot; the second is the superstitious zealot; and the third is the hypocrite. Stay free of all three unless you intend to lay the knife to the throat of holiness.

(a) *Do not ignore God's rule*

Liberal men try to stretch their freedom by saying the law is not a rule for Christians. But Christ baptized the law and gospelized it, both by preaching it as a rule of holiness in His sermons and by walking out His life according to that rule.

Any principle which takes away the standard for a righteous life may be indicted as a murderer of holiness. This is Satan's subtle way of surprising the Christian traveler. If he can make the saint so weary of his Guide that he sends Him away, it will not be long before he will wander out of heaven's way and fall into the roads of hell. The apostle tells us of a generation who, while they promise themselves liberty, 'are the servants of corruption' (*2 Pet. 2:19*). People who slip off the yoke of God's command under the pretense of liberty soon stoop under a far worse bondage – the heavy yoke of sin.

(b) *Do not walk by a false rule*

Anything contrary to God's Word is false. 'To the law and to the testimony: if they speak not according to this word, it is because there is no light in them' (*Isa. 8:20*). But we must not ever go beyond what is written – this is what Scripture calls 'righteous over much' (*Eccles. 7:16*). Remember, the man who has three hands is just as deformed as the person who has only one!

A curse is stored up for the man who adds to as well as for him who takes away from the word of Scripture. It is one of Satan's oldest designs to undermine scriptural holiness by extolling fictitious holiness. He knows too well that as the pot boils over and puts out the fire, he can quench real holiness by making men's zeal spill out into a false holiness. At last their fervor will disappear and be displaced by cold atheism.

Now the Pharisee has to eke out God's commands with the traditions of men; and his son and heir lives by holy orders, unwritten doctrines and rules for a more stern life than God ever thought about requiring. I warn you strictly – stay away from will-holiness and will-worship. God handed down a heavy decision against His chosen people concerning their strong will: 'Israel hath forgotten his Maker, and buildeth temples!' (*Hos. 8:14*). How can a person forget God but be devout enough to erect temples? Israel built them without God, for He counts Himself forgotten when people forget to live by His Word.

Holiness which is the product of our own heart is not holiness after God's heart. Jeroboam's great sin was that 'he offered upon the altar which he had made in Beth-el . . . in the month which he had devised of his own heart' (*1 Kings 12:33*). The penalty which falls upon such bold men is that God gives them over to real unholiness for pretending to have more holiness than they actually have.

God will not let His children be self-movers. It is a worse sin to do what we are not commanded than not to do what we are commanded by God. A citizen becomes a worse criminal when he presumes he can make the law out of his own head than when he does not obey the law which his ruler is carrying out. Because God is the only one who can declare holiness, we grab His royal scepter out of His hand every time we try to set up a holiness of our own.

(c) *Do not use only part of the true rule*

If you do not square every part of your life by the rule, the whole frame is distorted. 'Divers measures . . . are an abomination to the Lord' (*Prov. 20:10*). An honest businessman uses the same measure, according to the law, for all his transactions; and a holy man uses only one rule, the Word of God, for all his actions.

How hateful the Jews' hypocrisy must have seemed to God – they did not dare enter the judgment hall for fear of becoming unclean; yet they rushed in to wash their hands in Christ's blood! And the Pharisees observed the strict letter of the law in tithing 'anise and cummin' but ignored 'the weightier matters of the law, judgment, mercy, and faith' (*Matt. 23:23*).

How would you feel about a customer who bought a penny's worth of merchandise but turned around and stole a dollar's worth from you? Or the debtor who punctually paid trivial debts only to cheat you out of a larger sum? It is horrible wickedness to comply with Scripture in little matters as part of a scheme to commit great secret sins against God.

III. KEEP YOUR MOTIVE PURE

Do not ever think your righteousness can buy anything from God – heaven is not for sale. 'The wages of sin is death: but the gift of God is eternal life through Jesus Christ our Lord' (*Rom. 6:23*). God gives to us what He sold to Christ! Believers are only heirs of what God's Son has bought from the Father. By claiming anything of God in our own righteousness, we shut ourselves out from having any benefit of His righteousness. We cannot be in two places at the same time – if we are found leaning on our own house we cannot also be found abiding in Christ.

Satan's policy is to crack the breastplate of righteousness by beating it out farther than the metal can bend. And every time you trust in this distortion you destroy the very nature and purpose of the armour – your righteousness becomes unrighteousness and your holiness degenerates into wickedness.

Is anything worse than pride, such a pride which runs

rampant over the way which God Himself has made for saving souls? If you really want to be holy, be humble, because the two are clasped together. 'What doth the Lord require of thee, but to do justly, and to love mercy, and to walk humbly with thy God?' (*Mic. 6:8*). God has not asked you to earn heaven by your holiness but to show love and thankfulness to Christ who earned it for you. Thus we have insight into the way Christ persuaded His disciples to walk in holiness: 'If ye love me, keep my commandments' (*John 14:15*). It is as if He had said, 'You know why I came and why I am going out of the world – I lay down My life and take it up again to intercede for you. If you value these deeds and the blessed fruit you reap from them, prove it by loving Me enough to keep My commandments.'

When everything the saint does through Christ is offered up as a thanksgiving sacrifice to Him, then this is gospel holiness bred and fed by this love. Because Christ has loved us 'with love . . . strong as death,' our response is that of a bride: 'I will give thee my loves' (*Song of Sol. 8:6; 7:12*). And this bride explains what is in her expression of love: 'All manner of pleasant fruits, new and old, which I have laid up for thee, O my Beloved' (*v. 13*).

The saint in Solomon's Song had confessed her faith in Christ and had drunk deeply of His love for her. And now to return His love in thankfulness, she stirred herself to entertain Him with the pleasant fruits of His own graces, gathered from her holy behavior. She did not lay these fruits up to feed her pride and self-confidence but reserved them for her Beloved, so He could have all the praise.

IV. CONSIDER CHRIST AS YOUR EXAMPLE OF THE HOLY
    LIFE

If we look at low examples we cannot ever expect to rise above them; and the holiest Christian on earth is too low to be our pattern, because perfection in holiness cannot be found in the most sincere servant in this world. Even Peter, the foreman of the apostles, did not always walk according to the gospel – and those who insist on following this man inevitably will be led astray. The good soldier follows his platoon leader only when he himself marches after his captain. Paul commanded, 'Be ye followers of me, even as I also am of Christ' (*1 Cor. 11:1*).

A doctrine must be followed no further than it agrees with God's Word. The teacher of hand-writing not only provides ruled paper for the student but also writes him a copy in his own hand. Christ's command is our rule and His life is our copy. If you want to live a holy life you must not only do what Jesus commands; you must do it as He did. You must shape every letter in your copy – each action in your life – in a holy imitation of Christ. By holiness we are the very image of God's Son, representing Christ and holding Him forth to all who see us.

Now two things make one thing an image of another – first, likeness; and second, source. Milk and snow are both white but we cannot say they are images of each other because in neither is the likeness derived from the other. But a picture which is drawn line by line of a man's face can be called the image of that person. Thus true holiness is derived from God's Son, when the person sets Christ in His word and Christ in His example before him.

What a sweet way to keep the power of holiness! When you are tempted to walk toward vanity, look at Christ's holy walk and ask yourself, 'Am I like Him in my thoughts and in the way I spend my time? If He were physically living on earth right now, would He do what I am doing? Would He not choose His words more carefully than I do? Would silly speech come from His lips? Would He enjoy my friends? Would He spend a fortune pampering His body, and swallow enough food at one meal to feed hungry people for a week? Would He be fashion-conscious, even if that made His appearance ridiculous and offensive? Would His hands be busy with games that drive time away? Should I do anything that would make me unlike Christ?'

Sometimes we like to rationalize our practices by bringing in the name of some well-thought-of person who thinks they are fine. And so we are led into temptation. But Christian, if your conscience tells you Christ does not like certain things, put them down – even if the most eminent saint in the country practises them. The more you study Christ's life, the sooner you will be able to mend your own!

V. DEPEND ON GOD FOR HOLINESS

The vine grows fruit as long as it has a wall or a pole to run upon, but without this help it will be trampled under foot and come to nothing. If you want to practise the power of holiness, 'lean not unto thine own understanding' (*Prov. 3:5*). God is ready to help everyone who asks Him but does not guarantee help to anyone who will not depend on Him.

The Christian's way to heaven is like some beaches over which the sea flows every day and changes them so much that it would be dangerous for the traveler who had passed there a month ago to venture those same steps unless his guide went with him. Whereas earlier he had walked on firm land, now he might fall into devouring quicksand.

Thus the saint who moves along a smooth and level road may later face temptation on the same path which will destroy him unless help from heaven carries him safely through. Christian, I warn you – do not risk even a single step without your hand of faith leaning on your Beloved's arm. If you trust your own legs you will fall; use those legs, but trust His arm if you want to stay safe.

VI. CHOOSE SPIRITUAL COMPANIONS

Avoid unholy friends; they will ruin the power of godliness. Would you drink from the same cup as a man with an infectious disease? Well, sin is as contagious as the plague itself!

It would not make sense for a cleaner and a coal miner to live together. What one purifies, the other immediately streaks with heavy black grease. Stop pretending – you cannot be among unholy people very long without defiling your soul, which the Holy Spirit has made pure. He did not wash you clean to watch you run out and bathe in the world's most stagnant sins.

We should never choose an environment where we cannot hope to make the people better or hope to be made better ourselves. The Spirit of God said that Abraham 'sojourned in the land of promise, as in a strange country, dwelling in tabernacles with Isaac and Jacob, the heirs with him of the same promise' (*Heb. 11:9*). He did not move in with the natives of that ungodly land or compromise to win their acceptance, but dwelt with God's family, who shared the same promise that he himself cherished. Instead of trying to make friends or blend in with the heathen, then, Abraham was willing to live as a stranger among them.

Christians are a separated people. It was recorded of Peter and John, for example, that 'being let go, they went to their own company' (*Acts 4:23*). Believers should never join themselves with unbelievers. Paul had this principle in mind when he asked the Corinthians: 'Is there not a wise man among you,' but you must go to law 'before the unbelievers?' (*1 Cor. 6:5, 6*). And I ask you that same question. Is there not a saint anywhere in town whom you can share with, or do you have to be a part of an ungodly circle? No wonder your holiness is not growing stronger! When you inhale the atmosphere of wickedness it is like the east wind – nothing grows and prospers that breathes it in.

VII. BE ACCOUNTABLE TO A MATURE CHRISTIAN

A spectator sometimes sees more than the actor himself. And a man with an open-hearted friend who dares speak honestly has a wonderful source of encouragement for the power of holiness. Sometimes self-love blinds us so we cannot see a single fault; and at other times, self-condemnation makes us appear worse than we really are. Therefore, keep your heart soft and ready to receive a reproof with real meekness.

A person who cannot face plain dealing and straightforwardness hurts himself more than anyone else, for this reason – he seldom hears the truth. If you do not have enough humility to accept a rebuke you are 'a scorner' (*Prov. 9:8*). On the other hand, a man who does not have enough love to give a reproof in season to his brother is not worthy to be called a Christian and proves himself a 'hater of his brother' (*Lev. 19:17*).

David said he would take it as 'a kindness' for the 'righteous to smite' him (*Ps. 141:5*). He accepted reproof as if the brother had broken open a box of precious oil upon his head – a high expression of Jewish love. And his actions backed up his word. Indeed, both Abigail and Nathan knew Godspeed in their mission to reprove David. Abigail warned him about his treacherous intentions against Nabal and his family; and Nathan reproved him for his sin against Uriah. Whereas Abigail prevented the king from sinning by her reproof at the right time, Nathan forced him to come out of hiding and repent of the dismal murder he had already committed. And notice this – not only did these two saints prevail in their unpleasant errands but actually endeared themselves to David by being obedient to God and faithful to their friend. David took Abigail as his wife and Nathan as his private counselor (*1 Sam. 25; 2 Sam. 12*).

One reason many professing Christians fall and few stand is that only a small remnant of saints are faithful enough to fill the office of reproving brothers. They prefer to tattle the problem to others – they bring disgrace rather than help. When we gossip, we forfeit all hopes of helping the involved person. It is hard to make a Christian believe you have come to heal his soul after you have already wounded his name.

VIII. LOOK AT HOLINESS FROM THE VIEWPOINT OF DEATH

Do you know people who do not care what kind of foolish talk comes from their conversation; who think it does not matter what they do; and who, for all practical purposes, ignore God? These are the men who look down on Christians who deny themselves for the sake of the gospel. And they flash condescending smiles at zeal: 'Can these Christians not find a pace more comfortable than an outright gallop to get themselves to heaven?'

But the night will inevitably come when death will creep in close enough to show his grim face. When these presumptuous people see they have no choice but to go into eternity – ready or not – they face their sentence of life or death with quite a different attitude. Suddenly righteousness does not seem quite so repulsive as it did before.

Some professional clergymen may think their religious habits to be unbecoming attire while they are involved in everyday community life. But these same men are most ambitious to be buried in their full garb when they die. Although this is a formal portrait of vanity carried to the extreme, it does sketch a candid picture for us. Those who live loosely in this life will desire the covering of a religious habit as they enter another world.

A young man of pleasure confided to his swaggering

companion after they had both seen Ambrose triumphing over death: 'O that I might live with you and die with Ambrose!' Vain wish! Do you plant weeds when you expect to harvest wheat? Or fill your coffer with dirt and then look for gold when you open it? You can cheat yourself day and night and even rationalize that you might win; but you shall never mock God. At your death He will pay you in the same coin you treasured and hoarded all your life.

In a word, few people are so wicked and hardened that they are oblivious to the reality of death. It sobers them so much that they have to put away the thought of it before they indulge in sin one more time. Christian, let the knowledge of death be your companion through serious meditation every day and see if it does not make a difference by the end of the week as to who and what else goes with you.

IX. RELY ON GOD'S COVENANT OF GRACE

Do you realize that Moses' holiness came from the gospel instead of the law? His recorded acts of holiness are all attributed to faith. 'By faith Moses . . . refused to enjoy the pleasures of sin for a season; by faith he forsook Egypt' (*Heb. 11:24, 25, 27*). But so you too can lay hold on this covenant to preserve holiness, consider three particular truths concerning grace.

(a) *God empowers us to live a holy life*

'I will put my Spirit within you, and cause you to walk in my statutes' (*Ezek. 36:27*). A mother can take her child's hand to lead him but is not able to put strength into his legs to make him move. A captain can give his men a commission but not the courage to fight.

Because God has built His power into His promises, they are called 'exceeding great and precious promises.' God gave them for this very purpose, that we 'might be partakers of the divine nature' (*2 Pet. 1:4*). Thus we are pressed into holiness not only by God's command but by His promise: 'Having therefore these promises, dearly beloved, let us cleanse ourselves from all filthiness of the flesh and spirit, perfecting holiness in the fear of God' (*2 Cor. 7:1*). It is a wonderful trip when God travels with us and promises to pay all the expenses home.

(b) *God supplies fulness of grace in Christ Jesus*
The Father has stored up a rich and full treasure of grace in His Son to supply all your need. 'It pleased the Father that in Him should all fulness dwell' (*Col. 1:19*). *All fulness!* All fulness dwelling in Christ! Not fulness of a land-flood, which goes up and then back down; and not the fulness of a drinking vessel to serve only a man's own thirst. Scripture speaks of a fountain which lends its streams to others without lessening its own supply.

It is fulness whose only purpose is to be given away. Because the sun does not provide light for itself but for the lower world, it is called a servant to hold forth light to the earth. Thus Christ is the Sun of Righteousness, diffusing His grace into the hearts of His people. God poured grace into His lips, but it was not His to keep but to impart: 'And of his fulness have all we received, and grace for grace' (*John 1:16*).

(c) *God expects us to receive from Christ*
Every child of God has a right to this fulness in Christ; but this is not all – it is the instinct of the new creature to draw grace from Him as the fetus takes nourishment in the womb through the navel cord of its mother. So if you are hungry for more holiness, receive more grace from Christ.

When David remembered God's faithfulness in delivering him from distress and oppression he sent the mightiest messenger he could find to thank heaven – his determination to live a holy life. 'I will walk before the Lord in the land of the living' (*Ps. 116:9*). But he did not want anyone to assume this vow came from self-confidence, so he added, 'I believed, therefore I have spoken' (*v. 10*). First he exercised his faith in God for strength and then promised God what he would do.

X. GUARD AGAINST DISCOURAGEMENT

Depression is one of Satan's most dynamic weapons to divert you from God's purpose for your life. If he can scatter a little dejection here and there in your thoughts – and even in your prayers – he can convince you to remove your breastplate of righteousness because it is too cumbersome and will go against your material and temporal interests. Do not give in that easily! First let me describe some of the devil's weapons for wearing down the saints. Then I want to lend you a little help in making him drop his weapons at your feet. God wants you to know that because of the breastplate of righteousness He has provided, 'no weapon that is formed against thee shall prosper; . . . this is the heritage of the servants of the Lord, and their righteousness is of me, saith the Lord' (*Isa. 54:17*).

SATAN'S STRATEGY TO DISARM THE CHRISTIAN OF HIS BREASTPLATE

I. SATAN SAYS RIGHTEOUSNESS HINDERS PLEASURE

The devil works to picture a holy life with such an austere, sour face that a person could not possibly be in love with it. 'If you intend to be *this* righteous, then say goodbye to joy,' the deceiver skillfully counsels. 'People who do not have such straight-laced consciences enjoy all kinds of good times – but you are missing them all.' The truth is, Christian, if you want to see the countenance of holiness in its actual color and vitality, do not trust Satan's carnal talents to paint the portrait.

Now I agree that some pleasures are inconsistent with the power of holiness; and whoever purposes to live righteously must know what these are.

(a) *Pleasures which are in themselves sinful*

Godliness will not let you take in evil nourishment. Is a father cruel who warns his child not to drink rat poison? If you have surrendered to the new work of the Holy Spirit, I hope you can call sin by some name other than pleasure. Satan argues that conscience ties you up in holiness and restricts your rights. But saints in the church have always found that the bondage lies in serving such pleasures; freedom is being saved from them.

Paul regretted the time he had spent being 'foolish, disobedient, deceived, serving divers lusts and pleasures'; and he thanked Christ for delivering him out of that slavery by His gospel (*Tit. 3:3*). According to God's mercy He has saved us – not by forgiveness only but 'by the washing of regeneration, and renewing of the Holy Ghost' (*v. 5*).

The devil makes his victims expect pleasure in sin by whispering provocative promises to them. But the benefit of sin is similar to the luxury which an island in the West Indies offers. Luscious fruits grow there, but these delicacies are seasoned with intolerably scorching heat by day and a swarm of stinging pestilence by night. Thus it is impossible for dwellers to enjoy their delicious fruit because they can neither eat comfortably nor sleep well. This adversity made the Spaniards call the place 'comfits in hell.' And it is true – what are the pleasures of sin but sweets in hell?

Carnal pleasures do delight a sensual appetite but they are served with the fiery wrath of God and the restlessness of a guilty conscience. Such fear and anguish are sure to waste away the meager enjoyment they furnish for fleshly hunger.

[214]

(b) *Pleasures which are not inherently sinful*

Some comforts are not sinful in and of themselves – the sin lies in abusing them. This misuse happens in two ways:

(i) *Improper use of pleasure.* No one can live righteously without living soberly too. Godliness might allow you to taste of these pleasures as garnish but not to feed on them as solid meat. Sad to say, some live in pleasures as if they could not live without them.

Once the aroma of enticements rises to the brain and intoxicates a man's judgment, he is so enchanted that he cannot think of parting with them. When the Jews started to thrive on Babylonian soil, for example, they were willing to lay down their bones there rather than return to godliness in Jerusalem. A master never minds his servant having plenty of food and drink, but he does not appreciate it if that servant becomes drunk just when he has a responsibility to perform. Yet this drunken man can do his master's business about as well as a Christian overcharged with creature-comforts and worldly fascination can serve his God in holiness.

(ii) *Improper timing of pleasure.* Fruit eaten out of season is bad. Scripture speaks of 'a time to embrace, and a time to refrain from embracing' (*Eccles. 3:5*). In certain seasons the power of holiness will not allow something which is acceptable at another time.

The Lord's day is an example – all carnal pleasures are inappropriate then. God calls us to higher pleasures and expects us to put aside everything else so we can taste *His* goodness. 'If thou turn away thy foot from the sabbath, from doing thy pleasure on my holy day; and call the sabbath a delight, the holy of the Lord, honorable; and shalt honor him, not doing thine own ways, nor finding thine own pleasure, nor speaking thine own words: then shalt thou delight thyself in the Lord' (*Isa. 58:13, 14*). It is impossible to taste the sweetness of communion with God and honor Him in sanctifying His day unless you deny yourself carnal pleasures.

Suppose a king invited some of his poor subjects to feast with him at his royal table. Can you imagine how these guests would embarrass and dishonor their host and cheat themselves if they brought their own ordinary food into the court? Do glorified saints in heaven miss their carnal delights as they praise God and feed on the joys flowing from their face-to-face vision with Him?

In seasons of fasting and prayer, or in times when the church is suffering – when Christ is bleeding – the Christian needs to deny himself of pleasures and pay his debt of sympathy to his brothers and sisters. When one member of the body of Christ suffers we all suffer.

(c) *True pleasures in Christ*

While a holy life will deny certain pleasures to please God and edify the body of Christ on earth, it will never deprive the Christian of the *true* pleasures of creation. In fact, no one can experience pleasure in the deepest sense of the word until he has walked in the power of holiness. Let me amplify this truth in two ways.

(i) *The holy man has a more sophisticated palate.* A fly cannot find a drop of honey in the same flower where the bee has just fed. Nor can an unholy heart taste the sweetness which a saint savors in God's material provisions. The unbeliever relishes gross carnal pleasures and makes an entire meal of them; but a heart full of grace tastes something more. All Israel drank of the Rock, 'and that Rock was Christ' (*1 Cor. 10:4*). But did everyone who enjoyed the water's natural sweetness taste Christ in it? No, only a few holy men who had a spiritual thirst experienced Him in this way.

Samson's parents ate honey out of the lion's carcass as he did; but he took more satisfaction from it than they. He tasted the sweetness of God's providence which had first delivered him from that very lion – and then furnished him honey to eat.

(ii) *The Christian's cup contains more true pleasure.* Earthly pleasure reaches the righteous man refined into a purer substance, but the unholy person drinks the dregs of sin and wrath.

Dregs of sin. The more fleshly opportunities the carnal man sees, the more he sins with them; they are only fuel for his lusts to kindle upon. He runs as fast with his worldly enjoyments as the prodigal ran with his bags of selfishness clutched about him. None are so wicked as those fed by carnal pleasures. They are to the ungodly what manure is to the swine, who grows fat by lying in it. Unrighteous hearts grow dull and their consciences more senseless in sin because of these pleasures. But the comforts and delights God gives a holy person through what He has created turn into spiritual nourishment of the saint's graces and draw them forth into actions.

Dregs of wrath. The sinner's feast is no sooner served than divine justice spoils it with a heavy bill. The Israelites knew very little enjoyment of their meat from heaven because God's wrath fell upon them before they could swallow it.

The gracious soul, however, is entertained at a cost-free feast. No fear of approaching danger makes him spill any comfort or blessings. He can say with David, 'I will both lay me down in peace, and sleep: for thou, Lord, only makest me dwell in safety' (*Ps. 4:8*). God will not break our rest. As the unicorn healed the waters by dipping his horn in them so all the beasts could drink without danger, Christ has healed His children's pleasures – there is no death in the saints' cup.

(c) *Pleasures which are peculiar to the holy life*

The power of holiness is far from depriving us of joy. In fact, it provides us with other inward joys which the soul finds in the ways of righteousness and with which no one can interfere. Because these joys are inward and unseen, the world speaks ignorantly concerning them. They will not believe in such pleasures until they can see them – but they shall not ever see them unless they believe.

When the Roman soldiers entered the temple and marched into the holy of holies they did not find the kind of images they used to have in their own idolatrous temples, and so they jeered that the Jews must worship the clouds! Because the pleasures of holiness and righteousness are not visible and cannot be examined by the world's carnal senses, ungodly men laugh at saints as if they embrace only a vapor instead of the stately beauty of Juno herself.

Let these wicked men know that their own hearts carry something which could make them see the pleasures of a holy life as being more real than a tangible idol. The guilt of their unholy lives will bruise their consciences; and no whip on their backs nor pain in their flesh has to tell them – peace from a good conscience brings a joyful life that carnality cannot provide.

(i) *It is a life from God*. Whatever God creates is good and pleasant – and life is one of the choicest of His works. In this respect the silliest gnat exceeds the sun even in its brightest glory. And every creature, of course, enjoys life best when it is in good health. Now holiness is the ideal condition of the soul just as health is of the body; thus a holy life must be a pleasant life. Before sin spoiled Adam he lived a pleasant life in paradise. When a person is made holy, then, he begins to return to his primitive state and with it, to his primitive joy. Men often become dissatisfied with their station and rank in the world, but the fault is much more serious than an external problem. It lies deep inside the person himself. The shoe is a nice straight one, but the foot that wears it is crooked.

(ii) *It is a life with God.* A gracious soul walks in God's presence and keeps communion with Him. If you meet a saint you already know what kind of friends he has. 'That ye also may have fellowship with us: and truly our fellowship is with the Father, and with his Son Jesus Christ' (*1 John 1:3*). Holy men will not introduce you to questionable company; instead they will carry you to God, their one great source of life.

The conversation of a cheerful traveling companion entertains and relieves the boredom of your trip. But best of all, if this companion loves you dearly, you take delight in His company. What joy, then, must God supply to the saint He walks with! 'Blessed is the people,' said the psalmist, 'that know the joyful sound: they shall walk, O Lord, in the light of thy countenance. In thy name shall they rejoice all the day' (*Ps. 89:15–16*). The sound of the trumpet which called David's people to religious assemblies is called 'the joyful sound' because God especially demonstrated His presence to His people during worship. Heaven is where the Lord is. Surely, then, that portion of God's presence which the Christian has on earth in times of worship is enough to make his life full of joy.

How sweet to walk with God here below by His comforting presence – the same Almighty God who manifests Himself in all His glory above in heaven! This is something the world cannot match – God walking with His child as friend to friend, manifesting Himself and gently leading him along the way of holiness which will take him into heaven.

By contrast, the lusts of an unholy person sugar-coat his mouth with bits of frothy pleasures, but as soon as they are melted off his tongue and the taste forgotten, they show him the region of darkness waiting for him. They will take him there and leave him to repent of his dearly-bought pleasures in endless torment.

(iii) *It is the life of God Himself.* A holy life is the life of God, much like the life God Himself lives. Holiness is the life of His life. Now friends, do you not think God lives a life of pleasure? And what is the pleasure of His life but holiness?

God takes pleasure in the graces of His saints; but how much more in His own inherent holiness, from whence those graces, those beautiful beams of righteousness, were first sent forth! Thus you are doing something God Himself cannot do if you can wrest any true pleasure out of unholiness. And let me ask this – is it not the lowest of blasphemies for you to say that the path of righteousness is an enemy to true pleasure? In that accusation you are saying God Himself lacks joy, because true pleasure does not exist outside of holiness.

Even the devils who hate God with a perfect hatred dare not declare that He is without joy. They know God is 'glorious in holiness' and the Christian's bliss consists in sharing the same holiness which makes God Himself so blessed (*Exod. 15:11*). This, Christian, is the ultimate expression of happiness, either on earth or in heaven – the same thing that makes you glorious is what has made God glorious. Your joy and pleasure are the same substance which God delights in: 'Thou shalt make them drink of the river of thy pleasures' (*Ps. 36:8*). Mark those words – 'the river of thy pleasures.' God has His pleasures, and He causes saints to drink of them!

Whenever a king commands his servants to take a

visitor down into the cellar so he can drink wine with them, the person is highly honored by his host's generous gesture. But for the king to set the man at his table and let him drink his own wine is an even more cherished experience. Thus when God gives a man the creaturely pleasures of property, corn, wine, and oil, He entertains him in that common wine cellar. But when His grace and mercy beautify a soul with holiness, He gives the most precious gift the person can receive. He never clothes a man with the robe of righteousness unless He means to seat him at His own table in heaven's glory.

II. SATAN CLAIMS THAT RIGHTEOUSNESS WASTES PROSPERITY

Even if you did not falter at the first stone Satan hurled – the lie that holiness hinders pleasure – he has another in hand ready to throw at you. He is not such an inexperienced hunter that he goes into battle with a single shot; expect him to aim another at you as soon as he sees that he has missed you with the first one.

Here is how the second runs: 'You really should not get involved with this holy kind of life unless, of course, you are willing to lose everything you have worked hard to get. And do not forget, people are depending on you. Just look at the most prominent men in the world – did their wealth and affluence come from being holy? Why, if they had been as strict in their consciences as you are, and tied to the rules of a holy life, they could never have arrived at such success. Now if you want some of their prosperity the first thing you must do is to take off the breastplate of righteousness – or at least unbuckle it so it will hang loose enough to give your ingenuity some room. If you do not, you may as well close up shop, for all the profit you will show for your hard work.'

Although the devil's words are deadly weapons, he does

[221]

not have the last word in spiritual warfare – God does. Let us study four facets of it from His point of view.

(a) *Holiness, not riches, is necessary for happiness*
You can fly to heaven without a penny in your pocket but you will not get there at all without holiness in your heart and life. And wisdom urges you to take care of that more important requirement first.

(b) *Heaven is worth all the poverty in the world*
There is a remnant of people who gratefully accept God's gift of salvation, if only they can arrive at heaven's glorious city. And God does not have to bribe them with prosperity and a problem-free walk; they resolve to be holy at all costs. Do not even consider what you might be missing – if you loved God, you would abandon the whole world anyway rather than part with Him.

(c) *Holiness thrives on contentment in Christ*
A few clothes are plenty for a strong healthy man. And warmth from the blood and vital fluids within him is better than warmth from a heavy layer of clothing on the outside. How much better, then, is the contentment which godliness gives a Christian in poverty than the contentment – if such a thing exists in the world – which wealth gives the rich man?

'Godliness with contentment is great gain' (*1 Tim. 6:6*). The holy person is the only contented man in the world. Paul learned to be satisfied no matter what. And if you asked him which master taught him this hard lesson he would tell you it did not come from sitting at Gamaliel's feet, but at Christ's. 'I can do all things through Christ which strengtheneth me' (*Phil. 4:13*). When the holy person is at his lowest and poorest time, he can testify that his heart and his circumstances match each other.

The world would pronounce a man happy if he could sustain himself without borrowing from anyone or if he could pay cash for everything he bought. If this person were to grow hungry for a special food he would not have to send to the market for it; it would already be available to him in his own domain. Well, godliness is so rich that it is more than able to support out of its own storehouse the Christian's whole desire. The saint will never have to beg at the world's door or risk losing his holiness to have it.

(d) *People who pawn their breastplate pay a precious price*
The true cost of this 'bargain' appears in the sin of it and in the heavy curse which moves in upon the heels of that sin.

(i) *It is a great sin.* The devil would not waste his time tempting God's Son with a small sin. Instead, he spread out golden bait before Jesus and 'shewed unto him all the kingdoms of the world' and promised they would be His if only He would fall down and worship him (*Luke 4:5*). The design of this foul spirit's demand was to make Christ acknowledge him as lord of the world and to expect good things from his hand, and not God's.

Thus everyone who seeks the world's prizes through unrighteousness goes to the devil for them and does, in effect, worship him. He may as well go ahead and confess Satan as his lord, for the devil has been put by him into God's place. Would you not say it is better to have poverty from God than riches from the devil? What a daring sin – to take away God's sovereignty and bestow it on the devil!

(ii) *It is a foolish sin.* 'They that will be rich' – that is, by right or by wrong – 'fall into temptation and a snare, and into many foolish and hurtful lusts' (*1 Tim. 6:9*). What is more stupid than to steal something which is yours already? If you are a saint, everything in the world is yours. 'Godliness' has the 'promise of the life that now is, and of that which is to come' (*1 Tim. 4:8*). If riches will be good for you, then you will surely have them, but God is the judge; and if He sees that wealth will not profit your soul, then He will pay you another way. 'Let your conversation be without covetousness; and be content with such things as ye have: for he hath said, I will never leave thee nor forsake thee' (*Heb. 13:5*).

If God gives you wealth but later asks you to part with it for His name's sake, He hands you His bond along with His request to recover the loss with 'a hundredfold' advantage in this life, besides eternal life in the world to come (*Matt. 19:29*). Only a fool will part with God's promises for any security the devil can give.

(iii) *It is an expensive bargain.* A heavy curse always cleaves to unrighteous gain. 'The curse of the Lord is in the house of the wicked' (*Prov. 3:33*), but 'in the house of the righteous is much treasure' (*Prov. 15:6*). You may visit a righteous man's house and find no money, but you are sure to find a treasure. Yet in the wicked man's house there may be much gold and silver but never treasure – the curse of God eats up all his gains. *God's fork follows the wicked man's rake.*

The ungodly bring shame into their houses, 'for the stone shall cry out of the wall, and the beam out of the timber shall answer it' (*Hab. 2:11*). And what man who cherishes his life would live in a haunted house like this, even for tons of gold? The cry of his unrighteousness follows him into every room of the house and echoes until he can hear the stones and beams groaning under the weight of sin that put them there.

This sin is so hateful to the righteous God that not only the man who gathers unrighteous gain, but also the instruments he uses to advance his project, are cursed. Thus the servant who co-operates with his master's fraud collects God's wages too. 'I will punish all those that leap on the threshold, which fill their masters' houses with violence and deceit' (*Zeph. 1:9*).

III. SATAN THREATENS RIGHTEOUSNESS WITH HEAVY
   WORLDLY OPPOSITION

The third stumblingblock which the devil throws across
the path of righteousness is a shrewd kind of peer
pressure: 'Do you not realize you are about to lose the
respect of your friends and neighbors by leaving that
breastplate strapped on?' he taunts. 'And you know
Scripture says it is important for you to live peaceably with
your neighbors. Or do you like being mocked the way Lot
was among the Sodomites, and Noah in the old world?
You really should know by now that this holiness thing
breeds bad blood everywhere it goes. If you have it you
will bring the world's fists down on your head.'

Although this is a weak argument, it carries just enough
weight to amount to a dangerous temptation when it meets
a person with a tender disposition and a strong inclination
to peacefulness. For instance, Aaron probably stumbled
over this very stone in the building of the golden calf. He
did not start out to please himself but rather to appease a
restless people: 'Let not the anger of my Lord wax hot:
thou knowest the people, that they are set on mischief'
(*Exod. 32:22*). It is as if Aaron defended himself like this:
'I did not know what the people might do if I denied their
demands. All I did was pacify them to prevent more
trouble.'

Thus we see the need to be armed against this
temptation of Satan's. And a good way to begin is to
examine the following truths.

(a) *God controls all men*
Anytime He chooses, God can give you favor in the eyes of
those you fear the most. 'When a man's ways please the
Lord, he maketh even his enemies to be at peace with him'
(*Prov. 16:7*). Laban and Jacob furnish a good example.
Laban was full of fury when he chased Jacob with

unswerving determination to get revenge; but God met him on the way and changed his mind. The transformation made such an impact on Laban that he confessed to Jacob why his rage had turned into a calm: 'It is in the power of my hand to do you hurt: but the God of your father spake unto me' (*Gen. 31:29*). Laban had the ability to hurt Jacob but God would not let it happen!

When Mordecai denied Haman the reverence commanded by royalty, it appeared he had chosen the fastest way to stir up the king's temper – but his conscience would not let his knee bow. Yet after Haman had tried everything he knew to punish Mordecai, he himself was forced to inherit the gallows built for the steadfast Jew. And then God's sovereignty moved Mordecai forward to take Haman's place in the king's favor. God, who keeps the keys to kings' breasts, suddenly locked Ahasuerus' heart against the cursed Amalekite and opened it to let Mordecai into his throne room. Why, then, should we hesitate to be conscientious when God provides for His children's safety so faithfully?

(b) *There is more mercy in sinners' hatred than in their love*
Saints usually gain more good from the wrath of the wicked than from their friendship. David was moved to pray for God to make His way plain because his enemies reached out for him with hateful, destructive hands. Dependence on God is always safer than favor with the ungodly – which easily snares believers into compromise. Luther, for instance, said he would not have Erasmus' honor for everything in the world – the familiarity this man had with the great natural minds of the world made him anaemic in the cause of God.

The Moabites could not defeat God's people at arm's length, but after they had made alliances with the Israelites they subdued them. It was not their curses but their embraces which gave Moab that victory. Let me assure you – we can never lose the love, or inherit the fury of men, for a better reason than keeping our breastplate of righteousness fastened close to us.

(i) *When we lose man's love we gain God's blessing.* 'Blessed are ye, when men say all manner of evil against you falsely, for my sake' (*Matt. 5:11*). God's providence is a perfect roof over our heads to defend us from the storm of man's rage. But it is a different story when a saint is caught in sin and gives the ungodly opportunity to speak evil of him. Man reviles and God frowns. His Word does not open its shelter then to hide you from the assault of reviling tongues. But when the wicked hate you *for your holiness*, God is bound by promise to pay you love for their hatred and blessing for their cursing. Can we ever complain about man's disrespect when obedience and holiness advance us to a higher place in the King's favor?

(ii) *When we lose the world's love we gain its reverence and honor.* The people who will not love you because you are holy cannot help but respect and fear you for that same reason. But every time you give up a little holiness to gain false love from sinners, you forfeit the reverence which their consciences secretly paid to your life. Like Samson, a Christian walking in the power of holiness is greatly feared by the wicked; but if sin exposes an impotent spirit he is captured and falls under the lash of their tongues and the scorn of their hearts.

Poverty and a low class in society cannot make you contemptible as long as you keep on the breastplate of righteousness. *Majesty can reign in a holy heart even when it is dressed in rags.* For instance, the righteousness of David commanded reverence from Saul, and the king paid homage to his exiled subject: 'He wept, and said to David, Thou art more righteous than I' (*1 Sam. 24:16, 17*). And this is as it should be – carnal men must admit that they are overpowered by the holy lives of saints. And this shall happen as you behave in that distinctive and singular manner called for by God, doing things that even the best of our unbelieving neighbors cannot do. As long as Pharaoh's magicians matched the miracles of Moses they assumed they were as good as he was. But the plague of lice stopped them – even their mightiest skills could not perform what Moses had accomplished and they had to admit 'the finger of God' was in it (*Exod. 8:19*). Christian, you must always do more than the unbelievers, and your righteousness, as one in God's calling, must exceed theirs. Now this realization brings us to the application of all we have learned so far about walking in the power of holiness.

TWO PARTICULARS ON LIVING A HOLY LIFE

I. SIN AND HOLINESS DO EXIST AND DO OPPOSE EACH OTHER

We live in a generation which treats sin and holiness as the melancholy imaginings of timid men and women. Some even brag about being free from the tyranny of holiness and that they can curse, lie, and steal without being accountable to an unbending conscience. They rationalize that sin does not exist except in the mind. Thus these are even worse fools than the one David described: 'The fool hath said in his heart, there is no God' (*Ps. 14:1*). These people go further and shamelessly announce to the whole world that they are fools.

I am not mentioning these ungodly men merely to disprove them – that would be as senseless as proving there is a sun on a clear day because an insane person denies it. I just want to impress upon you the abominable times we live in.

What a deep sleep we have slept, that the enemy could

have come in to sow these tares among us! Maybe we took it for granted that such poisonous seed would not grow in our soil, where Christ's servants have worked so hard – at great cost – to clear it. Yet experience has proved that when disease invades a city it rages more freely in pure air than in polluted climates. And when a spirit of delusion falls upon a people who have enjoyed the gospel most, it grows to epidemic proportions.

It makes me tremble to see the weeds and nettles springing up in England, when for so long she was one of Christ's fairest, most fruitful garden plots. When men fall so far from the profession of the gospel, and become so blinded that they cannot tell light from darkness, are they not sliding backwards into atheism? This is not natural blindness, for even the heathen can tell the difference between good and evil; they can see holiness and sin without scriptural light to show them. No, this blindness is a plague of God which has fallen on them for rebelling against the light when they did have it.

II. IT IS POSSIBLE TO LIVE IN THE POWER OF HOLINESS

God would never command His people to do something without supplying the power to perform it. Even so, we must remember the distinction between legal righteousness and evangelical righteousness. Of course not all God's children have the same stature and strength – some walk in holiness much more easily than others. Yet there has never been a saint endued with new life from Christ who has not had both a true desire and some success in this matter of evangelical righteousness and who does not desire to do more than he is able.

A seed is tiny but contains the bigness and height of a mature tree inside; and it continually puts forth more and more strength as it grows to maturity. Thus in the very first principle of grace which is planted at conversion, is contained perfect and complete grace in a sense. That is, the desire is in him to grow up into that perfection which God has appointed for him in Christ Jesus.

In a word, Christian, when thoughts of the impossibility of having this holiness here on earth are suggested to you, reject them and send them straight back to Satan. He knows your efforts for holiness will prove him a liar. Purpose continually to be holy and keep your eye on God's promise to help. You need not be afraid either, 'for the Lord God is a sun and shield: the Lord will give grace and glory: no good thing will he withhold from them that walk uprightly' (*Ps. 84:11*). Mark those words 'grace and glory' – that is, 'grace *unto* glory.' God will keep adding 'more grace' to what you already have until your grace on earth merges with glory in heaven (*Jas. 4:6*).

REPROOF OF UNHOLY PERSONS
We live in the midst of a crooked and perverse generation. For this reason it is necessary for us to recognize three different types of unrighteousness which flourish all around us.

I. SOME PEOPLE ARE SATISFIED WITH THEIR UNHOLINESS
This is the natural state of every person on earth, but many are so far from walking in the power of holiness that their souls are paralyzed under the power of sin. Their lusts dictate and cut out all their work for them – and demand every hour of the day and night to get it done. It is a sad and wasted life which is spent on such beastly work as sin.

The apostle Paul linked 'the bond of iniquity' and 'the gall of bitterness' (*Acts 8:23*). Anyone who plants sin and unholiness and tries to harvest anything except bitter fruit for all his work claims knowledge beyond God Himself. For He guarantees that the natural fruit which grows from this root is 'gall and wormwood' (*Deut. 29:18*).

The devil, through centuries of artistic cookery, might baste the bitter morsel of unholiness with such clever forms of deception that you cannot taste the real flavor of it. But as Abner asked Joab, 'Knowest thou not that it will be bitterness in the latter end?' (*2 Sam. 2:26*). Hell will melt all the sugar the pill was coated with. And then – if not before – you will taste the true bitterness of what went down so easily. How many in hell today must be cursing their feast and their feast-maker too!

Do you think it eases the pain of the damned to count up the pleasures, profits, and carnal entertainment they got for their money on earth when they must pay for them through eternity with unspeakable torments? Surely it only deepens their agony to realize how cheaply they sold their souls and lost heaven – all because they decided the burden of holiness was a price too high to pay!

While the false economy of Satan's deception is not hard for Christians to see, very few people ever consider what is happening in eternity. They see sinners die every day in the middle of sin but do not think any more about them burning and roaring in hell than fish in the river wonder what happens to their fellows who snatched the dangling bait. Even though the captives are cast alive into the frying pan or boiling pot, their silly companions are ready to nibble at the very same hook. Even so, careless men and women eagerly pursue sinful pleasures and the wages of unrighteousness which have taken millions of souls before them into hell and damnation.

II. OTHERS HIDE BEHIND COUNTERFEIT HOLINESS

There are men who are just as unholy as the ones contented in sin – but these wear something like a breastplate, a counterfeit holiness to save their reputation in the world. 'Verily I say unto you, they have their reward' (*Matt. 6:2*). And what a measly reward! You are doing the devil a double service, and God a double disservice, to march into battle armed with hypocrisy. First you draw the prince's expectations towards you as a soldier who will attempt courageous duties for him. But then when you do nothing he sees only a traitor taking up the place of a faithful subject armed for victory. You do your prince more harm than the coward who stays home, or rebelliously runs over to the enemy's camp and tells him plainly what he intends to do.

Be serious, friends. If you are after holiness make sure it is true holiness. 'Put on the new man, which after God is created in righteousness and true holiness' (*Eph. 4:24*). Observe two phrases in that passage. Holiness is called the 'new man after God' – that is, according to the likeness of God. Such a sculpture is drawn from God's being, as an artist copies the face of a man. Also, 'true holiness' means a holiness of Scripture truth, not pharisaical and traditional doctrine; as well it means a holiness which has as its point of reference the heart, which is the seat of truth or falsehood.

In order to have true holiness then, the Christian must have righteousness and holiness in his heart. Many people have beauty of holiness which is like the attractiveness of the body – skin deep and all on the surface. If you tear open the most beautiful body on earth you will not find much except blood and stench; so also, when counterfeit holiness is exposed, it will have only an abundance of spiritual impurities and filth inside.

Paul assured the high priest: 'God shall smite thee, thou whited wall' (*Acts 23:3*). And if you are a hypocrite I must echo the apostle's warning: 'God will strike you as a painted tomb, because the whitewash of religion that you have applied to your profession of faith does not dazzle others into admiration of your sanctity as much as your rottenness will soon make you abhorred by everyone who sees you.'

III. MANY MOCK RIGHTEOUSNESS

Some men are so far from being holy themselves that they ridicule those who are. These think the breastplate of righteousness is so foolish that they laughingly point to the saint who wears it in his daily behavior: 'Look! There goes a holy brother, one of the pure ones!' But their mocking language does more than scorn the saint's holiness – it betrays the wickedness of their own hard hearts.

A further degree of ungodliness appears in mocking the holiness of another person rather than only harboring unholiness in oneself. How desperately wicked is that man who not only refuses to partake in the divine nature himself but cannot bear the sight of others choosing to follow the holiness of Christ. The very hint of holiness works up such a strong opposition inside the person that it causes him to vomit out the gall and bitterness of his spirit against it.

God's Spirit reserves the chair for this kind of sinner and seats him above all his brethren in iniquity. 'Blessed is the man that walketh not in the counsel of the ungodly, nor standeth in the way of sinners, nor sitteth in the seat of the scornful' (*Ps. 1:1*). In this case the scorner is set as chairman at the counsel-table of sinners.

Some read the word *scornful* as 'rhetorical mockers,' for there is indeed a devilish cleverness in some of these jeerers. Such scorners take pride in polishing the darts they shoot against saints. The Septuagint translates the phrase as 'the chair of the pestilent ones.' As the plague is the most deadly of diseases, so is the spirit of scorning among sins. Very few recover from this sin, for the Bible speaks of sinners almost synonymously with the dead.

God warns us not to waste our healing balm of reproof – 'reprove not a scorner, lest he hate thee' (*Prov. 9:8*). All we can do is write 'Lord, have mercy' on his door – pray for him, but do not try to reason with him.

Perhaps the saddest example of scorn is the mingling of mockers among godly people. Notice how God's Spirit interprets the sarcasm of Ishmael in Abraham's family: 'But as then he that was born after the flesh persecuted him that was born after the Spirit, even so it is now' (*Gal. 4:29*).

The world will not label malice as persecution unless it draws blood, but God wants the scorner to know ahead of time what his title will be at Christ's judgment – *persecutor*. The mockery of holiness is a serious sin because it carries the seed of bloody oppression in it. Those who freely move their tongues to ridicule and show their teeth in bitterness would bite into righteousness and tear it apart if they had enough power to do it.

As Ishmael persecuted his brother who was born after the Spirit, 'even so it is now.' This mocking spirit runs in the blood of all ungodly men, though God in His mercy rides some of them with a bit in their mouths. While this latter group will not open their hearts to Christ, the powerful conviction of truth makes their consciences agree with the conclusion of Pilate's wife: 'Have thou nothing to do with that just man: for I have suffered many things . . . because of him' (*Matt. 27:19*).

While there have always been mockers of holiness, the Spirit of God has prophesied that a special kind of scoffer will come on the stage in the last days. Those who laugh at righteousness used to be men and women who openly defied God and wallowed in wickedness – but the Spirit of God tells of a new gang that will mock holiness under the name of holiness. Some of them will be as ungodly as the former ones, but their evil is cloaked in religion. 'But, beloved, remember ye the words which were spoken before of the apostles of our Lord Jesus Christ; how that they told you there should be mockers in the last time, who should walk after their own ungodly lusts' (*Jude 17, 18*). And so we will not expect them only among heathens and criminals; Scripture gives us as clear a characterization as if they wore names on their foreheads: 'These be they who separate themselves, sensual, having not the Spirit' (*v. 19*).

One minister reads these words as 'sect-makers, fleshly, not having the Spirit.' Sect-makers – those who separate themselves! My heart trembles to see the mocker's arrows shot out of this window. These are the ones who say they must separate because conscience tells them they have a more pure worship than others; and they cannot stand to touch unclean people by joining their ordinances. Are these people actually mockers, and fleshly? Truly, if the Spirit of God had not told us this we might have gone into their tent last, as Laban did into Rachel's, not suspecting mockers of holiness to live there. If you are an atheistic mocker or a mocker of true holiness in the disguise of a false one, 'be not deceived, God is not mocked' (*Gal. 6:7*).

Neither will God let His grace be mocked in His saints. Remember what it cost the children who teased Elisha? 'Go up, thou bald head; go up, thou bald head' (*2 Kings 2:23*). Not only did they scoff at God's prophet with that nickname but they ridiculed Elijah's rapture into heaven. It is as if they had dared Elisha: 'If you believe your master is gone up to heaven, why do you not go up after him, so we may get rid of you both?' It is hard to realize that these children could sink to such depths of ungodliness – until we stop and remember where they came from – Bethel, a city of idolatry.

God dealt with Michal severely for despising David's

dancing before his Lord, an act which her proud spirit thought too common for her husband. Do you recall her punishment? 'Therefore Michal the daughter of Saul had no child unto the day of her death' (*2 Sam. 6:23*). Because in her thinking the praise of God was too lowly for a king, no heir ever came from her womb to wear a crown.

Further, it is a serious sin to mock a person who is in trouble. 'Whoso mocketh the poor reproacheth his Maker' (*Prov. 17:5*). To laugh at a saint's sin is a heavy wrong in itself. Because some sons of Belial enjoyed watching David fall into the temptation of adultery and murder, God charged them with blasphemy.

How much more critical, then, is it to deride a person for his holiness! Sin does carry some cause of shame, and gives ungodly hearts an occasion to reproach a man, especially a saint, for unbecoming behavior. But holiness is not only the nobility of a human being, but the honor of the most high God Himself: 'Who is like thee, glorious in holiness?' (*Exod. 15:11*). Thus no one can mock holiness without mocking God infinitely more, for there is greater holiness in Him than in all men and angels put together. Nothing dishonors God more than for someone to bruise His children's holiness.

When the Romans wished to assassinate a person's character they would pour contempt on him by commanding any portraits and statues of him found in the city to be smashed. Now every Christian is a living image of God and the more holy one is, the more like God. Thus if you scorn a saint you besmirch God's honor. A devastating, demonic wickedness in Old Testament heathens made them 'cast fire' into God's sanctuary and 'break down the carved work . . . with axes and hammers' (*Ps. 74: 6, 7*). The church saw this destruction and mourned, 'God, how long shall the adversary reproach? shall the enemy blaspheme thy name for ever?' (*v. 10*). How then must God view malice which is spent not on wood and stones but on the gracefully carved work of His Spirit – the holiness of His living temples?

EXHORTATION TO SAINTS

I. BLESS GOD FOR FURNISHING THE BREASTPLATE

Hundreds of people are destroyed by the devil every day because they do not have the breastplate of righteousness to defend their hearts against his murdering shot. If God had made you famous and rich in the world, but not holy, He would have given you nothing more than fuel for hell. How then can we forget to thank God for His precious breastplate of righteousness?

When an enemy approaches a city without walls or arms for defense, the wealthier that city the worse the destruction. And each time Satan comes to a man who has much of the world but nothing of God in his soul to defend him, he makes a miserable wreck of the person. He takes whatever he pleases and does whatever he wants with such souls. The devil's plundering possession is so thorough that the captive would not think of postponing or denying a lust. Although he knows what this fulfillment will cost him in hell, he goes ahead and damns his soul rather than stand against the burning demands of temptation.

Herod threw down half his kingdom at the feet of a malicious wench; and when she decided this was not enough, he sacrificed everything he had. But if the blood of John the Baptist cost Herod his throne in this life, surely it was nothing compared to the wages of divine providence paid immediately when he met death.

But let the saints humbly shout 'Hallelujah!' When God made you a holy man or woman He gave you gates and bars to your city. Now through His grace you are able to defend yourself with the continual comforts which heaven sends to withstand Satan's power. Once you were a timid slave to him but now he is under your feet. The day you became holy God firmly planted your foot on the serpent's head. Your lusts – mighty strongholds which gave him easy control – have been taken out of his hand. A town celebrates when the headquarters which commanded it are won back from the enemy. Satan has been dislodged and can never again set himself up as king of your soul.

In a word, when God made you a righteous person He began heaven in your soul. The moment you were born again, an heir to heaven was born as well. Think about the festivities that take place when a young prince is born as heir to the throne of even some tiny territory in God's vast creation. Do you not have even more reason to rejoice when heaven's glory is settled on you, especially as you recall in what realm your inheritance lay before you were adopted into God's family? Paul joins both of these aspects in a full doxology: 'Giving thanks unto the Father, which hath made us meet to be partakers of the inheritance of the saints in light: who hath delivered us from the power of darkness, and hath translated us into the kingdom of his dear Son' (*Col. 1:12, 13*). What a blessed change – stepping out of the devil's dark dungeon, where you were kept in chains of unrighteousness as a prisoner bound for hell, into the kingdom of Christ's grace, where the golden chain of righteousness around your neck tells Satan and the whole world you are the heir-apparent to heaven!

II. KEEP YOUR BREASTPLATE ON

Does a soldier have to be reminded to put on his armour when he heads into battle? Could he easily be persuaded to leave it off? Yet many have done this and paid dearly for their pseudo-boldness. Even if the weight of that armour becomes cumbersome it is better to struggle with it than to carry a deadly wound in the breast. If this piece falls off you cannot keep on the rest of your armour for long.

If you allow unholiness to penetrate, conscience will call your sincerity into question. It is true that Peter claimed uprightness only a short time after he had denied the Master: 'Lord, thou knowest all things; thou knowest that I love thee' (*John 21:17*). Even after he had it called into question by his Lord three times, Peter still vouched for his sincerity. But we must consider two things: Peter's sin was not deliberate; and much bitter sorrow intervened between his denial and the renewing of his repentance. It was so much harder, though, for David to clear sincerity to his conscience after he had deliberately sinned that he earnestly begged of God: 'Create in me a clean heart, O God; and renew a right spirit within me' (*Ps. 51:10*).

Again, the gospel shoe will not fit a foot that is swollen with sin and unholiness. It is impossible for you to wear it unless unrighteousness has been lanced by repentance and cut out by pardon. Consider this: are you fit enough to suffer joyfully or patiently for God the way you are today? No more than a diseased, bedridden soldier is to undertake a long march! Unholiness weakens the soul as much or more than sickness weakens the body and prevents it from enduring hardship.

David expressed keen sorrow for the unholiness in his life: 'O spare me, that I may recover strength, before I go hence, and be no more' (*Ps. 39:13*). He did not want to die until holiness ruled his heart again. Ungodliness is a poison which drinks up all serenity of conscience and inward springs of joy. If you throw a stone into a clear brook it will soon become muddy. 'He will speak peace unto his people, but let them not turn again to folly' (*Ps. 85:8*).

Carelessness in the walk of holiness dangerously

exposes your faith, which is kept in good conscience as a jewel is protected in a cabinet. Faith is an eye, and sin casts a hazy mist before it. To faith, a holy life is like pure air to the eye; we can see farther on a clear day. Thus faith sees further into God's promise when it looks through a holy well-ordered life.

Faith is a shield. Will a soldier drop his protection unless he has been seriously wounded? If faith fails, what will happen to hope, which cleaves to faith and draws strength from her as a nursing child takes nourishment from its mother? If faith cannot see pardon in the promise, then hope cannot look for salvation. If faith cannot claim sonship, hope will not wait for the inheritance. Faith informs the soul it has 'peace with God' and then the soul rejoices 'in the hope of the glory of God' (*Rom. 5:1, 2*).

Are you trying to use the sword of the Spirit? How can you hold it when unholiness has seriously maimed the hand of faith that must carry it? This sword has two edges – one side heals but the other wounds. With one it saves and with the other it damns. The Bible does not speak a single kind word to the person who practices sin. Now – think and then think some more – is any sin worth all this confusion which will inevitably strangle and smother your soul?

III. BE HUMBLE WHEN YOU ARE HOLY

From whichever direction pride tries to get in – like wind blowing open a door or window – shut it out! Nothing is more abusive to your holiness – it turns righteousness into hemlock and holiness into sin. You are never further from Christlikeness than when you are puffed up with the conceit of pride. When we see a man swollen with dropsy we can tell his blood is watery and sick even without a blood test. The more pride forces its way through your life, the less pure blood of holiness you have running in the veins of your soul. 'Behold, his soul which is lifted up is not upright' (*Hab. 2:4*). That word *behold* is like a sign painted on the proud man's door so everyone may know an ungodly person lives inside.

If you do not want to cripple the power of holiness, or question its existence, guard against pride. Have you ever felt like separating yourself from other saints because they are not as holy as you? Be careful – this stinks of Pharisaism. It is the nature of holiness to give brothers and sisters every advantage – first. 'In lowliness of mind let each esteem other better than themselves' (*Phil. 2:3*).

Or maybe you have noticed the germs of a disease called self-righteousness invading your thoughts; your heart leans hard on its righteousness until confidence boosts you to expect salvation because of it. Well, in that case I must warn you with the words of Constantine: 'Set up your ladder then, and climb up to heaven by yourself; because no one else has ever gotten there like that.' Do you really think you might be the only one in heaven who has bought your own peace? Go and measure that ladder by the holiness of God's gospel. If it is even one rung short you will be exactly that far short of heaven!

If you are depending on your own righteousness when it has shined in public places and your own holiness as it has walked in brightness, you have kissed your hand with your own mouth. You are guilty of giving the highest part of divine worship to a human, to the created sun of your supposed inherent holiness, something which God has appointed and reserved for the uncreated Sun of Righteousness alone – 'The Lord our righteousness' (*Jer. 33:16*).

You have only two choices as Scripture teaches them – plead guilty and renounce your humanistic endeavor or else give up life and salvation altogether. Now to help you keep down the insurrection of pride and conceit from holiness, take these thoughts of humility into serious consideration.

(a) *Meditate on the holiness of God*

A man who stands in a high place does not get dizzy until he looks down. If he allows a condescending survey of those who are less holy than himself, his head begins to spin. Looking up is the only cure for this disease. The holiest man in the world, once he sees God's infinite holiness, knows himself as he really is and is humbled. Isaiah's vision revealed God sitting on His throne surrounded by heavenly ministers covering their faces and crying, 'Holy, holy, holy, is the Lord of hosts.' But the heavenly scene also opened up to the prophet his own vileness; when he heard the seraphim crying 'holy' before God, he cried out 'unclean' regarding his own spirituality (*Isa. 6:3, 5*).

Job was another man who realized the impurity of his soul when he glimpsed God's holiness. 'Now mine eye seeth thee. Wherefore I abhor myself, and repent' (*Job 42: 5, 6*).In a darkened room we seem clean enough; but if we could surround ourselves with beams of God's glorious majesty and holiness, the sun's rays could not discover more specks of dust in the air than God's holiness would convict us of our sin. But the policy of pride is not to appear where it can be outshined; it prefers to go where it will be adored in the muted light of self-exaltation.

(b) *Meditate on the holiness of man's innocent state*

It is true – if you are a believer you have a principle of holiness planted in you. But what about the nature you had before Adam sinned? The Israelites who saw the second temple, but could not remember the first one, thought it was a splendid structure. Yet those who had also seen the walls of the first one, Solomon's Temple, had tears mixed with their rejoicing as they recalled its destruction. 'Many of the priests and Levites and chief of the fathers, who were ancient men, that had seen the first house, when the foundation of this house was laid before their eyes, wept with a loud voice' (*Ezra 3:12*). Let this remind us, then, of what man in all his glory fell into by Satan's design. In heaven you will realize the same pleasures Adam enjoyed in paradise, but many weary steps through obstacles of lust, temptation, and sin lie between you and the top of that hill.

The Christian's journey to heaven is a hard one to travel. 'If the righteous scarcely be saved, where shall the ungodly and the sinner appear?' (*1 Pet. 4:18*). The wise virgins had no oil to spare. Remind pride of that and watch its feathers fall.

(c) *Meditate on your own human inadequacy*

Paul had an effective method of waylaying pride when it tried to follow him too closely. He humbled himself by remembering how wicked he had been before salvation. And he dared not speak a word about his holiness before he had bolted the door on pride and recalled the whole story of the darkest chapters of his life. No enemy could have drawn Paul's picture with blacker colors. Again and again pride was battered by the apostle's description of himself: 'I am the least of the apostles, that am not meet to be called an apostle, because I persecuted the church of God' (*1 Cor. 15:9*).

Only after Paul had openly washed himself in the pool of his former sins did he mention his cleansing by God's mercy: 'By the grace of God I am what I am: . . . but I labored more abundantly than they all: yet not I, but the grace of God which was with me' (*v. 10*). He knew the best way to kill the weed of pride was to break up his heart and turn it inside out – to humble and abase himself for every abomination. Pride cannot easily survive in soil where honest humility plows through regularly. Pride is a worm which gnaws the very heart out of grace. Only bitter medicines break and kill a bag of worms gathered inside the stomach; sweet things nourish them. Christian, take doses of this bitter medicine as needed – humility and repentance – and with God's blessing, you will be healed.

But do not ever think this worm breeds only in young children and weak Christians. It is the most common disease of that age, yes. But mature Christians are not immune either. Old David, for instance, was infested with this worm when he ordered Joab to number the people. Have you ever found yourself secretly keeping score of the good works you have done and the sufferings you have endured for God, and enjoying a little muffled self-applause now and then?

8: Seventh Consideration: The Christian's Spiritual Shoe

And your feet shod with the preparation of the gospel of peace (Eph. 6:15).

T HIS verse presents the third piece of armour in the Christian's protection – a spiritual shoe, fitted to his foot and designed to be worn as long as he battles sin and Satan. '*And your feet shod with the preparation of the gospel of peace.*' Let us now study three distinct terms from Scripture concerning this shoe: first what is meant by the *Gospel*; second, what is meant by *peace*; and third, what the word *feet* means here, as well as the grace intended by the *preparation of the gospel of peace.*

1. What is Meant by the Gospel

Gospel, according to the meaning of the original word, signifies *good news* or *joyful message*. Usually in Scripture the word is reserved for the doctrine of Christ and His salvation. 'I bring you good tidings of great joy,' said the angel to the shepherds (*Luke 2:10*). And then he added, 'Unto you is born this day in the city of David a Savior, which is Christ the Lord' (*v. 11*). Thus *gospel* in the New Testament generally carries the connotation of *joy* and *good news*, and we shall use that same meaning here.

THE MOST JOYFUL NEWS IN THE WORLD
The revelation of Christ and the grace of God through Him is, without compare, the best news a sinner can hear.

[245]

It is such a unique message that no good news can come before it nor bad news can follow. God's mercy precedes His blessing to sinners: 'God be merciful unto us, and bless us; and cause his face to shine upon us' (*Ps. 67:1*).

I. GOD FORGIVES AND THEN HE GIVES

Until God mercifully pardons our sins through Christ He cannot look kindly on us sinners. All our benefits are but blessings in bullion until gospel grace – pardoning mercy – stamps them with salvation and makes them current. God cannot show any good will until Christ makes peace for us: 'On earth peace, good will toward men' (*Luke 2:14*). And what joy would it be, even to the sinner who inherited a kingdom, if he could not claim it from the joy and favor of God's heart?

II. NO BAD NEWS CAN COME AFTER ONE EMBRACES THE GOOD NEWS OF CHRIST

God's mercy in Christ changes the very nature of evil to the believer. All plagues and judgments that can come to the person baptized in the stream of gospel grace receive a new name. They arrive on a new errand of God's sovereignty and have a different taste to the Christian, as water running through minerals takes on a new flavor and a healing virtue that it did not have before. 'The inhabitant shall not say, I am sick: the people that dwell therein shall be forgiven their iniquity' (*Isa. 33:24*). The prophet did not say that they would not *be* sick, but that they would be so filled with the joy of God's pardoning mercy that they would not complain of being sick. *Affliction is too thin a veil to darken the joy of the good news of Jesus.*

The gospel message brings such joy that God opened a crevice to let some beams of this light in even to Adam. This is the news God used to comfort His people when things were at their worst and their lives were at the lowest ebb: 'Therefore the Lord himself shall give you a sign; Behold, a virgin shall conceive, and bear a son, and shall call his name Immanuel' (*Isa. 7:14*). 'But thou, Bethlehem Ephratah, though thou be little among the thousands of Judah, yet out of thee shall he come forth unto me that is to be ruler in Israel; whose goings forth have been from of old, from everlasting . . . *And this man shall be the peace*' (*Mic. 5:2, 5*).

This is the precious secret which God whispers, by His Spirit, only in the ear of those whom He embraces with special distinguishing love. 'In that hour Jesus rejoiced in spirit, and said, I thank thee, O Father, Lord of heaven and earth, that thou hast hid these things from the wise and prudent, and hast revealed them unto babes: even so, Father; for so it seemed good in thy sight' (*Luke 10:21*). 'Now we have received, not the spirit of the world, but the spirit which is of God; that we might know the things that are freely given to us of God' (*1 Cor. 2:12*). On the other hand, it is the pathetic but sure sign of a soul marked for hell to have the gospel hidden from him: 'But if our gospel be hid, it is hid to them that are lost' (*2 Cor. 4:3*).

This brings us to the characteristics of a joyful message, all of which are found in the gospel. Let us study five of these now.

PROPERTIES OF A JOYFUL MESSAGE FOUND IN THE GOSPEL

1. A JOYFUL MESSAGE MUST BE GOOD

Nobody is glad to hear bad news. Joy enlarges and opens the heart so it can go out and welcome its most special desires; but bad news always finds the door shut against it.

The gospel brings promises which herald the good that God intends for sinners, but threatenings are the native tongue of the law. While it cannot speak anything except judgment to sinners, Christ's gospel of grace smiles on them and smooths out the frowning wrinkles on the forehead of the law.

II. THE NEWS OF THE GOSPEL IS AS GREAT AS IT IS GOOD

If we hear insignificant news we will probably forget it. But if it is both important and very good, it causes rejoicing. The angel of the Lord said, 'I bring you good tidings of great joy' (*Luke 2:10*). It has to be *great* joy because it is *all* joy; the Lord Christ has brought news of such fulness that He left nothing for anyone else to add. If you think something might be missing from the gospel you must look higher than God, for He gives Himself through Christ to believers in the covenant of grace. We are fully persuaded the apostle Paul's argument will hold: 'All things are yours; and ye are Christ's; and Christ is God's' (*1 Cor. 3:22, 23*).

The gospel places our vessels close to the fountain of goodness itself; and surely we must have all if we are united to the One who has everything. Can any good news come to glorified saints which heaven does not give them? We have proof of that glory in the Word: 'Jesus Christ who hath abolished death, and hath brought life and immortality to light through the gospel' (*2 Tim. 1:10*). The sun in the sky hides heaven from us while it shows the earth to us! But the gospel enlightens both at once – godliness has the 'promise of the life that now is, and of that which is to come' (*1 Tim. 4:8*).

III. A GOOD MESSAGE MUST INTIMATELY CONCERN THE HEARERS

The audience must have a personal interest before an announcement can be good news. While we can be happy to hear about something good happening to another person, it affects us more when it is poured directly into our own hearts. For example, a sick man does not feel the joy of another's recovery as strongly as he would his own.

The gospel does not report what God has done for angels but *for us*. 'Unto you,' the angel said, 'is born . . . a Savior, which is Christ the Lord' (*Luke 2:11*). If angels rejoiced for our happiness, surely our benefit gives even deeper reason to be glad. It would be strange if the messenger who only brings the news should sing, but the recipient shrug it off indifferently. But be assured that these gospel tidings are for you, if you embrace Christ Jesus with arms of faith.

Now in a kingdom every subject, no matter how lowly, has a part in the prince; he is a common good to them all. And so is Christ to believers. The promises are laid out like a well-done portrait; they follow everyone who looks on them with an eye of faith. The gospel's joy is your joy if you have faith to receive it.

IV. SURPRISE ADDS MORE JOY TO THE GOOD NEWS

The glad message of the gospel was unheard of and unlooked for by the sons of men. It could never have entered into the heart of a human to conceive such news until God unlocked His own good pleasure and revealed the counsel of His will. During the reign of King Henry VIII a pardon was sent to a nobleman only hours before he was scheduled to be beheaded; and this sudden news was so unexpected that the man died for joy! The vessel of our human nature is so fragile that the wine of even such inferior joy sometimes shatters it. Yet divine tidings exceed 'natural news' as far as God's mercy surpasses the mercy of a mortal man, or as deliverance from eternal hell differs from temporal death, which is gone before the pain is barely felt.

V. GOOD NEWS MUST BE TRUE AND CERTAIN

This is not like rumor or hearsay which no one can trace back to the author. We have the gospel from God Himself, who cannot lie. The ruler of all heaven guarantees the truth of it: 'This is my beloved Son: hear him' (*Luke 9:35*). All the miracles of Christ confirmed the validity of the gospel. The skeptics who denied Christ's doctrine were nonetheless forced over and over again to acknowledge the divinity of His miracles, thus exposing the absurdity of their unbelief to the entire world. Jesus' miracles were to the gospel as seals are to a document. Unbelievers could not deny that God was in these miracles but they could not see Him in the doctrine. As if God would ever set His seal to an untruth!

Here is what fills up the joy of this good news – it will not deceive any who lay the entire weight of their confidence on it. 'This is a faithful saying, and worthy of all acceptation, that Christ Jesus came into the world to save sinners' (*1 Tim. 1:15*). The bridge which the gospel builds over the gulf of heavenly wrath, for sinners to pass from their sins into the kingdom of God, is supported by the arches of His divine wisdom, power, mercy, and faithfulness. And the believer need never fear until he sees these starting to bend or break. It is called the 'everlasting gospel' (*Rev. 14:6*). Even when heaven and earth are in ruins, not the least part of any promise from God will be buried in their rubble. 'The word of the Lord endureth for ever. And this is the word which by the gospel is preached unto you' (*1 Pet. 1:25*).

CLAIMS ON OUR COMPASSION OF THOSE WHO NEVER HEARD THE GOSPEL

Because a dismal night of spiritual poverty and blindness is stretched over whole nations, they are under a continual massacre from the bloody butcher of hell! And that soul-fiend makes easy conquest of people in darkness. He lays his knife to their throats and meets with no resistance because he finds them fast asleep in their ignorance – destitute of the only light which can reveal the way of escape from the destroyer.

Saints who have tasted the sweetness of gospel grace tremble at the pitiful condition of the ungodly – and may God forgive us for not weeping even more for them. We do not live so far from these people that we should not pity them, pray for them, and sincerely desire their salvation. And do not be deceived – failure to do these things smears us with the guilt of their blood, which is shed continually by the murderer of mankind.

While you cannot give these unlearned people a portion of your own salvation, remember that they are starving to death because they have never feasted on the Bread of Life. Some have even taken up the false hope that heathens can find Christ by knowing the sun, moon, and stars, by seeing the greatness of creation. Those with this view may seem to be kinder to the heathen, but I fear it will be shown in the end that they are the more cruel for not rather working and praying for the light of gospel preaching to arise in power in the nations.

When military personnel judge the defense of a camp to be adequate, reinforcements and aid often begin to arrive more slowly. And for this reason I wish Satan had not deceived so many in this same fashion. If such a wonderful lesson could be learned from the stars, we should by now have heard of some thus taught. Of course a star did lead the wise men to Christ, but a heavenly preacher opened that text to them; otherwise they would never have understood what they saw.

THE WORLD'S REJECTION OF THE GOSPEL
When the news of the Savior's birth was told in Jerusalem, it should have caused every heart to beat for joy, to see the

blessed Messiah fill the hope of every generation. But just the opposite was true – Christ's coming alarmed these men as if an enemy, not a Savior, had arrived.

But, one might reason, even though men faltered at accepting Christ's lowly birth and parentage, surely they would worship Him when the rays of His divinity started shining through all the miracles and wonders that followed this Man. When His own lips showed His authority and told the joyful message He brought from the Father, would they not thirstily drink in the salvation preached to them? No, they persisted in cursed unbelief and obstinate rejection of the Christ.

Although the Scripture, which the Jews seemed to adore, so fully testified for Christ that it accused them to their own consciences, they still refused Jesus. Christ warned, 'Search the scriptures; for in them ye think ye have eternal life: and they are they which testify of me. And ye will not come to me, that ye might have life' (*John 5:39, 40*). They did want life, but chose to lose it rather than come to Him for it.

Has the world changed much since then? Does Christ in His gospel meet with any kinder welcome today? The invitation He offers is still the same: 'Come unto me, all ye that labor and are heavy laden, and I will give you rest' (*Matt. 11:28*). The worst that Christ does to those who come to Him is to put them into a place of life and salvation; yet thousands somehow expect to hear better news from the world and relegate the gospel to a foreign language which does not concern them, at least for the present. They like to keep the gospel at a comfortable distance, assuming there will be time enough to take care of it when they are about to enter the next world.

But Christ's gospel has never been designed to accommodate carnal desires; it does not lure men with worldly honors and pleasures. If Christ had satisfied the craving of only a few lusts, even if it meant promising less in the world to come, the news would have been cheered by those who prefer the slurred stories of strong drink to the message of heaven itself.

What then will God do with this degenerate age we live in? I fear it will be strong judgment. If such a wonderful gospel is rejected, tragic news cannot be far off. God comes to men because He wants to; so why should He stay where He is not welcomed? It is high time for a merchant to pack up and leave when only a few people – or none – want his goods.

Do we not see the names of Christ's faithful messengers bleeding today under the reproaches and attacks aimed at them? Are not the most precious truths of the gospel almost covered with the mire of errors and blasphemies, which corrupt minds – hired by the devil himself – have thrown into the face of Christ and His gospel? And where is the man valiant enough to stop these foul mouths from spitting venom against the Lord Jesus? When opposition does come forward it is so faint that Christ's enemies are encouraged. Justice is so lightly sprinkled, like a few drops of mist on fire, that it actually increases the flame of their rage rather than quenches it.

But blessed be our God – there is a remnant of saints who believe and know Christ is precious – who gladly embrace His gospel and weep in secret for the contempt that profane men hurl at it. If there were not a few overcoming believers remaining among us, our crisis would be much more desperate than it already is. And if these saints had not hung on to Christ's legs through the years and with strong supplications begged Him to stay, His gospel presence would have been gone long ago. Even so, there are a few considerations concerning the world's

THE CHRISTIAN IN COMPLETE ARMOUR

attitude toward Christ's gospel that make our hearts wonder what God might do next.

I. ONLY A REMNANT EMBRACE THE GOSPEL

If it were put to a vote, would not thousands carry the decision to get rid of Christ and His gospel? History itself prophesies the future of such great odds. Each time God has withdrawn from a people, there have been a few holy ones mingled among the ungodly. Sardis, for example, had several names which had not 'defiled their garments', but the candlestick was removed nevertheless. All they had was a promise for themselves – 'They shall walk with me in white' – but no protection was pledged for the whole church (*Rev. 3:4*). God can pull down a house and at the same time provide safety for His saints whom He finds inside.

A few voices are easily drowned in the screams of a crowd and a dozen cups of wine are hardly tasted in a whole cask. Thus a remnant of Christianity sometimes can do little to save the wretched millions of unbelievers surrounding them. When disease controls a weakened body, nature tries with her utmost strength but cannot heal the sickness – perhaps her best efforts will only prolong life for a while. So then a few saints, shut up in a wicked age of Christ-despising men, may gain a reprieve from judgment. But if the unbelievers themselves do not choose to change, ruin inevitably will break in on them.

II. MOST OF CHRISTENDOM IS MADE UP OF OLD DISCI-PLES, NOT NEW CONVERTS

The womb of the gospel has been shut up from bringing forth souls in a solid work of conversion. Of course, if you count those who baptize themselves into new religious feelings with good intentions and wholesome opinions, there are plenty of 'Christians'. But in this age of withering professions of faith and an even weaker practice of holiness, it is hard to find a real convert!

Of course God is pleased to bring the pangs of new birth now and then in our churches so His despised servants may have His seal to confirm their ministry and stop the blazing scorn against the gospel. But its rarity certainly must be a solemn warning to this nation.

When we see a tree that used to stand thick with fruit yielding just a very few apples now and then on scattered limbs, we assume that tree is dying. Because of her fruitfulness, Leah encouraged herself that Jacob would cleave to her. On the contrary, will not God leave a people who have grown barren under His abundant covering of grace? The Lord Himself promises it: 'Be thou instructed, O Jerusalem, lest my soul depart from thee.' And if God removes His presence, His Word confirms the worst thing that can happen – 'I make thee desolate, a land not inhabited' (*Jer. 6:8*).

When our burials outnumber births, we must be losing the battle. There is a sad list of holy names taken away from us each day; but where are the ones who are being born to God? If the good ones leave and those who remain are becoming worse and worse, we have every reason to fear God is clearing the ground and making way for judgment!

III. DIVISIONS ARE FOUND AMONG GOD'S PEOPLE

Contentions always herald trouble. Christ sets up the light of His gospel to walk and work by, not to fight and argue under. We should not be too surprised, then, if He decided to put it out and end the whole dispute. If the tempest against the church had made Christians all row the same way – as the Galilean storm caused Christ's disciples to do – we could expect Jesus to come walking toward our trouble in mercy and get us safely to shore. But when we throw away the oar and start scuffling in the boat, while the wind roars all around us, we are more likely to drive Christ out than to invite Him in. And we are in far more danger then of sinking than saving the ship – and ourselves with it.

EXHORTATION TO UNBELIEVERS AND BELIEVERS

I. TO UNBELIEVERS

Be persuaded to receive the message of the gospel believingly into your hearts; it is the best news you can send back to heaven as a thanksgiving for those glad tidings of Christ. The announcement of your embracing Christ Jesus will be as welcome news to heaven as the message of salvation through Him is to you. 'Joy shall be in heaven over one sinner that repenteth' (*Luke 15:7*). The angels that sang Christ into the world will not lack for a song when you receive Him into your heart; for this is why He came.

God's Son descended when He came to earth, but now He ascends. His coming was an act of humiliation, but your salvation is His exaltation. *The highest created throne God can sit on is the soul of a believer.*

We can witness the celebration in heaven because of salvation by drawing a sample of the joy it caused in Christ while He was on earth. It had to be wonderful news to bring a smile to the face of the 'man of sorrows' (*Isa. 53:3*). Yet we read that when His disciples, whom He had sent out to preach the gospel, returned with news of victory, Jesus rejoiced in spirit and said, 'I thank thee, O Father, Lord of heaven and earth' (*Luke 10:21*). Of all the years of His life, that was the hour when Christ expressed His joy. The care of the Holy Spirit to record this passage lets us know how much Christ's heart was turned to the saving of souls. Thus, if we want to send any happy news to Him in heaven it should be of the ruling power which His gospel has over our hearts. This made Christ rejoice in the midst of His sorrows here on earth, and it must prove even more joyous to Him in heaven now, where His own sufferings are all healed, past, and gone.

Now if acceptance of the gospel is such glad news to Christ, imagine how distasteful the rejection of it must be. As He rejoices in spirit to hear that the gospel prevails, so He must be deeply angry when the unbelieving world pushes it away. In fact, Christ illustrated this truth in His parable of the servants and the supper. 'The master of the house' was 'angry' when His servants, sent to invite the guests – that is, to preach the gospel – returned with nothing but polite rejections. This so angered the master that he pronounced a dreadful doom upon every one of the people who refused the invitation: 'None of those men which were bidden shall taste of my supper' (*Luke 14:21, 24*).

Those unbelievers who would not come when the supper of the Lord's gospel was on the table had to go to bed hungry and die in their sins. As they shut the door of their hearts against Christ, His padlock of justice was eternally fastened to it. The only revenge Jesus takes against a man who refuses Him is to condemn him to his own desires.

The thing God tolerates least is contempt forced upon His grace. Although the Jews, for instance, have experienced many grievous consequences of their idolatries and other errors through the centuries, they have never suffered calamities more grave than those brought on by rejecting Christ. Under the former judgments their attitudes had softened somewhat; but the latter have hardened their hearts.

Unbeliever – if you will not have Christ now, you shall

not have Him later. You have had so many offers; why do you want to die without Him? Can you not see you are moving at full speed toward damnation? No one sinks quite so deep in hell as the man who stumbles at God's Son. The same gospel which brings you good news now will repeat itself on the day of judgment as the heaviest, worst pronouncement of condemnation you have ever heard.

II. TO BELIEVERS

'A feast is made for laughter,' Solomon wrote (*Eccles. 10:19*). I am sure God intended His children to be joyful in the feast of Christ's gospel. In the Old Testament, mourners were not allowed to sit at God's table. Since a saint's gloom reflects unkindness on God Himself, how can we recommend His satisfying love if it does not satisfy us? The world thinks the Christian life is depressing anyway, a dry meal where very little wine of joy is tasted. Why will you confirm their deception, Christian? Why should they have your example as evidence against Jesus and His Word, which promise peace and joy to everyone who comes to this table?

God forbid that your behavior, which should hold forth 'the word of life' and demonstrate the reality of it in the eyes of the world, ever disagree or throw doubt on His Word (*Phil. 2:16*). It is a gross error for Rome to teach that we cannot know Scripture as God's Word except by the testimony of the church. Yet a practical testimony from Christians' lives has great authority over the consciences of men to persuade them of gospel truth. They can believe it is good news when they can read it clearly in a cheerful life.

When unbelievers see Christians sad as they hold the cup of salvation in their hands, they suspect the wine is not so good as preachers say it is. If traders to the Indies returned poorer than they were when they began, it would be hard to convince others to venture to that place, regardless of how many golden mountains might tower there. Christian, do not give unbelievers reason to imagine, by seeing you limping through the race, that they must forfeit happiness if they become Christians and spend the rest of their lives in a house of mourning, with a team of losers.

Is Christ's gospel full of abundant life or not? Then do not go into debt with the world to soak up its carnal benefits; you need never leave God's house to be made glad. He has such a supply of joy that you could not possibly spend it all. Abraham would not take as much as a thread or a shoelace from the king of Sodom, lest he might claim he made Abraham rich. And a saint should be ready to refuse the world's joys and delights so the ungodly cannot chide, 'He drew his joy from *our* well.'

God's Spirit has cut out the channel in which He would have His saints' joy to flow. 'Is any merry? let him sing psalms.' In other words, the substance or reality of the saint's joy is *spiritual*. On the other hand, if he is afflicted 'let him pray' (*Jas. 5:13*). God has provided the means of expressing both our joy and our sorrow.

Just as a prince's recreation is not to be like a pauper's, a Christian's joy is not to be like the carnal man's. If ever there was a need for Christians to feed the lamp of their joy with holy oil – spiritual fuel from the gospel fountain – it is now. Many professing Christians today conform to worldly fashions, entertainment, and greed and even encourage others to join them in realizing their goals of carnal freedom. Their excitement for the world shows that the spiritual joy drawn from the wells of salvation does not satisfy them. If it did they would not drink from the contaminated pools which before were used only by those who had not drunk from Christ's cup.

Why do so-called Christians forsake the pure wine of gospel joy for the adulterated poison which the whore of the world smilingly holds out to them in her golden chalice? Is it because the message of the gospel, which once sparkled in the preached Word and furnished comfort to mourners, has now grown stale? Or has that stream of spiritual joy which has run through the lives of saints for so many generations, without mingling with the world's polluted pleasures, at last fallen into them and lost its divine nature? No, the gospel stays the same; and the joy it brings is as refreshing and restoring as it has always been. It will be lovely as long as God and Christ continue to be life, for it flows and is fed from their heart.

The problem is not in Scripture; it lies in those who say they hold to it. Those who insist they obey this gospel are not like holy men and women of earlier times. The world has grown callous and men's priorities and affections have chilled and become cold. Our palate is no longer chaste; it no longer prefers the heavenly foods served in the gospel. The cheer is as lively as ever but the guests are deadened by constant contact with the world. We have grown debauched in our judgments and corrupt in our principles; no wonder that our joys are carnal.

Error is a whore that lures the heart away from Christ and His spiritual joys. Once the mind is confused by error and begins to malign the truth, it affects the heart, poisoning it with carnal affections. And carnal affections only keep company with gross and carnal joys. Here, then, is the root of the misery of our times.

Satan has played his game cunningly among us in that he has often changed his instruments into angels of light and made gullible souls think they might find more grace and power in this artificial light than in the revelation God provides. But then he trips men and with clever maneuvering of their fleshly lusts, makes them fall so far as to accept the pleasures of the world as the full and only payment of his promises. I hope this display of the devil's mis-shapen plot will make you love the gospel even more and stay in its everlasting arms as long as you live.

Christian! Bless God for the good news of the gospel; and never listen to anyone who tells you of any substitute, unless of course you want to put down truth and take up a lie bursting with deadly venom. Let it make you careful to draw all your comfort from the gospel's breast. When a carnal person wants to have a good time he does not reach for the Bible or run to the promises and walk in quiet meditation on them. And it certainly does not bring him any happiness to think of Christ in heaven. Instead, he buys trivial, soul-wasting books and looks for carousing companions to help him kill time and satisfy his restless hunger with provisions from the pit of hell. The sort of good news that interests him is that from the market place: business gossip; what he will profit from his herd, his crops, or his stocks and bonds; and what new things he can spend his money on.

Where does your road lie, Christian? Where does your soul lead you for joy? Do you go to the Word and read what Christ has done for you on earth, and what He is doing for you in heaven? Is the throne of grace the place to which you resort for good news from that far country where all your treasure lies and your best friends live? Are you listening for the next promise Christ's peace will whisper to your heart? If so, you are not carrying your name for nothing – you are a real Christian.

Erasmus said that when a true student gets tired from studying he refreshes himself with more studying, but in an easier and more readily pleasurable subject. Thus after the true believer's spirit is weary from the more severe

[261]

exercises of Christianity like fasting and prayer, he can recover at the feast of God's love in Christ, where he sees his water turned into wine, and the tears that his sins have covered his face with, all washed away with the blood of Christ. When fear makes the saint falter with the realization of God's justice and judgment of sin, the meditation of sweet gospel promises revives him. He finds his healing in the same Word where he met his wound; and where he had sorrow, he receives Christ's joy.

2. What is Meant by Peace

Peace is a comprehensive word. 'We looked for peace, but no good came,' the prophet said (*Jer. 8:15*). Peace brings good with it, as the sun furnishes light for the world. When Jesus expressed what He wanted most for His disciples, He wrapped up all the happiness His large heart could hold and sent it in this blessing: 'Peace I leave with you, my peace I give unto you' (*John 14:27*). Now peace in its greatest latitude, if it is not counterfeit, will always grow from this gospel root. True peace, then, is the blessing of the gospel, and only of the gospel. The blessing of reconciliation with God is the first type of peace we shall examine.

PEACE OF RECONCILIATION WITH GOD

I. NEED FOR PEACE WITH GOD

Open acts of hostility between nations announce the start of a war. Similarly, despite the fact that he shoots short (though such misses are against his will), man sends whole barrages of sin and unholiness at God. Even the most mature saints recall their old life before converting grace gave them a new one: 'We ourselves also were sometimes foolish, disobedient, deceived, serving divers lusts and pleasures' (*Tit. 3:3*). In other words, being in bondage to

Satan, we were willing to fight against God and take the side of His only enemy.

There is not a single part or faculty of the unconverted man that does not resist and fight against God. 'The carnal mind is enmity against God,' Paul instructed (*Rom. 8:7*). And if war boils over in the mind, there cannot be peace in the lower parts of the soul either. By nature the enmity against God is seated in the superior faculties of the soul. Common soldiers are often more interested in the personal benefits they receive from the battle, whereas officers are concerned about the principles at stake, and go into the fight full of contempt for the opposition. Thus, inferior faculties seek only the satisfaction of their sensual appetite in the excitement of sin, while the superior faculties of the mind come forth more directly against God to oppose His sovereignty. In fact, if it were possible to take away God's life itself, there is enough hatred in the carnal mind to execute that plot.

Not only is man in arms against God, but God is against wicked man also. 'God is angry with the wicked every day . . . he hath bent his bow and made it ready. He hath also prepared for him the instruments of death' (*Ps. 7:11–13*). God has set up His royal standard in defiance of all the sons and daughters of Adam, who are traitors to His crown. And He has taken the field as with fire and sword against everyone who rebels against His Word. God gives sufficient testimony of His wrath by revealing how He judges sinners – they are crushed to death by His righteous foot, a fate suited to their viperous master in sin.

At every door where sin enters, the anger of God meets it there. Because each faculty of the soul and member of the body is used as a weapon of unrighteousness against God, so every one, even to the tip of the tongue, receives its portion of divine wrath. And just as man is sinful all over, so he is cursed all over – inside and outside, soul and body alike. Curses and punishments are written over him so closely together that there is not room for one more to be added to those God has already written.

In a word, the Lord's displeasure against sinful man is so fiery that all creation must share in it. Although God takes aim at man, and levels His arrows primarily at him, yet they wound other creatures as well. God's curse, then, blasts the whole creation for man's sake; and part of the misery of man is paid to him through the fallen creation, through all the forces and creatures of the natural world which originally were ordained to minister to man and to provide contributing drops in the filling of his cup of joy.

We can compare God's plagues to an enraged army which spoils all the enemies' land – destroying their supplies, poisoning their water, and burning their homes. Nothing escapes the fury of it. The very bread we eat, air we breathe, and water we drink are poisoned with God's curse, so that even the oldest, healthiest living man will eventually die.

All these expressions of God's violence against sin, though, cannot be likened to hell any more accurately than a handful of soldiers can be compared to an entire army. God does nothing but skirmish with sinners here – He sends only a sampling of His judgment to let them know they do have an enemy who is alive, who sees everything they do, and who can overpower them any time He pleases. Only in hell does God unleash the full fury of His judging power, for there He will punish sinners 'with everlasting destruction from the presence of the Lord, and from the glory of his power' (*2 Thess. 1:9*). This, then, establishes the fact that there *is* a quarrel between God and man.

II. PEACE ONLY BY THE GOSPEL

God's Word first presents man with the articles of the

gospel peace treaty and then becomes the instrument, through preached and published Scripture, to effect this blessing.

(a) *Scripture presents the articles of peace*

The gospel is God's heart in print; and its precious promises are heaven's truths translated into man's language. In them are the purposes of love and mercy agreed upon by the Father, Son, and Holy Spirit for the recovery of lost mankind by Jesus. These are promises which are exposed to the view of our faith so we may believe them, and know the Father empowered His Son to preach His peace and then to purchase that peace by death on the cross. Finally, God sent the Holy Spirit to seal these promises to everyone who would believe Jesus' letter of credentials (the confirming miracles and the Bible's testimony), and receive Jesus as Savior by faith unfeigned.

The guilty man is surrounded on every side by a deluge of wrath – with no hope or help – until the gospel, like a dove, brings the olive branch of peace and tells him the tide has turned and the flood of wrath poured upon him for sin has fallen upon Christ. Because Christ was made a curse for us, the gulf which hindered our journey to God has been absorbed, and where the great sea once appeared we now find safe dry land called 'a living way,' by which every believing and repenting sinner can cross over (*Heb. 10:20*). Jesus offers Himself as the bridge to change for us the justice of God into His love and favor. 'Being justified by faith, we have peace with God through our Lord Jesus Christ' (*Rom. 5:1*).

We are entirely indebted to Scripture for the discovery of these truths of justification and peace. Philosophers like Cicero and Aristotle share only a deep silence on the subject – they are not able to tell the sinner how he can find peace with God. And neither is this reconciliation to be found in the covenant God made with Adam, which shuts up the sinner in a dark dungeon of despair and tells him to expect nothing but the wrath which a just God will measure out to him.

Paul acknowledges that only Christ brings 'life and immortality to light through the gospel' (*2 Tim. 1:10*). It lay hidden in the womb of God's purpose until the gospel came and led us into the knowledge of it, as the sun's light reveals what was there before but could not be seen without its light. Therefore God's supply of peace is called not only 'a living way' but 'a *new* and living way which he hath consecrated for us' – so new that the heart of man never knew a single thought of it until the gospel opened it: 'I will bring the blind by a way that they knew not; I will lead them in paths that they have not known' (*Heb. 10:20; Isa. 42:16*).

(b) *The published and preached gospel effects peace*

Before peace can be completed between God and man, both must agree on the following: God pardons and the sinner must accept and embrace peace on God's terms. But how can this be done? The heart of man is so deeply rooted in its enmity against God that it requires a strength equal to that which can tear up mountains and carry rocks from one place to another in order to pluck the heart from that evil soil. The preached gospel is God's mighty tool to accomplish this feat. 'I am not ashamed of the gospel of Christ: for it is the power of God unto salvation,' Paul declared (*Rom. 1:16*). It is the chariot in which the Spirit victoriously rides when He enters the hearts of men – called 'the ministration of the spirit' (*2 Cor. 3:8*). He makes the heart new as He framed the world at first – by His spoken word.

This is the day of God's power in which He makes His

people willing and causes them – who had seeds of war sown in their natures – to become His friends. Unheard-of power! It is as if the sound of an army's beating drum could carry such an amazing influence as to make the enemy's soldiers throw down their arms and seek peace from the one they resisted with such rage and fury. Such a secret power accompanies the gospel. It not only strikes the sinner's sword out of his hand while it is stretched out against God, but cuts the enmity out of his heart as well – and brings the stoutest rebel to his knees, humbly craving the peace published in the gospel. It makes a sinner so obedient to the call of God in the gospel that he suddenly forsakes and forgets the close embraces of his beloved lusts, so they cannot keep him apart from God a moment longer.

III. WHY GOD EFFECTS PEACE BY THE GOSPEL

It is God's choice to reconcile sinners to Himself by Christ. 'Having made peace through the blood of his cross, by him to reconcile all things unto himself; . . . And you, that were sometime alienated and enemies in your mind by wicked works, yet now hath he reconciled in the body of his flesh through death, to present you holy and unblameable and unreproveable in his sight' (*Col. 1:20–22*).

Some say God did not know any other way to do it. But how pitiful is any attempt of created understanding to fathom the unsearchableness of God's omnipotent wisdom – to say what He can and cannot do! Yet we can say, in full reverence for the Majesty of heaven, that God could not have found a better way of exalting His own glorious name and purchasing sinners' peace, than by reconciling them to Himself by Christ the precious Peacemaker.

This mysterious exchange has in itself the ability to solve all the difficulties of the enmity between man and

God, and for wonder it exceeds even God's workmanship in creating the world. Now this creation is so perfect and glorious that it tells every creature that its Maker is God, a knowing which puts the atheist to shame in his own conscience because he will not believe. Even so, the plan of reconciliation excels the creation of heaven and earth as greatly as the watch surpasses the crystal which covers it. Indeed God intended, by this way of drawing sinners to Himself, to cause both angels and saints to admire the mystery of His wisdom, power, and love in it – from now through eternity.

When at last all angels and Christians meet together in heaven, the whole beautiful counsel of God will be unfolded to them! At that time we shall see how the seas of unbelief were dried up and what rocks of impossibilities were cut through by the omnipotent grace of God, before a sinner's peace could be secured. We shall learn how the Father worked to bring it all to completion. Surely we will be swallowed up in adoring the abyss of His wisdom, who laid the foundation of all this peace according to the eternal counsel of His own will! As the sun exceeds the strength of our natural vision, the glory of God's peace will stretch beyond our capacity to understand it.

This, then, is the masterpiece which God drew on purpose, for its rare workmanship, to beautify heaven. When Christ returned to the Father He did not take any of this world's crowns or silver or gold with Him. Of course men risk their lives every day for these riches, but what are earth's treasures to heaven? Earth's glories suit heaven no better than the beggar's scraps do a prince's table, or a patched threadbare coat suits a royal wardrobe.

No, the Lord Christ came for a much higher purpose than anything the world could ever design; He undertook to negotiate peace between God and rebels who justly earned divine vengeance. And God knew no one else beneath His Son trustworthy enough to transact it. So Jesus stayed here long enough to complete His Father's business and then carried the joyful report of His finished work back to heaven. But now let me proceed to several more detailed reasons why God adopted this method of reconciliation by the gospel.

(a) *God expresses perfect hatred of sin and perfect love to sinners*

Nothing demonstrates mercy like forgiveness. To receive a reconciled sinner into heaven is not so great an act as to reconcile the sinner in the first place. The terms are very different, for there is every reason to expect the first but no reason to expect the latter. When God performs the act of reconciliation, He causes the sinner to see His hatred of sin written on His face of love. And this is necessary, if we consider how hard it is for our corrupt hearts to conceive of God's mercy without a shameful reflection on His holiness.

When God said, 'I kept silence,' what did the wicked man conclude about Him? God's Word answers: 'Thou thoughtest that I was altogether such an one as thyself' (*Ps. 50:21*) – that is, 'You assumed I tolerated sin as much as you do.' Now if such a plain text of God's longsuffering mercy is glossed over to tarnish His holy nature, how much more will a sinner subject His forgiving mercy to abuse? Some stare for so long at the consoling truth of mercy that they are unwilling to look up and see any of God's other attributes.

Now in reconciling Himself to sinners by Christ, God has some formidable ways of convincing them of His implacable hatred of sin. It is true that the Bible says sin finds no favor in God's heart; it confirms the torment of a guilty conscience which hunts down peace and cries out

[269]

damnation to its prisoner. Scripture also describes the fiery judgments of this world, and the furnace heating for unbelievers in eternity shows how furious God's heart burns with wrath against their sin. All these are convincing arguments. But when we see the Father plunge the fatal knife of anger into the heart of Jesus even during His pain and supplications, and force His life out of His body, this shows God's hatred of sin more than all the tormenting screams of hell.

The backs of the entire damned population of hell are not broad enough to bear the total weight of God's wrath at once, for it is infinite and they are but finite. And if this were possible, they would not still be writhing in that dark prison for non-payment. But look at the One who carried the complete curse of sin on His back. The sufferings of condemned sinners are infinitely *extensive* because they are everlasting; but Christ's were infinitely *intensive*. He paid in one sum what they will be paying for ever, yet never finish.

The whole curse of sin met in Jesus, as all streams run to the ocean – a collection of all the wages of sin and death merged in Him. 'The chastisement of our peace was upon him; . . . and the Lord hath laid on him the iniquity of us all' (*Isa. 53:5, 6*). But take another step and consider God's unspeakable love for His beloved Son as He watched Him – alone – enter the stage of bloody tragedy. Be still here and know the painful price both God and His Son paid for you to be one with Him. I think you are at the highest stair God's Word can lead you to ascend into the meditation of His love.

Picture a father who has only one son – and can have no more – sending that child to prison and with his own lips sentencing him to death. And then, to guarantee the execution be completed with the most horrible torment possible, he watches his child's death with eyes brimming not with grief but with anger. If you study this parent's countenance you conclude that surely he hates his son or the sin he committed. This is what you see in the Father towards His Son, for it was God, more than men or devils, who caused Christ's death.

Jesus knew the warrant for His death was signed and sealed by His Father's hand, for He prayed, 'O my Father, if this cup may not pass away from me, except I drink it, thy will be done' (*Matt. 26:42*). Yet the spirit of the Man of Sorrows rejoiced in obeying God and His blood was the only wine which made the Father's heart glad: 'It pleased the Lord to bruise him' (*Isa. 53:10*). When Christ suffered death on the cross, God was pleased – not because He did not love His Son and not because He had disobeyed Him, for Jesus never once disappointed God. But God hated sin, and in His determination to exalt His mercy toward sinners, He satisfied His justice on His only Son.

(b) *God purchased our peace by Christ so He could protect Christians from pride*

Pride is the stone that made angels and man stumble and fall. And in order for man to stand up again, God rolled that stone away and laid aside that weapon with which His children harmed themselves. To protect His family from future batteries of hell at this door, then, God chose such a secure way of saving them that when the prince of this world comes to tempt with pride, he cannot find anything in them to respond to his offer. We wonder how pride, of all sins, can grow since its only root is traced to man's imagination and flights of fancy. Yet it flourishes like a mushroom or moss among stones, where little or no soil is there for the root to attach itself to. In this gospel way of reconciling sinners by Christ, God makes Satan haul in that soil from outside.

Do you want peace with God? You cannot expect to find it in penance. 'The chastisement of our peace was upon him' (*Isa. 53:5*). Be assured you will never be your own peacemaker! That is Christ's name, and He did this work by Himself: 'For he is our peace, who hath made both one' (*Eph. 2:14*) – Jew and Gentile at one with God, and at one with each other.

Is it righteousness you want? Then you must not appear before God in your own clothing. Someone else has provided righteousness for you: 'Surely, shall one say, in the Lord have I righteousness and strength' (*Isa. 45.24*). In a word, do you desire to have a right to heaven's glory? Certainly your silver and gold are not good enough to buy it. The price cannot come out of your pocket; it must come from Christ's heart. He has bought it for us, not with silver and gold but with His precious blood, an inheritance coming down as freely as a father's estate upon his children (*Eph. 1:14*).

God chose to give this treasure of reconciliation to humble us, so our haughtiness might bow and God could be exalted in our day of salvation. 'The bread of God is he which cometh down from heaven, and giveth life unto the world' (*John 6:33*). And notice why God chose that method to feed His children in the wilderness: 'Who fed thee in the wilderness with manna, which thy fathers knew not, *that he might humble thee*' (*Deut. 8:16*).

Let us examine this humbling process more carefully. Naturally we assume that the Israelites would have become wise as well as humble when God Himself fed them with 'angels' food' (*Ps. 78:25*). Yet man is proud and wants to be his own provider; he does not enjoy a meal sent in by charity, at another's expense, nearly so much as he does food which he earned by himself. This pride made the children of Israel wish for the onions of their Egyptian gardens – inferior food but food bought with their own money instead of brought to them by God.

(c) *God's reconciliation to sinners was aimed at a more perfect union than He had with Adam*

God would never have allowed His first workmanship to be so scarred by sin if He had not planned to build a more magnificent structure out of its ruins. Because He intended to print man's happiness in the second edition with a more perfect type than the first, He used Christ as the only fit instrument to accomplish this design: 'I am come that they might have life, and that they might have it more abundantly' (*John 10:10*). He did not come to give the dead and damned a bare peace – naked life – but a more abundant life than man ever had before sin separated him from God.

It was Christ who filled the second temple with a glory greater than the first – Christ in the second creation of man who lifts his head above his first happiness. Just as Adam was a pattern to all his seed – what he was, they should have been, had he remained innocent – so Christ is a pattern to all His seed of that glory which they will be clothed with: 'Beloved, now are we the sons of God, and it doth not yet appear what we shall be: but we know that, when he shall appear, we shall be like him; for we shall see him as he is' (*1 John 3:2*). Our earthly bodies will be 'like unto his glorious body' and our souls like His glorious soul as well (*Phil. 3:21*). Meanwhile, the status of a reconciled sinner in Christ surpasses Adam's first condition because of the redeemed person's union to God and his communion with Him.

SUPERIORITY OF OUR NATURE IN CHRIST TO THE NATURE OF ADAM

I. THE RECONCILED SINNER'S UNION WITH GOD

(a) *It is nearer*

The union is nearer because God and man make one person in Christ. And of course Adam in all his glory never heard of such a mystery as this. He was in a covenant of friendship with God – that was the finest gem in his crown – but he could not claim the blood kinship which the reconciled person has with God. This comes only by the marriage of the two natures, divine and human, in the person of Jesus Christ. And this union is the foundation of another, the mystical union between Christ and every believer. In this union the saints and their Head become one in Christ, 'for as the body is one, and hath many members, and all the members of that one body, being many, are one body: so also is Christ' (*1 Cor. 12:12*). The church, then, is nothing but Christ displayed. This union leaves not only Adam, but also the angels themselves, beneath every reconciled sinner.

At first Adam was made only 'a little lower than the angels'; but God has lifted the reconciled saint above them both, for Christ did not take upon Himself 'the nature of angels' but 'the seed of Abraham,' and made 'the elder serve the younger' (*Ps. 8:5; Heb. 2:16; Gen. 25:23*). Even angels minister to the lowliest saint, their Master's chosen heir.

(b) *It is stronger*

The closer the stones stand together the stronger the structure. The union between God and Adam in the first covenant was not strong enough to keep Adam from falling, while God's glory stood whole and unshaken; but the union is so close and strong between God's Son and His saints that Christ cannot be Christ without His members. 'Because I live, ye shall live also,' He promised, implying that our life is bound up in His (*John 14:19*). By this Jesus meant that it would be as easy for Him to be put out of heaven as for us to be kept out!

The church is called Christ's 'body, the fulness of him that filleth all in all' (*Eph. 1:23*). A body is not complete without every member and joint, no matter how small and apparently insignificant, and each one in its wholeness too. The saints' grace is Christ's glory. And although His essential glory as God is not deficient in any way – He does not need Christians to make that glory more complete – we see Him in His place as head of the church and there in a sense His glory is filled up every day as His chosen ones are called in and grow up to their appointed stature in Him. From this perspective, then, Christ does not have His fullness until the saints have their perfection and grace in heaven's glory.

II. THE RECONCILED SINNER'S COMMUNION WITH GOD

Communion comes from union; 'the nearer, the dearer.' The closer you are to a person, the dearer he becomes to you. If the reconciled sinner's union with God is stronger than Adam's was, then his communion must be sweeter as well. The communion of a husband and wife, for instance, is fuller than that of friends because their union is more intimate. God's oneness with Adam was like a friend with his ally, but with the forgiven Christian it is like a husband with his wife: 'Thy Maker is thine husband' (*Isa. 54:5*). Now there is a double portion of benefit peculiar to the reconciled sinner's communion with God.

(a) *Christ is the foundation for building closeness with God* Of course Adam was a son of God, but he was kept at a farther distance than the reconciled soul is. Although he was the son of God by creation, the Son of God was not yet the Son of man by incarnation; and this is the only door where the believer's cherished oneness with God comes in.

Every time the Christian lifts up his eye of faith to God he sees his own nature standing there at the throne in the person of Jesus Christ. Now if the patriarchs ran home with joyful news to their aged father at the sight of Joseph at Pharaoh's right hand, in the regalia of royal power and honor, what an abundant message faith carries to the saint after each vision of love in communion with God: 'Cheer up, my soul; I see Jesus Christ, your nearest kinsman, in glory at God's right hand. Do not be afraid any longer, for He has "all power . . . in heaven and in earth"; and His blood makes you so kin to Him that He cannot forget you unless He hides from His own flesh!' (*Matt. 28:18*).

The lower a king stoops to the least subject, the more familiar he becomes to them all. It was a wonderful condescension when the almighty God, who has no equal, first made man and then entered into such a friendly covenant with him. Yet in God's new covenant He descends from His throne and exchanges His majestic robes of glory for the rags of man's frail flesh. He leaves His palace to dwell for a time in His creature's humble cottage; and while there He suffers persecution even from the hands of those He has come to save.

When His years on earth are over He returns to heaven, not to complain how He has been abused and to align divine troops against His tormentors, but to make heaven's palace ready for those who once hated Him but now are full of His grace.

Yet Christ does something more. In order for those on earth not to fear His reclaimed royalty might crowd them out of His heart, He proves He is the same in the zenith of His honor as He was in the depth of His humiliation. And He demonstrates this unchangeableness by going back to heaven's glory in the same clothes He had borrowed from their nature. Thus God's Son makes those clothes part of His glorified life and gives a pattern of what the saints' own bodies will be like in the kingdom. None of this identification of Christ with man was present in God's dealings with Adam.

(b) *Christ's pardoning mercy and bleeding love sweeten communion with God*

Adam did not have this lump of sugar in his cup – he knew about the love of a giving God, but was a stranger to the mercy of a forgiving God. The reconciled sinner experiences both.

A father's love is a great comfort to an obedient child, but this demonstration of tenderness cannot be compared to the compassion of a father toward his rebellious child. Certainly the prodigal who is received again into his father's arms has more reason to return that father's love than the brother who never left home. Without a doubt, then, God's pardoning mercy and the love of Christ which procured it are the sweetest, most wholesome fruit a saint here on earth can meditate upon.

But who can conceive of the splendid music which glorified saints will make on this note of God's mercy and love? Surely the song their harps are tuned to is 'the song of the Lamb' (*Rev. 15:3*). The saints' fulfilled celebration in heaven's glory is a composite of all the finest ingredients possible – so arranged by the hand of God that not one of them can be left out; and the taste of one cannot be lost in another. Yet pardoning mercy, and the unsurpassable love of God through Christ, give a sweet topping to the feast and can be tasted above all the rest.

WHY YOU SHOULD SEEK PEACE WITH GOD

We know God's peace is worth having, or else He made a mistake when He directed the angels to sing 'Glory to

God . . . , and on earth peace' (*Luke 2:14*). And if the sinner's peace with God is not of the highest price and value, Christ Himself was deceived – He has little to show for the flow of heart-blood. But this we cannot believe.

Yet to see how freely God offers this peace and pardon through Christ, and men's indifference toward that offer, an ill-informed person might be tempted to think it some cheap and shoddy merchandise which God is trying to unload and that that is why God is so ready to give and man so reluctant to take. Who is the wicked counselor who hardens a man's heart from reaching out for the mercies God has for him? None but the devil can hate God and you so much.

Think about this, sinner – what answer will you send to heaven when God calls His ambassadors home, never to extend or renew His peace treaty again? Satan's quarrel with God is too advanced for him to give you a second glance. Besides, can he give you armour to quench the fiery blast of God's judgment? How could he, when these burning bullets are embedded inside his own heart, causing unspeakable torment? And will he send sympathy when at last you have destroyed yourself by following his advice? Of course not – no more than the ravenous wolf pities the sheep after he has torn her into pieces and drunk her blood.

So that you can never say you did not understand how to find peace with God through the gospel, carefully weigh these next four thoughts.

1. CONSIDER WHAT IS BEING OFFERED – PEACE WITH GOD

This peace is both indispensable and comprehensive. You cannot be happy with anything less than peace but you do not need anything more than peace to fill you with true joy. Of all the varieties on God's spiritual menu, His serving of peace can least be spared. If you take this away the feast is spoiled, even if a brightly garnished outward peace replaces it at the center of the prince's table.

Sinner, listen to me! Is not this controversy between you and God like a swollen toad at the bottom of your cup of honey? Your sins are unpardoned and you are condemned to die for them, no matter how much you may be dancing in the shadows of your prison. What would you think about a man who spent his last hours before being hanged playing at his favorite sport? Truly God is merciful if He stays your execution one more day!

I confess, when I see a man whose life proves him an unforgiven sinner, and whose pleasure comes by dressing in expensive clothing and entertaining with the prideful air of affluence, I am amazed that he cares neither about God nor himself. How much longer do you think the Lord will watch him pile up all this trash around himself before He tosses a torch to the bottom of it?

A creditor is provoked to disgust when he watches his debtor living high on his borrowed money but never thinking about getting free of debt. How much more serious it is, then, for God to see sinners spending what He has given, leading lighthearted lives but ignoring the reality of making peace with Him in whose debt-book they are so deeply deficient.

It would have been foolish had the Jews planted fields, painted houses, and played in the streets after Ahasuerus had sealed the warrant for their annihilation. Instead, they did all they could to have that bloody command reversed. Now you are worse than an unconscious drunk in an alley of waste if you skip through life carrying in your conscience the sentence of death from God's own mouth.

When Sir Thomas More was in the Tower he refused to trim his beard and reminded others of the controversy between the king and himself for his head; until that issue could be settled, More vowed, he did not intend to waste any time shaving! Certainly all the cost and effort you invest to make yourself happy is a waste until you find out what will become of both your body and soul.

The first thing you need to do is make peace with God. An old saying sums it up like this: 'He who gets out of debt grows rich.' The reconciled soul can never be poor. As soon as peace is complete, a free trade is opened up between the person and God. Once you are pardoned you may sail to any port that lies in God's dominion and be welcome there. All His promises stand open with their rich treasure. Take in as much as your faith can afford – no one will stop you. As a man may draw the wine of a whole barrel through one tap, so faith draws comfort of the whole covenant out of this single promise – reconciliation.

Now through this doorway of reconciliation you enter into communion with God in all His ordinances. This way, you can walk in agreement with God in any direction, whereas your presence once made His heart draw back as one would at the sight of an enemy, ready to fight sin with judgment. 'The smith and his penny are both black.' That is what you were like in the company of your dead works before you were reconciled to God in Christ. But now your voice is sweet to Him; and your 'countenance is comely' (*Song of Sol. 2:14*).

Everything God has is yours – His horses and chariots belong to you too, as Jehoshaphat informed Ahab. Even when the most dangerous enemy makes you afraid, you know where to find a friend who will always be on your side. God's providences, in fact, may seem like bees that fly here and there, some moving in ways that apparently contradict others, until it is impossible for you to trace their free course. But they all work for your good! And your soul is the hive where they will ultimately unload the sweet fruit of their labor, although it may be night – the evening of your days – before you find it.

In a word, then, if you are reconciled you stand just a step away from heaven: 'Whom he justified, them he also glorified' (*Rom. 8:30*). You will be there as soon as death tears the veil of your flesh, which is all that separates you from the fullest glory of God in Christ.

II. CONSIDER WHO OFFERS YOU PEACE – THE HOLY GOD

It is hard to decide which is the greater wonder – for God to offer peace or for you to reject it. It is not unusual for a condemned man to prostrate himself at the feet of his prince and beg for his life. But it is a mystery to see this traitor open the dungeon door and find his prince standing there for no other reason than to urge him to accept his pardon.

Practically speaking, self-love is often the main motive for this apparent self-denial. For example, a father who stoops to gain his child back is loving himself, for that child carries much of his parent's own life within him. And a ruler's safety may be so intertwined with the traitor's life that he cannot execute him without jeopardizing his crown.

But neither of these conditions forced God to seek peace for His saints; it is the child of free condescending love. How can you expect to live if you deny a gift like that? If the poorest neighbor in town comes to make peace after he has wronged you, would not your conscience always bother you if you turned him away? How, then, can you look God or conscience in the face if you refuse peace at God's hands? He has absolute and flawless power over your life. And His offer of peace is not extended because His sword is broken and He has no alternative. He is not at a disadvantage. He brings this peace when His justice could have already fastened you up in chains of darkness among the damned.

III. CONSIDER HOW GOD OFFERS YOU PEACE

(a) *He offers peace sincerely*

Take comfort – know it is the 'God of truth' who offers you peace without fraud or betrayal. He has never shed the blood of war in the name of peace or given a person over to the sword of His anger after peace has been given. 'If we confess our sins, he is faithful and just to forgive' (*1 John 1:9*). God's promises are not 'yes' and 'no' like the devil's, who arranges them so he can receive credit both ways. No, the heart of God can be seen as through a crystal window in these promises; they are all 'yea and amen' in Christ (*2 Cor. 1:20*).

(b) *He offers peace affectionately*

God's heart is preoccupied with tender ways to show mercy to sinners, and this compassion appears to us in three ways.

(i) *In making a way for reconciling sinners to Himself.* Men will stretch their minds to the utmost to achieve the desires of their hearts. And God has invented such a unique way of reconciling sinners to Himself that even angels must study this mystery of divine mercy, that they might know 'the manifold wisdom of God' (*Eph. 3:10*).

(ii) *By the early revelation of reconciliation to the sons of men.* No sooner had the first man rebelled against his Maker than the Lord's heart relented toward him and would not let the sun go down on His wrath. In the very same day that man sinned, God preached peace in the seed of the woman (*Gen. 3:15*).

Little did Adam think that God had such a message for him when he first heard Him coming toward him. 'Adam, where art thou?' sounded like the voice of an avenging God to his guilty ears – yet that sound proved to be the call of a gracious Father who wished to ease His child's throbbing conscience with the compassion and grace He had conceived toward him (*Gen. 3:9*). Surely, surely God's heart was overflowing with this mercy or else it would not have burst out so soon.

(iii) *In the ordinance of the gospel ministry.* One might think it would have been enough for God to print His thoughts and purposes of mercy in Scripture and confine them to that book. For instance, when governments publish a law they expect every citizen to find it, read, and fully obey. They do not send a person throughout the land persuading people to submit. Yet this is exactly what God does. He sends out ministers for the purpose of convincing sinners to be reconciled to God. Observe these details concerning God's ministers:

The persons God sends to preach. Although angels do minister to the heirs of salvation, they are still foreigners to our nature. Instead of choosing them to preach the gospel, God sends men – humans with like passions – whose nature puts them under the same limitations and temptations as others. Because these men know their own hearts they can freely tell us the baseness of ours. And the fire of God's anger which has scorched them for their sins can point out the danger we are in because of the same kind of ungodliness. On the other hand, the pleasant aroma that God's love in Christ has left on their lives invites us to feast upon that same abundance.

The qualifications required in God's gospel ministers. 'The servant of the Lord must not strive, but be gentle unto all men, apt to teach, patient, in meekness instructing those that oppose themselves' (*2 Tim. 2:24, 25*). God does not intend anything to be in the preacher to prejudice the sinner's judgment or harden his heart against the offer of grace. For example, if the servant is proud and demanding, how can people know his master is meek and patient?

[283]

The gap should not be made any wider than it already is – indeed, the one who takes the bird must not frighten it. Besides, sinners are never pelted into Christ with stones of hard, provoking rhetoric, but drawn and wooed into Him by heart-softening exhortations.

The commission God gives His ambassadors. The two main parts of God's calling involve its *largeness* and its *strictness*. First, *largeness* says, 'Go . . . and preach the gospel to every creature' (*Mark 16:15*). 'Offer peace to everyone,' Jesus was saying. 'Make no difference – rich or poor, hardened sinners, old sinners or young ones. Invite them all, for I have room for every person who will repent and believe.'

God's *strictness*, on the other hand, emphasizes the seriousness of delivering His message faithfully. Paul trembled at the very thought of laziness: 'Woe is me if I preach not.' And Christ reached deep into His own heart to persuade Peter: 'Lovest thou me? . . . Feed my sheep' (*John 21:16*). It is as if He had said, 'Peter, you are crying and feeling guilty because cowardice made you deny Me; but there is still a way to demonstrate your love – feed My sheep. Do this and stop worrying about that traitor of the past.' Once again, Christ showed more care for His sheep than for Himself.

The joy God expresses when sinners accept His peace. Joy is the highest testimony which can be given to our peace. Love is to joy as fuel is to fire. If love gathers only a few scraps of kindling – only small desires in the heart – then the flame of joy that comes out of it will not be very hot. Now because God takes such great joy in pardoning sinners, His affection is also great in His offer of peace. In fact, the motive which prevails with God to forgive the ungodly is that 'he delighteth in mercy.' 'Who is a God like unto thee, that pardoneth iniquity, and passeth by the transgression of the remnant of his heritage? he retaineth not his anger for ever, because he delighteth in mercy' (*Mic. 7:18*).

If you ask a fisherman why he stands with his hook in the water all night he will tell you it is because he enjoys fishing. Now you know why God waits for sinners – months, years – preaching to them; He delights in forgiving them by His grace and mercy. Now and then a government official will pardon an offender more to please others than himself; but God forgives to make His own heart glad. Thus when Christ came to reconcile sinners to God, His ministry was called 'the pleasure of the Lord' (*Isa. 53:10*).

God's pleasure was so great in Jesus' mission of reconciliation that He was satisfied only by the death of His Son. 'It pleased the Lord to bruise him' (*Isa. 53:10*). Earthly fathers deeply mourn the death of a child, yet God's joy at this violent act of procuring peace came forth because a way was being made for sinners to be held in His arms. As you see how much God wants you to come to Him, I ask you to think about one more matter before you decide whether to accept the way of His peace or slide down your own way to hell.

IV. CONSIDER WHAT HAPPENS WHEN YOU REFUSE GOD'S PEACE

Determination of war or peace is usually the result of the most mature counsel and deliberation possible. What are you doing, then, when you break off God's peace treaty? Are you not merely making more work for repentance when it shall be to no avail? But just in case you are not faithful enough to God and your soul to let your conscience speak freely in this matter, I will do it for you – and tell you exactly what you do when you reject peace.

First, anyone who refuses a pardon either denies he has

[285]

done wrong or, which is worse, stands to defend it. Your actions say you do not wish to be friends with God and, for all practical purposes, you intend to continue the fight between the two of you. Amilcar was such an enemy to Rome that when he died he made his son Hannibal heir to his hatred. Is it not enough that you have fought so long here on earth against your Maker? Or will you keep up the quarrel in the next world also, where there is no more possibility to put an end to it than to eternity itself?

Further, you are throwing the greatest possible contempt upon God – as if His love and anger were such minute trivia that they cannot tip the scale of your thoughts either toward trust or toward fear. In a word, you are consenting to your own damnation and casting yourself into the mouth of God's flaming judgment.

You realize, of course, that the Lord is under oath to destroy you if you die like this. Death is His trap-door to let you down to hell's dungeon; and once you are there you will have plenty of time to cry for your choice, though here you take no such trouble to make God your friend. The very memories of His offers of peace will be like salt and vinegar, which your accusing conscience will continually baste you with as you roast in the fires of hell. If you are a sinner, this language grates on your nerves, I know; but it is not nearly so horrible as the sound of gnashing teeth in hell.

I have read of a foolish and cruel law among the Lacedemonians, that no one could be told any bad news concerning himself. Instead, each one was left to discover any such news on his own. Sad to say, many among us today would be more than happy if such a law shut ministers' mouths and kept them from scaring sinners about the wages of sin and death. Most ungodly men are more offended by talk of hell than by the sinful state that is pushing them into it.

[286]

When can we ever show God's love to sinners if we do not do it right now? In hell there will not be anything else love can do for them – because it is the worst sort of plague-house, we will not be able to write on its gate, 'Lord, have mercy on them that are inside.' No, those who pray for their salvation now, and cry out for their lost condition, must one day vote with Christ for the damnation of the unrepentant, even if they are their husbands, wives, and children. Be careful, sinners – *now* is the acceptable time to make peace with God before you wake up in hell with the hearts of God and your loved ones hardened against you.

HOW TO FIND PEACE WITH GOD

I. FACE THE ENMITY BETWEEN YOU AND GOD

Wherever you go, an angry God surrounds you; His wrath is like a big cloud full of curses hanging overhead, ready to empty them upon you. This truth must be pressed home. Men may admit they are sinners, but they will not go so far as to rank themselves among the enemies of God.

Like thieves, sinners will confess some minor flaws but carefully avoid anything that might suggest a need for judgment. 'Sinner' is an accepted name. After all, who does not sin sometime? But admission of open enmity with God brings them too near the sight of the gallows. They are like the Jews who demanded that Rabshakeh not speak the Hebrew language 'in the ears of the people' for fear of scaring them (*Isa. 36:11*). They insisted that he speak in a foreign tongue instead. Sinners, too, prefer the truth not to be spoken so plainly within the hearing of their conscience. They would much rather have their ears tickled than to know the worst.

You might own all the empires of the world, and have

[287]

nations creeping to your feet, as the animals came to Adam; and your lease on life might be twice as long as Methuselah's span to enjoy all this, without one cloud of trouble. But if you lack peace, I would rather be the worm under your shoe or the toad in the ditch than you in your palace. Just one small thought of approaching death and the torment waiting for you can immediately destroy all your present happiness.

This refusal to accept God's peace on gospel terms makes the great leaders of the world – in fact, *all* unreconciled sinners, high and low – go to their graves as bears go down a hill – backwards. One glance forward might cause them to die of fright as they see where they are going. They are headed there without a breastplate, the persuasion of peace with God.

What should you do next, then? Shut yourself up as a condemned sinner, apart from flattering friends who would lullaby your soul into senseless security – the cradle which the devil rocks souls in, to their utter destruction. Instead, send for those who dare to be faithful, like Samuel, to tell you every word God has against you, hiding nothing.

Read your own sentence with your eyes on the Word; take your condemnation from God's mouth, not from man's. 'There is no peace, saith my God, to the wicked' (*Isa. 57:21*). Meditate on that Scripture until it cleaves to your soul like a plaster to a sore and draws out the core of pride and carnal confidence which have hardened your heart. By this time the anguish of your own spirit will prompt you to want peace with God more than anything else in the world. This is what God has been waiting to hear from you.

II. MAKE SURE YOUR MOTIVE IS RIGHT

Nothing is so hateful to God as buttery words of peace in

the mouth while cold war remains in the heart. Be careful not to harbor shallow purposes when you ask God for peace, for He sees right through every one of them. Now God has never changed His mind about anyone whom He pardoned and took up into the chariot of peace with Him, because He has never been deceived as men sometimes are by false brethren. When Joab killed Amasa, the latter did not pay attention to the sword in Joab's hand (*2 Sam. 20:9, 10*). But God looks straight to the heart to see what is in its hand; therefore be sure you are clear in your own mind as to your true motive.

Now God does let you come over to His side because it is secure. No one has yet made peace with Him unless this motive was a factor. If Jacob, for instance, could have been safe at home he would never have run to Laban. Every person is routed out of his own self-confidence in some way before he surrenders to God. Just be careful that this is not all you are aiming at; God does not permit peace when nothing more than self-love draws up the treaty. For example, a man caught in a storm might be forced under the roof of his worst enemy for shelter without having any change of heart whatsoever. Two things, then, are more important than self-preservation as you look for peace.

(a) *Reconciliation must seek to honor God*
If God could not be glorified in our peace more than in our damnation, it would be a selfish thing for us to desire it. But He is no loser in His acts of mercy: 'Help us, O God of our salvation, *for the glory of thy name*: and deliver us, and purge away our sins, for thy name's sake' (*Ps. 79:9*).

God is free to choose what pleases His own heart the most and what exalts His name. And we see from Scripture that He loves 'mercy, and not sacrifice' (*Matt. 12:7*). He is satisfied more in the mercy shown to one sinner than in the blood of all the damned who must be

[289]

sacrificed to His justice.

But God has a higher purpose in sinners' damnation than their suffering: He enhances the glory of His mercy in those children who are saved. This, then, is the lovely prism God delights in – and judgment is only a shadow to it.

You may seek peace with God when your heart is ready to heap honor on Him, for praise is a motive God will not deny. 'This,' Abigail said to David, 'shall be no grief unto thee, nor offence of heart unto my lord' (*1 Sam. 25:31*). She meant he would never regret that he had been kept from shedding blood. Thus the saint's prayer is, 'Lord, when I stand in heaven among men and angels praising You for pardon and grace, You will not be sorry that mercy kept You from spilling my blood and damning my soul to hell.'

It is plain to see today that many who pursue peace expect God to pardon them, although they care nothing for His honor and remain totally ignorant of Him and of His Son Jesus. They want God to make peace with them while they make war with Him and His Word. Like a thief at the bar, this kind of person implores the judge to spare his life by whatever means, right or wrong, legal or illegal. What difference does it make as long as he is pardoned? Does this man consider the honor of the judge? Well, do not be deceived, because God will not make war among His own attributes to make peace with you.

(b) *Reconciliation must seek to have fellowship with God*
Suppose God should confide, 'I am your friend – I have commanded that you will never go to hell. And My hand holds your discharge so you can never be arrested for indebtedness to Me. But as for fellowship, do not expect any. I am through with you now and you will never know Me better.' If you heard the Father say this, how excited

would you be about your peace? Even if the tormenting fires were put out, the anguish of a hell would remain in the dismal darkness without God's presence.

Absalom saw no middle ground between seeing his father's face and being killed. 'Let me see the king's face; and if there be any iniquity in me, let him kill me' (*2 Sam. 14:32*). 'If I am not worthy to enjoy my father's love and presence,' he pledged, 'I do not want to live.' On the other hand, an ungodly heart gropes for peace without any longing after fellowship with God. Like the traitor, he is ready to promise the king anything, if only he will save him from execution.

III. SURRENDER YOUR REBELLION AND SUBMIT TO GOD'S MERCY

God will not talk with you as long as your sword is in your hand. 'Come now, and let us reason together, saith the Lord' (*Isa. 1:18*). And notice when the negotiation really begins: 'Put away the evil of your doings' (*v. 16*). Only then are you on the path which leads to peace.

(a) *God is a great God*

The Almighty Lord is far too glorious to meet with His lowly creatures on equal terms. A king can arrive at peace with a fellow ruler, or he may be able to achieve it by force. But all that king has to do to conquer a rebellious subject – one helplessly bound in chains – is to order him hanged for treason. The great God wants you to understand that. Let those haggle and set stipulations who can resort to their own strength and live without peace. But as for you, sinner, I hope you do not think you are in any position to meet God in battle. The only way to conquer Him is on your knees, as you fall on your face and confess, 'Lord, my life is Yours. I will be Your prisoner and choose to die by the hand of Your justice rather than keep fighting against Your mercy.'

The man who lays down his life at Jesus' feet will soon rest in His arms: 'Humble yourselves in the sight of the Lord, and he shall lift you up' (*Jas. 4:10*). But although the high and lofty One will stoop to take up a penitent sinner into the embrace of His forgiving mercy, He will not dishonor His sovereignty by reasoning with a man who stands up and argues with Him. There is one red letter in God's name – He 'will by no means clear the guilty' (*Exod. 34:7*).

(b) *God's nature is holy*

Sin is what made God turn from His children. How can you hope to make peace with your Father, then, if you hold sin – the source of all this contention – in your heart? God is more than willing to be reconciled with you, but you cannot expect Him to be one with your sin, too. What assurance does He have of your love if you will not renounce the one thing that seeks His life?

Sin is deicide. As long as it rules, God refuses to consider peace. And they cannot reign together; you must choose which you will have. Do not be deceived, either, by presuming you can send lust away for a while and then call it back when the controversy is over. God shall not be mocked like that – He stands up to His promise: 'Let the wicked forsake his way, and the unrighteous man his thoughts: and let him return unto the Lord, and he will have mercy upon him; and to our God, for he will abundantly pardon' (*Isa. 55:7*). Do you see how complete God's Word is? It leaves no place for sin to hide – we must forsake *all*. This absoluteness implies a deliberate choice and a decision not to invite sin in again.

(i) *To forsake sin is to make a deliberate choice.* Some people's sins forsake them – the unclean spirit goes but is not driven out. Maybe the occasion to sin ceases or the person's physical ability to obey sin's commands is lacking. Either way, there has been no true forsaking of sin. But holy determination and indignation to break with sin – when surging temptation is most demanding – this is forsaking. For example, when David's enemies surrounded him he began to resist and repel them in the name of the Lord. And Moses' praiseworthiness is in his forsaking the court of Pharaoh – not when he was old, like Barzillai – but when warm blood yet rushed in his veins.

(ii) *To forsake sin is to leave it without reserving any thought of returning to it.* When a man leaves on a business trip he has not forsaken his house; he fully intends to return to it. But if a man packs everything he owns, locks the door, leaves, and moves into another place, we say that he has forsaken that house. If a drunkard is sober now and then, this does not mean he is not still a drunkard. The person forsakes his sin when he throws it out and bolts the door, purposing never to open it again. 'Ephraim shall say, What have I to do any more with idols?' (*Hos. 14:8*).

Before pardon can be sealed, the person must do more than put away one or two certain sins; he must forsake the whole way of sin. A traveler might shift from one path to another and still be going the same direction – he can leave a deep, rugged road for a more comfortable one. That is what happens when a man steps over into a more acceptable path because his gross sins are making his conscience uneasy. But all he gets is a smoother way to hell than his crude neighbors are taking. To forsake the way of sin, you must turn aside and leave the road altogether. You must change your direction. In a word, it is necessary that you forsake even the most hidden path in sin's way – even what lies behind the hedge – 'and the unrighteous man his thoughts.' Otherwise you are knocking in vain for pardon at God's door. Forsake all sin or do not bother to forsake any; when you save one lust you lose one soul.

If men are so bent on getting to hell, why must they be so polite and precise about it? Compromising with sin is ridiculous. It is as absurd as the condemned man's request on his way to the gallows – he asked to avoid a certain street for fear of catching the plague! What good will it do if you arrive in hell by way of ignorance and spiritual pride rather than by the avenue of open profanity?

What lust is so valuable that it is worth burning in hell for? When Darius escaped from Alexander, he threw away his heavy crown so he could run faster. Is lust so precious that you cannot leave it behind rather than fall into the hands of an angry God? This is foolish reasoning.

IV. HUMBLY RUN TO THE THRONE OF GRACE AND ASK
GOD TO GIVE YOU PEACE

Carry with you the faith that God is more ready to give peace than you are to receive it. Do not ever place your confidence in repentance or reformation, though; this would be a sinful bargaining with God. He does not await a peddler coming to make deals with Him, but a humble suitor to make supplication to His love and grace.

It is just as blatant an error, however, to presume upon God's *absolute* mercy. This is to take hold of the sword by the blade and not by the handle. People who do this will find death and damnation in the very mercy which would have saved them if they had accepted it the way God gave it – through Christ. 'Let him take hold of my strength, that he may make peace with me' (*Isa. 27:5*). And where is God's saving strength but in Christ? The Father has laid strength upon His Mighty One who is 'able also to save them to the uttermost that come unto God by him' (*Heb. 7:25*). Do not let natural reasoning mislead you – it is not God's absolute power or mercy that will help you, but His *covenant strength and mercy in Christ*. Take hold of Christ and you hold God's arm.

Indeed the Father's essential goodness is a powerful persuasion to rely on the promise in Christ for pardon, when the person considers that God's very nature is forgiving and merciful. But if there were no promise to apply this mercy to sinners through Christ, the fact of God's goodness would be only cold comfort. After all, He could have damned the whole stock of Adam and not impaired His goodness in the least.

It is certainly no blot to the almightiness of God's power that He does not do everything in the spectrum of His divine ability. He could make more worlds if He wanted to; but He is no less powerful because He does not. And He could have saved the fallen angels with the sons of lost man had He thought such a design was fitting. But, having brought forth no promise for such a thing, the essential goodness of God affords the devils little hope that He will do it.

Yet God's goodness continues. Those who, out of simple ignorance of the gospel or proud reasoning away from it, reject God's way of making peace through Christ's satisfaction and then depend on God's absolute mercy and goodness at the last day will, it seems, find as little benefit from this Christless mercy as the devils themselves have found. And their final destination will only confirm the futility of neglecting such a great salvation through the blood of God's Son.

Suppose a prince freely makes a law to govern his people and then takes a solemn oath to maintain and enforce it. Could a criminal condemned to die by this law expect any lenience by appealing from the law to the goodness and mercy of his prince? If some through the course of history have saved their lives this way it is because their ruler was either imprudent in making the law or unfaithful in keeping his oath. Neither of these faults can be imputed to our infinitely wise and holy God.

Now the Lord has enacted a law, called the law of faith, for saving sinners through Christ; and He is under an oath to make it good both in the salvation of everyone who believes on Christ and in the damnation of everyone who does not. To make sure this plan works perfectly, God has given His Son an oath to be faithful, trusting Him as a priest to procure redemption and as a judge to pronounce the sentence at the great day of victory or condemnation.

So do not let anything draw you away from placing complete confidence in Christ the Son of the Most High – God and man in one Person – who laid down His life to atone for the sin of the whole world. Now He offers this blood as a price for you to carry in the hand of faith to the Father for pardon and peace.

Even if false teachers should come and call you from one Christ to another, from Christ outside you to a Christ within you, know this direction is not from God. The mouths of these reputed saints may quote Scripture, but their design is as dangerous as it is clever. When someone calls you from a Christ without to a Christ within, strip the doctrine of its pleasing disguise. In plain English, the false teacher calls you from trusting the righteousness of Christ (His objective work done for you and made yours by faith for your justification) to trusting in an alleged work of the Spirit within you. Now you are not a new creature in Christ – you are not saved – if you let go your hold on the living Christ to rely on something within yourself – on some creature, even if it is the 'new creature'. Unless your conscience has already been given over to believing a lie, you can tell that this 'new creature' is only a vein of gold enclosed in much dirt and imperfection; and these outward trappings will never fully be purged until you have been put into the refining pot of the grave.

Look to yourself, Christian – it is a matter of life and death. Of course you must prize Christ's grace within you. As well, it is true that you do not have any if you do not value it above all the mountains of gold the world piles up. But do not even trust this grace of Christ for salvation; if you do this you are prizing something created by God above God Himself. Let me put it this way. A bride does well to treasure her husband's picture which he has given her to keep, especially if it is a good likeness, and even more if it has been drawn by his own hand. But how ridiculous it would be if she goes so far as to slight her husband for the sake of the picture. If she needs clothing or food or money, she is both foolish and dishonorable if she goes to the picture instead of to him.

The saint's grace is called 'Christ within' because it is His picture, and makes the saint so much like Christ. It deserves to be cherished for the resemblance it bears to the holiness of Christ, who drew it on your heart with the finger of His own Spirit. But what tragedy it would be if you turned your back on the Lord Jesus Christ Himself, to whom you are married by faith, and expected comfort and happiness and heaven not from Him but from the grace He has given!

EXHORTATION TO THOSE WHO ALREADY HAVE PEACE WITH GOD

1. DO NOT MAKE PEACE WITH SIN

Sin is what broke your peace with God in the first place; so now let your peace with Him begin a war with sin that will never end. Surely you cannot forget the inestimable damage you have suffered because of it. In fact, every moment you enjoy God's sweet love should be a catalyst to keep revenge burning in your heart against that cursed enemy who separated you from Him for so long.

Now that God has, I hope, won your heart by His pardoning mercy, you have been brought to love Him dearly because He loved you first. How then can you possibly watch patiently as lust bursts from its trench – your heart – and openly defies your Father and His grace in you? Is your spirit not greatly disturbed to see pride and unbelief mocking God from under the roof of your own soul?

Christian, there is only one way to stop the invasion of sin. To steel your heart against all compromise with evil you must carry the Savior's blood into the battle with your hand of faith. Just as the sight of Caesar's bloody clothing held up by Antony angered Roman citizens against his murderers, meditation on Christ's wounds will enrage your heart against lust.

Remember how sin murdered the precious Lord of glory, laid Him in an obscure grave, and sealed it with a curse which we sinners deserved – a seal stronger than anything man could devise. It could never have been broken by any power less than Christ's own almighty arm!

Alexander's military victories could not compare with his daring feat of avenging the death of Philip, his father. As soon as he came to the throne he killed the murderers upon his father's tomb! In the same way, you should never rest until you have triumphed over every drop of lust which shed our Savior's blood. Until you do this you continue to consent to the same cruelty which was spent on His gentle life. This, then, is the 'honor' which 'his saints' shall have – God has put the two-edged sword into our hands to execute vengeance on sin.

II. BE RECONCILED TO OTHERS

God expects it. And you have every reason to pardon your brother for God's sake – He forgave you for His pure mercies' sake. Thus in pardoning you are doing no more than you already owe your fellow man; but when God forgave you He owed nothing except wrath. And you need not think you are dishonoring yourself, even if you forgive the poorest beggar in town. Your God stooped even lower when He reconciled you to Himself – the high and lofty One – by persuading you to accept His forgiveness.

No, when you are full of revenge you are condescending not only beneath your heaven-born nature but beneath your human nature too. Only the devil, and those who bear his image, are implacable enemies. Hell-fire is all that is unquenchable. 'The wisdom that is from above is . . . easy to be entreated' (*Jas. 3:17*). Do you call yourself a Christian and still carry this hell-fire within? When we see a child of gentle parents acting in anger, we wonder where he got such an ungodly disposition; his mother and father were not like that. Well, who taught you to be unmerciful, Christian? You did not learn it from your heavenly Father.

III. TRUST GOD FOR YOUR NEEDS

If God has made peace with you and has forgiven your sins, you can always afford to trust Him completely for everything you need. Two things will help your faith as you exercise it.

(a) *God gives His children more than they will ever need*
When God pardoned you He gave you His Son. And 'how shall he not with him also freely give us all things?' (*Rom. 8:32*). When a father gives his son the whole orchard, it is absurd for the child to ask for one apple. 'All things are yours,' and 'ye are Christ's' (*I Cor. 3:21, 23*), God assures the Christian.

On the other hand, a wise father may bequeath a huge estate to his child – but not let him control any more of this inheritance than he can manage properly. In the same way, God gives believers a right to all the comforts of life, but His infinite wisdom proportions out smaller amounts for their actual use according to the needs of each soul. Thus if you should have much less than someone else, this does not mean God loves that person more, but that He cares enough to supply according to your ability to profitably use. We pour a drink according to the size of the cup; the wine which fills the whole cup would be spilled if poured into a smaller vessel.

(b) *God gives these temporal things even to those to whom He denies His peace*

Though unbelievers will soon stumble into hell, His providence reaches them while they are still on earth. Does He really feed these unclean ravens? And cause His rain to fall on their fields, too? Then how can He neglect a believer? If the king regularly feeds the traitor in his prison cell, surely the child in his castle shall not starve either.

In a word, if God in His providence takes such good care of the ungodly, if He 'so clothe the grass of the field' – a symbol of wicked man – 'which today is, and tomorrow is cast into the oven, shall he not much more clothe you, O ye of little faith?' (*Matt. 6:30*).

IV. ENDURE AFFLICTIONS PATIENTLY

Do not be disappointed when God allows a cross or affliction to come into your life. If He has brought you His mercy first, you can trust His kindness when He brings you His rod – you have the sugar to sweeten the bitterest cup.

When the prophet Samuel came to Bethlehem, 'the elders of the town trembled at his coming, and said, Comest thou peaceably? And he said, Peaceably' (*1 Sam. 16:4, 5*). Thus if some heavy affliction settles upon the believer for a time it might make him afraid until he knows why it has come. Now if you have made peace with Him the fear is over – you can be sure the affliction has come only on an errand of God's mercy.

Christian, what can ever separate you from the joy of peace with God? Are you afraid of men's anger? Maybe you have many enemies – and mighty ones at that. Let them express all the rage they can. Is God among them or not? Does He borrow their vengeance to pour it out on you? If not, you are worrying for nothing. And *you wrong God* by not sanctifying His name in your heart, the One whose mercy is able to protect you from their fury: 'If God be for us, who can be against us?' (*Rom. 8:31*). Even if they surround you, there is no more need to fear them than wispy straws in the wind. But *you wrong yourself* also; for as long as you stay underneath such a paralyzing fear of man's passion, you can never taste the true sweetness of God's love.

Maybe you are poor and sick and in trouble. Will God's reconciling mercy keep you from whispering discontent against Him – and stop envious glances toward the prosperity of the wicked? Remember that you have a wonderful treasure which they cannot claim, even at the height of all their worldly glory: 'I might be poor and sick, but because of God's mercy I have His peace.' If this word is taken thoughtfully it will change everything – the happiness of the prosperous sinner into mourning and your sorrow, Christian, into joy.

V. LET HOPE FEAST ON HEAVEN'S GLORY

Comfort yourself in this truth: if you are at peace with God now on earth it will not be long until you will celebrate His love in heaven with Him: 'And whom he justified, them he also glorified' (*Rom. 8:30*). Now before you think this news is too good to be true, here is encouragement for you: *Heaven's number of glorified saints is made up of justified sinners.* There is no more of one than the other.

Are you justified by faith? Then rejoice with your fellow saints in the hope of the glory of God. It lies before you. Every day brings you closer to it, and nothing can keep you back from getting there. Not even your sins, which you fear the most! The One who paid the full price at your conversion will find enough mercy in His heart to pass by the petty debts which Satan's subtlety and your own weakness have charged against you. You were an enemy when God canceled the first debt, but now you are His friend. God guarantees that He will provide for your latter obligations as He does not intend to lose His first expenditure.

Christ died to make enemies of God become friends with Him; and He lives now to bring us together with Him in heaven. 'For if, when we were enemies, we were reconciled to God by the death of his Son, much more, being reconciled, we shall be saved by his life' (*Rom. 5:10*). Paul was saying, 'Can you believe God has taken people who were bloody enemies into a place of peace and favor with Him? Surely, then, it is easier for your faith to proceed logically from reconciliation to salvation than from hostility and enmity to pardon and peace.'

If Christ could obtain reconciliation by His death, when He was at His weakest and at the lowest point of His humiliation, how much more can He save those whom He has reconciled from His powerful throne in heaven? He uses the 'keys of hell and of death' freely to open and shut doors of peace as He pleases – all for the favor of a believer (*Rev. 1:18*).

VI. WITNESS TO OTHERS

The Father's house is still not full; 'yet there is room' (*Luke 14:22*). Is there not someone you love enough to tell about God's mercy in Christ? The carnal husband lying beside you, the children of your womb, neighbors you see every day – if they should die as they now live, their precious souls are lost for ever. Yet these spiritually blind people think no more of the torment coming upon them than the simple sheep wonders why the butcher is sharpening his knife just before slitting her throat.

The more unmerciful sinners are to their own souls, the more you need to show compassion toward them. We take the best care of those who are least capable of caring for themselves. If a friend's illness became so serious that he could not help himself, would you take care of him or watch him die? Suppose a child were condemned to death but did not intend to try to get a pardon – would you do everything you could to help him rather than see his days end in such a waste? In a word, if your neighbor locked himself up in a room to commit suicide, would you break down his door to prevent him?

Where is that holy violence that is needed to save souls? People see parents, husbands, children, and neighbors going to hell before their eyes and do not even ask them *why*. For the Lord's sake, be more merciful to the souls of sinners. You have found the feast; will you let others starve, not knowing where the table is?

Go and invite everyone you see to God's house. This is what David did: 'O taste and see that the Lord is good' (*Ps. 34:8*). And do not be afraid that you might send God more guests than He wants – He protests that He desires more: 'Ye will not come to me, that ye might have life' (*John 5:40*). Further, God threatens those who prevent sinners from making peace with Him by flattering them with a false peace, called 'strengthening the hands of the wicked, that he should not return from his wicked way, by promising him life' (*Ezek. 13:22*).

What an acceptable work it is to win men to Christ! A doctor is never angry with a man who brings a patient to him, because through the cure his dedication and skill will be publicized. And this is the great design Christ has had for a long time, and prayed for – 'that the world may believe' that God sent Him (*John 17:21*). His aim in gathering in souls by the grace of the gospel is 'to take out . . . a people' from the heap of sinners 'for his name' (*Acts 15:14*) – to choose a peculiar people, show mercy on them, and allow His glorious name to be exalted.

PEACE OF CONSCIENCE

Peace of reconciliation reconciles a man to God; but peace of conscience reconciles him to himself. Since man broke peace with God he has not been able to be a friend to his own conscience. This second kind of peace is so necessary that the person cannot taste the sweetness of reconciliation with God, or of any other mercy, without it.

Peace of conscience is to the soul what health is to the body. Even a suit of gold cloth does not feel comfortable on a diseased man's shoulders. And neither does anything seem joyous to a distressed conscience. When Moses brought good news to the troubled Israelites in Egypt 'they hearkened not' to him 'for anguish of spirit' (*Exod. 6:9*). Hannah went up to the festival at Jerusalem with her husband but 'she wept, and did not eat' (*1 Sam. 1:7*). Thus the wounded soul goes to the sermon but does not partake of it; she hears many precious promises but cannot receive the life they offer.

A royal banquet spread before a deeply troubled man does not make him happy; he would rather go off in a corner by himself and cry. 'A wounded spirit who can bear?' (*Prov. 18:14*). Diseases which are incurable are called the physician's reproach. And the spiritual perplexity of an accusing conscience puts all the world to shame for their vain attempts to apply a cure.

Peace of conscience is the blessing of the gospel and only of the gospel. *Conscience knows Jesus, and the gospel of Jesus*; it refuses to obey anyone or anything else. Two particular themes will demonstrate this truth – first, what satisfies the conscience; and second, what applies this satisfaction to the conscience.

I. WHAT SATISFIES THE CONSCIENCE?

Sin causes the convulsions of horror which distort and torment a person's conscience. If this little word – but such a deadly plague – could ever be blotted out of men's minds, the storm would soon be stilled and the soul would immediately become a calm sea, quiet and smooth, without the least wave of fear to disturb its face. But sin is the Jonah which stirs up the tempest; wherever it comes, war is sure to follow.

When Adam sinned he drank away this sweet peace of conscience in one unhappy swallow. No wonder it almost choked him as soon as it was down his throat – 'and they knew that they were naked' (*Gen. 3:7*). Now, whatever is to bring true peace to the conscience must first prostrate this Goliath of sin before the war can end and peace can heal.

It is true – the poisoned head of sin's arrow which burns and throbs in the sinner's conscience is guilt. It robs the person of his rest by giving the alarm that judgment is coming and punishment is inevitable. Because that man dreads what will happen when this infinite wrath of the eternal living God comes for him, he lives in fear and agony of that expectation.

Now if you want to comfort a conscience which roasts on the burning embers of God's anger, kindled by his own guilt, you must first quench those coals and present the news that God forgives sin and that He will make reconciliation with sinners who repent and believe. Nothing but this gospel can offer the man true peace with his own thoughts. 'Son, be of good cheer,' Jesus said to the palsied man. 'Thy sins be forgiven thee' (*Matt. 9:2*). Not 'be of good cheer because your *health* is given' (although that was restored too); but 'your *sins* are forgiven.'

It would not help a condemned man on the road to execution if you put a fragrant rose in his hand and advised him to smell the flower and feel better about everything. He would still see the gallows just ahead. If a messenger from the prince should press a pardon into his hand, though, he would be overcome with joy. But this is the only thing that could change the man's heart. Anything short of pardoning mercy is as insignificant to a troubled conscience as that flower would be in a dying man's hands.

Conscience is God's sergeant to arrest the sinner. Now this sergeant does not have any power to release his prisoner on any private arrangement; he must receive official notice that the debt has been fully paid or the creditor completely satisfied. Only then can conscience free his prisoner.

(a) *The source of God's peace covenant*

There is no other way a man's sins can be forgiven and his soul reconciled to God except by the gospel of Christ. Here alone is the covenant of peace to be read between God and sinners; here is the sacrifice to purchase the pardon. If the serpent-bitten Israelites had looked on anything else besides the brazen serpent they would not have been healed. And neither will the sin-bitten conscience be eased by looking on anything but Christ in the gospel promise.

Both the priest and the Levite saw the wounded man, but would not go near him; he could have lain there and died in his own blood for all they cared. Only the good Samaritan poured oil into his wounds. It is not the law, but Christ by His blood, that bathes and cures the wounded conscience. Not all the drops of oil in the world are worth anything for healing – only what God has stored up in His gospel vial.

The Jews offered up an abundance of sacrifices, but the blood of all those animals put together never quieted a single conscience or purged a sin. The 'conscience of sins' – that is, guilt – would have remained unblotted had it been separated from the spiritual significance of these sacrifices (*Heb. 10:2*). And the apostle wrote out the reason: 'For it is not possible that the blood of bulls and of goats should take away sins' (*v. 4*). There is no redeeming relationship between sin and the blood of beasts, even if it could swell into an ocean. Man's sin deserves man's death – eternal death of both body and soul in hell. This is the price God has put on the head of every sin.

But the gospel brings joyful news of a fountain of precious blood, the blood of Jesus Christ who freely poured it out upon the cross and 'obtained eternal redemption for us' (*Heb. 9:12*). This is the only door where all true peace and joy can enter the conscience. This is why God tells us to anchor our confidence, and take our comfort, here and nowhere else. 'Let us draw near with a true heart in full assurance of faith, having our hearts sprinkled from an evil conscience' (*Heb. 10:22*).

(b) *The office of conscience*

God appoints conscience to judge man's spiritual status, good or bad, forgiven or unforgiven. If his condition is good, then conscience acquits and comforts; if evil, it accuses and condemns. Therefore the Bible calls the accusing conscience the evil conscience.

The evil conscience condemns the sinner to God's just punishment for sin; but a person who has been sprinkled by the blood of Christ and has had this offering applied to his heart by the Spirit is free to enjoy pardon and reconciliation with God. In the law, sprinkling meant the person was cleansed from all legal impurities. Therefore we understand the essence of David's prayer: 'Purge me with hyssop, and I shall be clean' (*Ps. 51:7*) – that is, 'apply the blood of Jesus to my troubled conscience as priests used hyssop dipped into a beast's blood to cleanse the leper. The sin which stains my conscience will be washed off and I can have peace, as if I had never sinned.'

The Holy Spirit alludes to this sprinkling of blood when He says: 'come to Jesus, the mediator of the new covenant, and to the blood of sprinkling, that speaketh better things than that of Abel' (*Heb. 12:24*) – 'better things' in the conscience. The guilt of Abel's blood, sprinkled upon Cain's conscience, spoke damnation and hell; but the blood of Christ sprinkled in the conscience of a penitent sinner speaks pardon and peace. Thus it is called 'the answer of a good conscience toward God, by the resurrection of Jesus Christ' (*1 Pet. 3:21*).

An answer, of course, implies there has been a question; and an 'answer toward God' presupposes a question which God has asked. His question to the sinner is this: 'What will you say when you stand doomed to damnation by the curse of My righteous law? Why should you not die the same death pronounced against every sinner of all time?'

Now the man who has heard of Christ and has taken Him into his heart by faith is the only one who can answer this question in a way that satisfies both himself and God. The Holy Spirit, through the apostle Paul, formed and fitted the answer for the mouth of every believer: 'Who is he that condemneth? It is Christ that died, yea rather, that is risen again, who is even at the right hand of God, who also maketh intercession for us' (*Rom. 8:34*). Because this confession is a response which God will not reject, Paul represents all Christians when he rejoices in its invincible strength against the enemies of our salvation: 'Who shall separate us from the love of Christ?' (*v. 35*). The apostle continues to challenge death and devils, with all their attendants, to step forward and do the worst they can against believers armed in God's breastwork. Finally he leaves the battle, filled with the holy confidence that none of them – no matter what they do – can ever hurt Christians: 'I am persuaded, that neither death, nor life, nor angels, nor principalities, nor powers . . . shall be able to separate us from the love of God, which is in Christ Jesus our Lord' (*Rom. 8:38, 39*). In a word, the Christian fastens all his flags of allegiance to Christ and places all his confidence in Him. If I have spent much time on this subject, my brothers, it is because it is the richest vein in the whole mine of gospel treasure.

II. WHAT APPLIES SATISFACTION TO THE CONSCIENCE?
Conscience is a lock which is not easily opened. Even if the key fits, a weak hand cannot make it turn in the lock. Thus when a mere man holds the key of comfort, conscience refuses to open; its doubts and fears will not be resolved until there is a work of God's Spirit.

Conscience is God's officer; and although the debt is paid in full from heaven, this official will not let the soul go free until the Spirit of God authorizes and brings a divine warrant. 'When he giveth quietness, who then can make trouble? and when he hideth his face, who then can behold him?' (*Job 34:29*). Now follow me as I demonstrate why an abundant peace of conscience cannot be found apart from the gospel and the working of the Holy Spirit.

(a) *Only the gospel presents God's Spirit as the Comforter*
The comfort of the Holy Spirit rests in the satisfaction of Jesus Christ. After He had shed His blood and paid the full price of the sinner's peace with God, He returned to

heaven and asked His Father to send the Comforter. Now Christ could not have made this request, nor could His Father have granted it, unless His death had protected God's justice from receiving any damage when believers received comfort from the Spirit. Christ told His disciples this: 'If I go not away, the Comforter will not come unto you: but if I depart, I will send him unto you' (*John 16:7*).

Now the Spirit was sent to believers as soon as Jesus appeared in the heavens with His blood as an intercessor. But you may be wondering how Old Testament saints could have had this peace and comfort since they lived before Christ's return to heaven – even before He came to earth the first time. Well, they found comfort in the same Person who bought their pardon. They were forgiven through the blood of Christ, who was a Lamb slain from the beginning of the world; and they were comforted by His Spirit. All their pardons were sent out on the credit of Christ, who even then stood ready to lay down His life in the fullness of time, and it is on that same credit that the Holy Spirit's comforts came to them.

Thus you can see that the Spirit is a comforter because of God's gospel covenant; He could never have spoken a word if it had not been for this gospel promise. Therefore when the Father sends Him to comfort He comes in Christ's name, who has stood in the gap between Him and sinners – that is, for His sake and at His request.

What does the Holy Spirit say when He comforts? The joyful news He brings is gospel intelligence: 'He shall not speak of himself; but whatsoever he shall hear, that shall he speak' (*John 16:13*). In other words, His teaching will not bring new light, different from what shines in the gospel but He will teach the same truth Christ preached.

When the Spirit comforts, the ingredients of His soul-reviving refreshments have been gathered from the gospel garden: 'He shall glorify me: for he shall receive of mine, and shall shew it unto you' – that is, Christ's death, His worthiness, His resurrection, ascension and intercession, the promises purchased and sealed with His blood (*v. 14*).

(b) *The Holy Spirit has power to comfort*

The gospel supplies sufficient power to satisfy the most troubled conscience in the world – the full satisfaction which Christ's precious blood has made to God for sinners. But if a person were left to understand and profit from this plan by himself, he might have to remain in the pains of scorched conscience because not one drop of cool balm has come to heal it. But just as God's love and wisdom provided a Savior to purchase eternal redemption for us, He also sent a Comforter to apply purchased redemption to us. This divine work is called appropriately 'strong consolation' (*Heb. 6:18*).

Christ showed His strength when He unhinged the gates of the grave and made His way out of that dark prison by His glorious resurrection. By this demonstration He was 'declared to be the Son of God with power' (*Rom. 1:4*). And it requires no less power to break open the dungeon where the guilty conscience lies confined. In fact, the same stone is upon the sinner's conscience to keep him from being resurrected to comfort as was on Christ's tomb to keep Him from being resurrected to life. Remember, though, that the strongest seal on Jesus' grave was not the stone which man rolled upon Him, nor the seal the Jews tried to fasten the grave with, but the curse of the law for sin which divine justice attached to Him. Not even the angel who rolled away the stone could have removed such a curse.

Suppose we could look in on the grave of this distressed conscience, where guilt has buried it, and sense the hell in its dread and fears. 'I am damned,' is the language ringing continually in his own ears. But what keeps his conscience here? Why can he not be lifted out of this pit of horror? You pour out the ointment of comfort in vain, for God's curse sticks like a dagger in his heart; and His anger weighs like a mountain of lead on the sinner's conscience. Unless you can take away this curse and anger, peace and comfort are impossible – the same gravestone rests on both.

But the Comforter comes to tell you good news. The same Spirit who kept Jesus from seeing corruption in the grave, who restrained death from feeding on Him, who quickened His dead body and raised Him not only to life but to immortality – He is the One whom Christ calls to satisfy your sorrowing conscience for His love's sake.

This blessed Holy Spirit has all the characteristics of a comforter. He is so pure and holy that He cannot deceive; He is called 'the Spirit of truth' (*John 14:17*). If He says your sins are forgiven, you can believe Him; He will not flatter. If it were not so He would have told you, for He can chide as well as comfort – He can convince of sin as well as of righteousness. And the Spirit of God is so wise that He cannot be deceived; He never knocks at the wrong door nor delivers messages to the wrong person, but knows the exact purpose which the heart of God holds for each person on earth. 'The Spirit searcheth all things, yea, the deep things of God' (*1 Cor. 2:10*).

These 'deep things of God' which the apostle mentions are God's counsels of love which lie deep in His heart until the Spirit draws them out and shows them to men and women. And He also knows perfectly the frame of man's heart. It would be strange if the cabinet maker did not know every secret compartment in the cabinet. Despite their long study, neither man nor the devil have anything even approaching a full knowledge of that little world, the microcosm of man's soul. But as in everything else, God knows this field perfectly and cannot be deceived.

In a word, God's Spirit is so irresistible that no one can stand against the power of His peace. For example, the pardon Nathan took to David was not all that he had hoped for; so David begged the Comforter to ease his pain. He went on his knees and prayed hard to have his lost joy restored and his softened heart established by the free Spirit of God. You might baffle man, and through your own melancholy manipulation, even evade the truths which Christians bring for comfort; but when the Holy Spirit Himself comes, all disputes will end. Satan cannot pull rank or his false logic on Him. Confusion vanishes and our fears with it, as darkness disappears before the sun. The Holy Spirit overruns the heart so sweetly and forcefully with a flood of joy that the soul can no more see sin and guilt than Noah could see ant hills when the whole earth was under water.

REPROOF TO THOSE WHO DENY THAT PEACE OF CONSCIENCE IS THE BLESSING OF THE GOSPEL

I. SOME DENY THE ASSURANCE OF SALVATION

If we could not know in this life that we are children of God, the uncertainty would shatter the vessel He molded to hold our joy and peace. It is not possible, of course, to have peace with our own consciences apart from the knowledge of our peace with God: 'Being justified by faith, we have peace with God through our Lord Jesus Christ: By whom also we have access by faith into this grace wherein we stand, and rejoice in hope of the glory of God' (*Rom. 5:1, 2*).

If the gospel cannot settle the question of whether you will go to heaven or to hell, you can forget about inward peace. In that case you may as well describe a saint's spiritual groping in the words of John: He 'walketh in darkness, and knoweth not whither he goeth' (*1 John 2:11*). A gospel like this could be called a gospel of doubt and fear rather than the gospel of peace.

Is that which is near the bottom of the law's curse upon sinners to be made the topmost part of the blessing which the gospel brings to Christians – that their 'life shall hang in doubt'; and they shall 'fear day and night,' and 'have none assurance' (*Deut. 28:66*)? God forbid! Men teach from a premise of foolish boldness when they so disfigure the sweet face of the gospel that they make Christ speak His precious promises as doubtfully to His saints as the devil lures his followers with vague enticements. Because their hypocrisy makes them question their own salvation – with good reason – they must therefore seal up the wells of salvation from sincere believers and then blame the gospel for their own doubt.

But there is a mystery of iniquity at the root of this false and uncomfortable doctrine. These religious leaders are similar to Judas, a thief who carried the money. Proponents of this teaching deposit more gold and silver in their treasury than Judas ever thought about putting in his. Although the doctrine of gospel grace brings peace to sinners' consciences, these men preach a superstitious fear which keeps ignorant parishioners pouring more and more money into their purses in pursuit of comfort. And the worst part of it all is that this principle of 'give-to-get' lies so near the heart of their religion that the gospel, heaven, and even Christ Himself must all bow to it.

II. SOME IMAGINE FOOLISH THINGS ABOUT THE GOSPEL AND ITS PEACE TO THE CONSCIENCE BECAUSE OF THE ABSENCE OF THAT PEACE IN SOME WHO PROFESS THE GOSPEL

Some people profess to believe the gospel but have no

more peace and comfort than they who are still strangers to it. In fact, they may be even more troubled in spirit than ever before.

Not everyone who confesses belief in the gospel is a Christian – but this is not God's fault. He does not lavish His eternal treasure upon everyone who knows the facts of salvation. The Spirit of God is too shrewd to sign a blank cheque.

Ministers offer the peace of the gospel to all who will accept it. But this peace refuses to stay where it meets an insincere heart. 'If the house be worthy, let your peace come upon it: but if it be not worthy, let your peace return to you' (*Matt. 10:13*). Just as the dove returned to the ark when it found the earth under water, so God's Spirit takes His comfort back to heaven from a soul still swimming around in sin, soaking in lust and worldliness.

(a) *Many are sincere but ignorant of the gospel's doctrines*
If light, joy, and comfort are missing from a sincere person's conscience it may be because his understanding is still dim. But the ignorance of the artist does not discredit the art – there is much more in art itself than the achievement of one artist. Fulness of comfort in principles of the gospel is an attainable reality, but not every Christian has yet attained to the 'riches of the full assurance of understanding, to the acknowledgment of the mystery of God, and of the Father, and of Christ', as the way in which 'their hearts might be comforted' (*Col. 2:2*).

(b) *Some do not walk in gospel doctrine*
There are those who do understand the doctrine of salvation by faith in Christ – the only foundation to build true comfort of conscience on – but they neglect to walk carefully by the gospel and deprive themselves of sweet peace from God's promises: 'As many as walk according to

this rule, peace be on them' (*Gal. 6:16*). When peace is absent, then, can we blame the gospel? No matter how superior the pen is, even in the hand of a skilled scribe, it will not write on wet paper. It is not the pen's fault, nor the hand's – the problem is the paper.

If the heart of a saint – no matter how famous and respected – is defiled by a lust which has not yielded to repentance, God's promise will not speak peace. This person has become a disorderly walker, and no joy and peace can reach him in his self-made prison. The Spirit knows how to use His rod of correction.

(c) *Many misunderstand the meaning of peace*

As for those who walk as close to the gospel as they can but still see no comfort, they may have peace and not realize it. The saint's joy is not a giggling lightheadedness like the world's; true joy is real. The parlor where the Spirit of Christ entertains the Christian is an inner room, not a porch next to the street where everyone who passes by can smell the banquet. 'A stranger doth not intermeddle with his joy' (*Prov. 14:10*). Christ and the Christian may be having supper within, even though you have not seen a single dish go in, or heard the music which sounds so splendid to believers. You might assume this soul does not have peace because he has not hung out a conspicuous sign on his countenance announcing the peace which he has inside.

On the contrary, sometimes there is never more inward peace and comfort in a saint's heart than when his face is covered with tears. If you should hear a Christian moaning and sobbing about his sins you might go home thinking that Christianity is a melancholy, dismal religion. And yet the one you pity would not part with his sorrow for all the giddy joy the world gives away. There is a mystery in these tears which human understanding cannot resolve.

Anguish of heart stems from guilt of sin and dread of God's anger because of it. Yet another kind of sorrow flows, not from fear or guilt but from awareness of the sin which remains in the soul and provokes the saint to dishonor God, who has freely loved him and forgiven his sins. This, then, is the sorrow which sometimes makes Christians seem sad or uncomfortable when all the time their hearts are as full of the assurance of God's pardoning mercy as they can hold. Their grief is like a summer shower, melted by the sense of God's love, like the warm sun. And it leaves the soul, like a garden of sweet flowers, refreshed by the gentle rain which falls upon it.

In a word, some saints who have embraced the gospel still may lack rest in their conscience. And while they might be troubled for a while in their spirits, all true believers have peace of conscience in three ways – the price, the promise, and the seed.

(i) *In the price.* The gospel puts into the hand that price which will certainly suffice to purchase peace – the blood of Jesus. We say, 'Anything is gold which is worth gold' – that is, which we can exchange anywhere for gold. Such is the blood of Christ – it is the peace of conscience because the soul that has it can exchange it for peace. Thus God cannot ever deny a prayer like this one: 'Lord, give me peace of conscience – here is Christ's blood to pay for it.' And whatever pays the debt can surely guarantee the receipt as well.

Peace of conscience is simply a seal under God's hand that the debt due to divine justice has been fully paid. If the blood of Jesus has purchased the greatest gift – salvation – it can pay for peace too. If there were medication which could infallibly produce health, we would say that the sick man has health as soon as he swallows this tonic, although he might not necessarily feel it immediately. It will come in time.

(ii) *In the promise*. A bond is as good as money in the bank. Now if God is determined to give peace to His children, who can stop Him? 'The Lord will bless his people with peace' (*Ps. 29:11*). This psalm shows what great things God can do; it is no harder for Him to create peace than to speak the word. 'The voice of the Lord is powerful; the voice of the Lord is full of majesty' (*v. 4*).

Now God promises to bless His people with both outward and inward peace. It would be a sad peace to have quiet streets but the cutting of throats inside our homes. Yet it would be even worse to have peace both in our streets and houses but war in our guilty consciences. Therefore Christ purchased the peace of pardon to obtain peace of conscience for His forgiven ones; and then He willed it to us in the promise: 'Peace I leave with you, my peace I give unto you' (*John 14:27*). There He both writes and executes His own will – to give out with His hands what His love has bequeathed to believers. There is no fear, then – His will shall be performed to the fullest, seeing that He lives to get that done by the power of His Spirit.

(iii) *In the seed*. 'Light is sown for the righteous, and gladness for the upright in heart' (*Ps. 97:11*). It is planted in the believer when principles of grace and holiness are dropped into it by the Spirit of God. Thus it is called 'the peaceable fruit of righteousness' (*Heb. 12:11*). It sprouts up as naturally from holiness as any fruit does from seed of its own kind. It is true that this seed ripens into fruit sooner in some than it does in others – spiritual harvest does not take place at the same time in everyone. But here is the security – whoever has a seed-time of grace in his heart will also have his harvest-time of joy.

God would not be keeping His promise if even one saint

should go without his reaping time. 'He that goeth forth and weepeth, bearing precious seed, shall doubtless come again with rejoicing, bringing his sheaves with him' (*Ps. 126:6*). Now if you think the gospel might be defective because a certain Christian's peace has not matured, know this – it is on the way, and when it does come it will be everlasting. *Do not focus on how the saint begins but how he ends.* 'Mark the perfect man, and behold the upright: for the end of that man is peace' (*Ps. 37:36*).

III. SOME SEARCH FOR PEACE OUTSIDE THE GOSPEL

Men are deceived if they try to heal their consciences with anything besides the refreshing ointment of the gospel. They turn away from the waters of living comfort which flow from this fountain opened in the gospel by Christ to draw peace and comfort from wells they have dug themselves – either a carnal cistern or a legal cistern.

(a) *A carnal cistern*

Sinners collect a wide variety of self-deceiving remedies to cure the fear of God's fury in their guilty consciences. If these people are awakened even slightly by Scripture their hearts become chilled from a few serious thoughts of their lost condition and they resort to the same alternative Felix chose. As soon as Paul's sermon sickened Felix's conscience, he hurried to get rid of the preacher and the disturbing noises he was making: 'Felix trembled, and answered, Go thy way for this time' (*Acts 24:25*).

Thus many turn their backs from God and run as fast and as far as they can from anyone or anything that irritates their already inflamed consciences and reminds them of their sad plight. One poor man, for instance, refused to attend funerals and even dyed his gray hair because he could not cope with thoughts of death. Yet this cowardly strategy was all this man had between him and a hell on earth in his conscience.

Other people have such a strong conscience that its light glares on them day and night, even though they calculatingly avoid all contact with Scripture, saints, and sermons. These men and women are so constantly haunted by their own guilt that they not only go 'from the presence of the Lord,' as Cain did, but apply all their energy to building 'a city' and giving their consciences the slip in a crowd of worldly business (*Gen. 4:16, 17*).

Diversion, then, is the great hungry beast that swallows up every thought of heaven and hell. Busy people are devoted to such complex projects and pressing schedules that conscience rarely finds the chance to speak a word. Besides, conscience is as offensive among sinners as Joseph's dream was among his brothers. So the unwelcome message of truth drives men to bribe their consciences with the worldly promise of profit.

But even that most sophisticated ploy to avoid gospel light is too weak to work without flaw; so sinners often invite Saul's harp and Nabal's feast to drown their cares and lull their raving consciences to sleep. Thus many soak their spiritual awareness with crude pleasures of sin; and while it sleeps in senseless stupidity they can sin without limit. But this is the height of help which a carnal recipe can give the sinner – a sleeping pill which dulls the senses of conscience for awhile, affording him a short season to forget; for the horror of his condition soon comes back to smother his peace more persistently than ever.

God keep you from such a cure for the troubles of your conscience! It is a thousand times worse than the disease itself. Undoubtedly it is better to have a dog that barks incessantly to betray a thief than to have one that sits still and lets us be robbed before we know danger is anywhere near.

(b) *A legal cistern*

Other people, thirsty for peace, have no relief except from

their own morality; they bless themselves by performing a good deed each time a qualm comes over their consciences. The cordial drink which they use to revive themselves is not drawn from the satisfaction of Christ's death but from the righteousness of their carefully disciplined activities. This wine has not been pressed from the precious intercession Christ makes in heaven but from their earthly prayers for themselves. In a word, even though the sparks of agitation kindle in their consciences – and this is inevitable with so much combustible matter for a roaring fire – it is not Christ's blood but their own tears with which they try to extinguish it.

Well, no matter who you are, if you build up peace of conscience with wood, hay, and stubble, I accuse you of being an enemy of Jesus Christ and of His gospel. If any herb grew in your own garden that could heal your wounded conscience, why did God prescribe such a rare balm compounded with the blood of His only Son? Why does He call sinners away from everything else except Himself? You can know this: either Christ was an imposter, and the gospel a fable – and I hope you are not such an infidel, worse than Satan himself, to believe that – or else you are not taking the right method of healing your conscience and obtaining peace for it.

Now as for laying a sure foundation for solid peace in your heart, you cannot complete it without prayers and tears – I mean repentance. But by themselves, these remedies will never provide peace with God. Peace of conscience is nothing more than the echo of pardoning mercy which brings the soul into sweet rest as its pleasant music sounds in the conscience. This echo is only the same voice repeated; so if tears and prayers and good works cannot purchase our peace of pardon, they cannot effect the peace of comfort either. Remember what I have said –

you cannot have inner peace without these; but you cannot have it by them alone.

A common wound will hardly heal unless it is wrapped up from the open air and kept clean; yet these measures do not cure it – the medicine does. I do not want you to stop praying and serving; just do not expect peace to grow only from their root. If you do rely on this you isolate yourself from any benefit of true peace which the gospel offers. One resists the other like two famous rivers in Germany, whose streams will not mingle when they meet.

Gospel peace will not merge with any other peace. You must drink it pure and undiluted or not at all. Speaking for himself and for all other sincere believers, Paul testified, 'We are the circumcision, which worship God in the spirit, and rejoice in Christ Jesus, and have no confidence in the flesh' (*Phil. 3:3*). He was declaring, 'We do not fall behind in any holy duty or service. No, we go beyond them, because we worship God in the spirit; but even this is not the tap where we draw our joy and comfort. We rejoice in Christ Jesus, not in the flesh.' Thus anything which opposes Christ and our rejoicing in Him, Paul calls flesh.

Indeed there are many who do use the balm of the gospel's mercy for the healing of a wounded conscience but they do not follow the scriptural order in applying it. Instead, they snatch a promise presumptuously and ravish it rather than wait for Christ's consent. Too often they are like Saul, who was in such a hurry that he could not wait until Samuel came to sacrifice for him but went to work first, disobeying God every minute that he served.

Impulsive people do not wait for God's Spirit to come and sprinkle their consciences with the blood of Christ according to the gospel; they do it themselves by applying the comfort of promises which do not pertain to them at present. For example, what would you think of a man who refused to wait for his doctor's prescription but rushed to the pharmacy and started mixing the medicine himself? Yet this is what every person does who sprinkles himself with the blood of Christ and blesses himself in the pardoning mercy of God before he turns away from sin.

Let every profane person know this. Just as the blood of the paschal lamb was not applied to the Egyptians' doors, but to the Israelites', neither will the blood of Jesus be sprinkled on the obstinate sinner but on the sincere penitent. That blood was not put on the threshold of the Israelites' doors where it might be walked on, but on the sideposts, where its mark became sacred. Neither is Christ's blood reserved, then, for anyone who continuously practices sin. This would be pouring out the most holy sacrifice to be trampled on. Remember, David had to confess his sin with shame before Nathan could comfort him with news of pardon.

CHARACTERISTICS OF GOSPEL PEACE

Let this doctrine be a touchstone to try the truth of your peace and comfort. Since Satan has his counterfeit comfort as well as counterfeit grace, we must seriously consider some characteristics of the peace which Christ speaks to His people from the gospel.

I. GOSPEL COMFORT IS POURED INTO A BROKEN HEART

Gospel comfort can be known by the vessel that contains it: 'I dwell in the high and holy place, with him also that is of a contrite and humble spirit, to revive the spirit of the humble, and to revive the heart of the contrite ones' (*Isa. 57:15*). And Christ's commission from the Father also restricts His comfort to such people: 'The Spirit of the Lord God is upon me: because the Lord hath anointed me

[323]

to preach good tidings unto the meek; he hath sent me to bind up the brokenhearted' (*Isa. 61:1*).

Thus we see the order of the gospel in comforting the soul. As in needlework, the somber, dark background is laid before the beautiful colors are stitched in. As the sculptor cuts and carves his statue before covering it with gold, so the Spirit of Christ begins in sorrow by reproving of sin and ends in joy by delivering from fear. He first cuts and wounds, then heals and overlays the soul with peace and comfort.

I hope you do not think I limit the Holy One of Israel in working to the same degree and measure in everyone. But in all cases the humbling work of the Spirit must convince a person before peace and comfort come to empty the soul of false confidence which she has stored up. Then the heart becomes like a vessel whose bottom has been beaten out until all the water spills out. It hates sins it once loved. The hopes which pleased and sustained her are gone and the person is left in a desolate and solitary condition.

The soul realizes that nothing stands between it and hell except Christ; and rather than die she cries out to Him, willing to follow His direction. The soul is like a patient who is thoroughly convinced of her doctor's personal skill and care. This is what I call 'the broken heart'.

I beg you, though, not to rest until your conscience answers some questions. Was your wine once water? Does your light arise from darkness? Is your peace the product of soul-conflict and trouble? Did you bleed before you were healed? If so, bless God who has turned your mourning into dancing.

On the other hand, if you drank wine before your pots were ever filled with water; if your morning dawned before there was evening; if your peace was settled before your false peace was broken; if your conscience was sound and whole before it was lanced and drained of pride and carnal confidence – you may possess short-lived peace. But Jesus denies all this to be *His* cure. It requires far more power to work true godly sorrow than false joy. You would be happier mourning from the distress of a troubled conscience than dancing around the devil's idol of peace.

II. GOSPEL PEACE IS GIVEN TO OBEDIENT SERVANTS

(a) *In a way of obedience and holiness*

'As many as walk according to this rule, peace be on them' (*Gal. 6:16*). Now 'this rule' is the holy walk of the 'new creature' according to God's Word (*v. 15*). The principles of grace planted in the believer's soul are as appropriate to it as the agreement between the eye and light.

It is not enough for a person to be a new creature and to have a principle of grace in his heart – he must actually *walk* by this rule. If he fails there will be no true peace in his conscience. And we know there cannot be any real peace except what the Comforter brings to the saint. It is scripturally sound that He who commands us to 'withdraw from every brother that walketh disorderly' surely will withhold His comfort from disobedient walkers (*2 Thess. 3:6*).

Now if you prefer a carnal lifestyle do not ever say that the Spirit brings comfort to you. He would not wish you good speed in such an evil course. No, He withdrew His comfort the moment you turned away from walking on His holy path. All the peace you pretend to have is illegitimate; and you have more reason to be ashamed of it than to glory in it. It is nothing to be proud of when the wife gives birth to a baby when her husband is abroad and could not have fathered the child. It is even worse for you to claim comfort when the Spirit of Christ will not own it.

(b) *In a way of service*

'Now the Lord of peace himself give you peace always by

[325]

all means' – that is, He will bless every proper means and opportunity to fill your soul with inner peace (*2 Thess. 3:16*). Thus the person who never seeks God but brags about personal peace causes sober Christians to question the truth of his testimony. Of course God is able, by special ministry of His Spirit, to bypass the saint's labor of hearing, praying, and meditating; but where did He say He would do that?

Why should we expect peace without seeking God? We would not think of harvesting before plowing and sowing. If we were like Israel in the wilderness, where the opportunities were taken away, and if we strove against pride and laziness, then I would not be surprised to see comforts falling on the soul as thick as manna around Hebrew tents. But God no longer rained bread once the Israelites grew corn to make their own bread. Neither will the Lord comfort by a miracle when the soul may obtain it through the ordinances: worship, preaching, the Lord's Supper, and so on. God certainly could have taught the eunuch Himself and satisfied him with a light from heaven. Instead, He sent for Philip to preach the Word, no doubt to honor the ministry of His gospel.

III. GOSPEL PEACE STRENGTHENS AND RESTORES THE CHRISTIAN

This peace makes the Christian strong enough to fight against sin and Satan. The saint is revived when he tastes only a little of this honey, but what a slaughter he makes of his spiritual enemies when he has had a full meal! He can go into battle like a giant refreshed with wine – no one can stand before him.

Peace also strengthens the Christian to work. Paul, for instance, remembered God's mercy and the awareness of His love glowed in his heart until it infused him with a zeal for the gospel above his fellows. This same kind of peace made David pray hard to drink again of this wine which had been locked up from him for so long. 'Restore unto me the joy of thy salvation; and uphold me with thy free Spirit. Then will I teach transgressors thy ways; and sinners shall be converted unto thee' (*Ps. 51:12, 13*). His fervent longing for the sweet taste of this wine was not the main reason he asked for peace – he desired power to do God's work.

I would urge you to look very carefully to see what peace has done in your own life. Are you humble or proud because of it? Do you walk more closely to the gospel? Where do you stand in worship? Do you cherish communion with God – or do you feel formal and lifeless? In a word, can you show that grace and peace both grow in your spirit? Or does one decrease because you pretend to have the other? By this you can know whether your peace comes from the peace-maker or the peace-marrer, from the God of truth or from the father of lies.

IV. GOSPEL PEACE COMFORTS THE SOUL

Gospel peace strengthens the soul when it has no other comfort to mix with it. It is a beverage rich enough by itself and does not need any additional ingredient. In a similar way David's devotion singled out God: 'Whom have I in heaven but thee? and there is none upon earth that I desire beside thee' (*Ps. 73:25*). If David had God – His love and favor – he had everything he needed. Thus the Christian's peace pays him the greatest dividends of joy when outward enjoyments contribute least, indeed nothing but trouble.

'But David encouraged himself in the Lord his God' (*1 Sam. 30:6*). You know when that was. If David's peace had not been sound it would have been hard for him to think of God in the middle of all his other heartaches. 'Great peace have they which love thy law: and nothing shall offend them' (*Ps. 119:165*). This is what distinguishes the saint's peace from that of the worldly person and the hypocrite.

(a) *The worldly person's peace*

His peace is drained to the dregs as soon as disgrace or poverty tilts his cup. When all the man sees is darkness instead of light, Christ comes to contrast His peace to that of the world: 'My peace I give unto you: not as the world giveth, give I unto you. Let not your heart be troubled, neither let it be afraid' (*John 14:27*). He was preparing His disciples for His departure, which He knew would be a severe test for their peace.

It is as if Christ had said, 'If the peace you have from Me lies in the same things the world's peace is made of – money, ease, and carnal happiness – you will have every reason to mourn at My funeral. No, you can expect trouble and persecution. But always be assured that the peace I leave with you is not in houses but in hearts. My comfort does not lie in silver and gold, but in pardon of sin and in hope of glory. And the peace which the Comforter, who will come from Me to dwell in you, will give you, will outlive all the world's joy.'

No father ever left such a legacy to his children. Of course many death-bed farewells have wished peace for the family; but no one except Christ could send a Comforter and cause peace to stay in human hearts no matter what might happen.

(b) *The hypocrite's peace*

Sometimes a man pretends to take comfort from God instead of from people, possessions, or situations. He seems to have joy in Christ and the precious promises of the gospel; yet when the real trial comes and he loses all earthly comforts, his true colors are seen and God indicts him for spiritual forgery.

What about you? Does your peace go with you only as far as the prison door? Or the hospital bed? It is easy to be confident of salvation as long as your health is good; but as soon as death is in sight, does your conscience point out the serious symptom that your peace is a mere pretense?

I know that affliction is a trying time. Even the most sincere Christian may, for a season, be beaten away from his artillery and Satan seem to capture his confidence. Some precious saints have been carried down the stream of violent temptations so far that they question whether their former peace was from the Holy Spirit the Comforter or from the evil spirit the deceiver. Yet there is a vast difference between the two.

(i) *They differ in their causes.* The darkness which sometimes comes upon the sincere Christian's spirit in deep distress comes from the withdrawing of God's countenance of light. But the horror of the deceived man's torment proceeds directly from a guilty conscience which prosperity and preoccupation have lulled to sleep. As God's hand upon this man awakens his numb conscience, it reveals the falseness of his profession of faith. It is true that the saint's conscience may justly accuse him of carelessness or compromise through strong temptation, but it cannot accuse him of a hypocritical motive behind his whole spiritual walk.

(ii) *They differ in the things which accompany them.* Lively workings of grace are visible even as the Christian sorrows. The less joy he has from awareness of God's love, the more earnestly he will grieve for the sin which clouded that joy. The farther Christ is gone out of his sight, the more he clings to his love for the Savior and cries after Him with the prayer of Heman: 'Unto thee have I cried, O Lord'; his heartfelt supplication rises to God early in the morning hours (*Ps. 88:13*).

The most fervent prayers are sent to heaven from the troubled spirit, while deep-rooted affection rises to God, desiring His face, and His favor. No child banished from his father's presence ever desired his angry parent's embrace more than a troubled saint longs to have the light of God's countenance on him once again. He searches his heart, studies the Scripture, and wrestles with God for grace to restore his comforts and his peace. The hypocrite, on the other hand, does not want love or grace and holiness for the intrinsic excellency in them; he views these qualities only as tickets for escaping the tormentor's hand.

(iii) *They differ in the issue.* The Christian is like a star in the heavens that wades through the very cloud which hides his comfort for a time. But the hypocrite is like a meteor which blazes through the air and then drops into a ditch, where it is soon quenched. Or, as the Spirit of God distinguishes them, 'The light of the righteous rejoiceth: but the lamp of the wicked shall be put out' (*Prov. 13:9*). In this Scripture the sincere Christian's joy is compared to the light of the sun which climbs higher and higher, even though it is hidden from the eye by many clouds. Finally it breaks out even more gloriously than ever and rejoices over the mists that seemed to obscure it.

But the joy of the wicked, like a candle, wastes and spends itself as it is fed with the fuel of outward prosperity. In a short time it will fail and the deceived man's comfort is snuffed out, past all hope of ever being lighted again.

The Christian's troubled spirit has also been compared to a person who faints; it is only a temporary situation and he will soon recover. A sickness rises in a holy man's heart because of his sin. 'Innumerable evils have compassed me about: mine iniquities have taken hold upon me, so that I am not able to look up; they are more than the hairs of mine head: therefore my heart faileth me' (*Ps. 40:12*). Yet before the Psalm ends this believer deeply groans in prayer and once again acts in strong faith toward God: 'Yet the Lord thinketh upon me: thou art my help and my deliverer' (*v. 17*). But once the hypocrite's hope begins to falter, it dies: 'The eyes of the wicked shall fail, and they shall not escape, and their hope shall be as the giving up of the ghost' (*Job 11:20*).

PEACE OF LOVE AND UNITY

Nothing but the gospel can knit the hearts and minds of men together in solid peace and love. Next to reconciling us to God and to ourselves, Christ personally designed this blessing to fill up the saints' happiness. Otherwise God would need to make a heaven for every Christian to live in by himself.

The ministry of John the Baptist, the preface to the gospel, was divided into two parts: to turn many of the children of Israel to the Lord their God and 'to turn the hearts of the fathers to the children' (*Luke 1:17*) – that is, to make them friends with God and with one another. This is the natural effect of the gospel wherever it is sincerely embraced – to unite the hearts of men and women in a powerful love and peace.

Isaiah prophesied of this strange metamorphosis which would happen under the gospel: 'The wolf also shall dwell with the lamb, and the leopard shall lie down with the kid' (*Isa. 11:6*). Men and women who have selfishly clung to decades of dissension will agree and rest in one another's embrace. This phenomenon is impossible, of course, without the power of the gospel working in those who believe.

The prophet continued, 'For the earth shall be full of

[331]

the knowledge of the Lord' (*v. 9*). It is in darkness that men attack one another with furious vindictiveness, but when gospel light streams in they soon put away their swords. The sweet spirit of love will never permit hatred to persist where she dwells; and this blessing is so peculiar to the gospel that Christ has chosen it as the badge to identify true Christians: 'By this shall all men know that ye are my disciples, if ye have love one to another' (*John 13:35*). A nobleman's servant is marked out from others by the color and cut of the coat he wears; and Jesus says that strangers can distinguish Christians from all others by their love for one another, which they ascribe to Christ and His gospel.

If you want to determine the qualities of a particular kind of wine, you must taste it not only after it has been refined from its impurities, but before merchants can dilute it. So then the best way to judge the gospel and its fruit is to taste it when it was received and accepted with the most simplicity – free from doubt or dilution (and without a doubt then, the period to examine is that of the early church). Or, secondly, we can taste it when it has its full effect on the hearts of men – in heaven. In both instances, this peace will appear as the natural fruit of the gospel.

I. ONENESS OF HEART AMONG THE FIRST CHRISTIANS

Christ's peace caused saints in the early church to live and love as if each one had forsaken his own heart to enter his brother's bosom. They forsook personal investments to keep their love whole and took bread from their own table to feed hungry brothers and sisters. Even when love to their fellow Christians was the costliest, these believers were not resentful. They 'sold their possessions and goods, and parted them to all men, as every man had need; and they, continuing daily with one accord in the temple, and breaking bread from house to house, did eat their meat with gladness and singleness of heart' (*Acts 2:45, 46*).

Tertullian reported that the love of Christians in primitive times was so notorious that heathens pointed them out: 'See how they love one another!' These believers were happier when they gave up all they had in charity than when they filled their pockets with worldly profit. Thus if saints of today have less love and peace, the blame does not lie in the gospel but squarely in their own attitudes. The gospel is as full of peace as it ever has been; but Christians today can fall very far short of manifesting its spirit.

II. THE PERFECTION OF THIS PEACE AND MUTUAL LOVE
   IN HEAVEN

After the promises concerning peace are fully realized in glory, then this sort of peace will be one of heaven's chief adornments. In the world, peace reminds us of a budding flower in springtime. On a warm day it opens a little, but as the cold night comes its petals shut tightly again.

The 'silence' in this lower heaven – the church on earth –is only for 'the space of half an hour' (*Rev. 8:1*). Even though there is love and peace among Christians, differences arise which drive back the sweet spring. But in heaven it is full blown and continues that way throughout eternity. Not only is the wound of contention healed; a scar is not to be seen on the face of heaven's peace to disfigure its beauty. Now let me show you specifically how the gospel knits men's hearts and minds together in peace.

HOW THE GOSPEL ALONE KNITS THE HEARTS OF MEN IN PEACE

I. THE GOSPEL SETS FORTH POWERFUL ARGUMENTS FOR
   PEACE AND UNITY

The cords of love which draw and bind souls together are

not woven in nature's loom; they are textured only by divine revelation. Thus Paul confidently exhorts Christians 'to keep the unity of the Spirit in the bond of peace' (*Eph. 4:3*).

The apostle then reminds God's people that 'there is one body,' not a philosophical or natural entity but a mystical one – the church – which consists of many saints (*v. 4*). If it is not normal for one member of a man's body to battle another, when they are all preserved in life by their union together, so much less in the mystical body.

Again, there is 'one Spirit' who quickens all true saints, and He is to the whole body of Christians as the soul is to the whole man (*v. 4*). Now it is a strange violence against nature for members of a man's body to war against one another and drive out the soul, which gives life to them in their oneness. Surely it would be even more perverse for Christians to force the Holy Spirit to leave because of their contention and strife. A wider door cannot easily be opened for Him to go.

Further, the apostle persuades Christians to preserve unity because of the 'one hope of your calling' – the bliss which we all hope for in heaven (*v. 4*). There is a day coming – and it cannot be far away – when we shall lovingly meet in heaven and sit at the same feast together, with no envy at what is on our neighbor's plate. Full fruition of God will be the feast, and peace and love the sweet music that accompanies it. How senseless it is, then, for us to fight on earth when we shall feast together in heaven. Now it is the gospel which invites us to this feast and calls us to this unity. Other truths are engraved on the same holy invitation and command – 'one Lord, one faith, one baptism' (*v. 5*) – but I shall leave these for your own study.

II. THE GOSPEL TAKES AWAY THE CAUSES OF STRIFE

Two main causes of division exist among the sons and daughters of men – the curse of God and their own lusts.

(a) *The curse of God*

Hostility among men and women is part of the curse which lies upon mankind because of apostasy. We read, for example, how the ground was cursed for man's sake – 'thorns also and thistles shall it bring forth to thee' (*Gen. 3:18*). Yet an even greater curse fell when one man became such a briar that he spilled the blood of another. The stinging nettles which come up so thickly in man's quarrelsome nature today give clear evidence of the power of God's curse. Some people suppose that the rose must have grown without thorns in paradise. Surely if man had not sinned, he would never have become the prickly thorn that even the most spiritual person is in our time!

The first man born into the world proved to be a murderer; and the first man who died went to his grave by that bloody murderer's hand. The power of God's curse on man's nature appeared in Cain's malicious heart as irrevocably as the fig tree was withered by Christ's curse. God was justified in mingling a perverse spirit among those who had expressed a false spirit to Him; they deserved to have their language confused and their relationships with each other tainted by strife and struggle because of disobedience to God.

Once the staff of 'Beauty' – which represented God's covenant with the Jews – was broken, then the staff of 'Bands' – which signified the brotherhood between Judah and Jerusalem – was severed also (*Zech. 11:10, 14*). When people break a covenant with God they cannot expect peace among themselves.

A curse, as we know, is a decree of God which condemns rebellious men and women to something evil;

and before there can be any hope of peace among men this curse must be reversed. Only the gospel can do that, for there is 'no condemnation' to the person who is in Christ Jesus (*Rom. 8:1*). The curse is gone and there is no arrow in the bow of threatening; that was shot into Christ's heart and can never enter into the believer.

Sometimes God may discipline His people, however, by permitting them to receive unbrotherly unkindness from one another's hands, a sharp rod in His chastisement to make them realize the seriousness of disobeying Him. Even so, the curse has ceased and God's true people live under a promise of peace and unity.

(b) *Lust inside hearts*

The internal reason for contention and strife among men is the lust which dwells in them. This is the root which bears all the bitter fruit of rivalry in the world: 'From whence come wars and fightings among you? come they not hence, even of your lusts that war in your members?' (*Jas. 4:1*). Lust breaks peace with God, ourselves, and others.

If we note a 'fiery vapor' wrapped up in the clouds we expect thunder and lightning to follow. And if lust is in the heart it will eventually vent itself, even if it tears up peace in a family, in a church, or in a kingdom. Now before there can be a foundation for solid peace the unruly lusts of men must be conquered. What peace and quiet can abide when pride, ambition, envy, and jealousy continue to dictate men's choices of behavior?

But please do not think it is enough merely to restrain these unruly passions and forcibly bind them up. If peace does not rise from the hearts of men, a truce is worth nothing. The chain which ties up the mad dog will wear out in time; and so the cords which seem to bind men together will snap if they are not tied with heartstrings and the cause of the quarrel taken away.

Now the gospel, and only the gospel, can form a plaster to draw out the very core of contention from the heart. The apostle Paul testifies how he and his brothers were healed of malicious attitudes: 'We ourselves also were sometimes foolish, disobedient, deceived, serving divers lusts and pleasures, living in malice and envy, hateful, and hating one another' (*Tit. 3:3*). And then Paul writes in some detail how that healing came: 'But after that the kindness and love of God our Savior toward man appeared, not by works of righteousness which we have done, but according to his mercy he saved us, by the washing of regeneration, and renewing of the Holy Ghost' (*Tit. 3:4–5*). He was saying, 'If this love of God to us in Christ had not appeared, if we had not been washed by His regenerating Spirit, we would still be paralyzed under the power of our lusts.'

Mortification is a work of the Spirit. 'If ye through the Spirit do mortify the deeds of the body, ye shall live' (*Rom. 8:13*). *And the gospel is the sacrificing knife in the hand of the Spirit*, the 'sword' God uses to kill sin in the hearts of His people (*Eph. 6:17*).

(c) *Grace for Christlikeness*

Just as the gospel lays the axe to strife and digs it up by its bitter roots, so it fills the hearts of men who embrace it with principles leading to peace and unity. Some of these tenets are self-denial, longsuffering, and gentleness. Self-denial prefers that another be honored before himself. Longsuffering is that which makes one not easily provoked. And if gentleness is pushed by a wrong, it holds the door open for peace to come in again.

We can see a whole bundle of these sweet herbs growing in one bed: 'The fruit of the Spirit is love, joy, peace, longsuffering, gentleness, goodness, faith, meekness, temperance' (*Gal. 5:22, 23*). Now this fruit does not crop

[337]

up in just every hedge, but only from gospel seed. Cedars in the forest would never have fitted perfectly together in the temple unless they had first been cut and carved for that purpose. And neither could trees have formed themselves into such beauty; this construction was the work of men gifted by God for that very reason.

Thus it is impossible for men and women, with all their skill and tools of morality, to square and frame their hearts so lovingly as to become one holy temple. This is the work of the Spirit, and He uniquely completes it with the instrument of the gospel, partly by cutting off the rough knots of our boorish natures by His mortifying grace, and partly by carving, polishing, and smoothing them with the power which flows from Himself.

THE DIFFERENCE BETWEEN THE PEACE OF SAINTS AND THE PEACE OF SINNERS

I. PEACE AND LOVE AMONG WICKED MEN

Worldly persons cannot experience true peace and love because they are strangers to the gospel which joins hearts together. What then can we call their peace? In some it is a mere organization or outworking of a desire to belong to a group. 'Say ye not, A confederacy, to all them to whom this people shall say, A confederacy' (*Isa. 8:12*). At other times people rally around a common hatred of the saints rather than love among themselves. And like Samson's foxes, they unite to do mischief to others rather than good to themselves. Two dogs can stop their scrapping long enough to chase a passing rabbit; but when the hunt is over they resume their fighting as fiercely as ever. 'And the same day Pilate and Herod were made friends together: for before they were at enmity between themselves' (*Luke 23:12*).

The peace and unity of others is founded upon a base

lust which ties them together. Thus we see a group of 'good fellows,' as they call themselves, gathered around their liquor in an abundance of false contentment with one another. And like a pack of thieves, they call out, 'Come with us; cast in thy lot among us; let us all have one purse' (*Prov. 1:11, 14*). Here is unity, but only because the members are brothers in sin.

Again, many people are drawn together by something other than hatred and theft; for while they have never known the power of the gospel, there is a measure of mutual love expressed. And for this ability to express compassion they are deeply indebted to the gospel, because it often civilizes and softens even where it does not sanctify. Yet this is a unity so fundamentally defective and incomplete that it does not deserve the name of true peace.

(a) *The peace of the wicked is superficial*

In the peace of ungodly persons lusts are chained from open war, but hearts are not changed into inward love. Unregenerate men are like the animals in the ark; even though they were kept at peace for a time, they retained their wild nature.

(b) *The peace of the wicked is unsanctified*

While unbelievers seem to experience peace with one another, they have no peace with God; and peace with Him is the only way to remove the curse. In other words, their peace proceeds from unsanctified hearts. And only the renewed heart can sanctify unity.

Centuries ago a heathen said that true love and friendship can appear only between good men, but unfortunately he did not know what makes a good man. When God's mercy intends to accomplish oneness, He first makes the people new. 'And I will give them one heart, and I will put a new spirit within' (*Ezek. 11:19*). Genuine peace is a fruit of the Spirit – it inevitably sanctifies before it unites.

Finally, we see that every part and purpose of the sinner's love is carnal, not spiritual. Augustine pitied Cicero for not having Jesus Christ in his life far more than he admired him for his eloquence. This, then, is what draws a heavy black line through the carnal man's peace and unity – there is nothing of God and Christ in it.

Do carnally-minded people aim at the glory of God? Is it Christ's command which binds them together? No, there is a still voice involved – but it is not God's. Their own relaxation or fleshly favor is the primary motive. Peace and unity are such welcome guests, and pay so well for their lodging, that they motivate men with no grace at all to keep up an external peace among themselves. In a word, the peace of the wicked will not last long because it lacks strong cement. Stones may lie together for a while without mortar, but not for long. *The only lasting cement for love is the blood of Jesus.*

II. THE SIN OF MINISTERS WHO STIR UP STRIFE

The gospel of peace is a strange text to preach contention from, yet Paul speaks of this very thing: 'Some indeed preach Christ even of envy and strife' (*Phil. 1:15*). These men seem to have forgotten that their Lord who sent them is Himself the Prince of peace! Their work is not to blow a trumpet of confusion or sound an alarm to battle but rather to call for a joyful retreat from the dreadful fight against God and one another.

There is a war which ministers are to proclaim, however – a war against sin and Satan; but Christians are not ready to march out to combat the devil and his forces until they agree among themselves. What would a prince do to that captain who stirred up strife among his soldiers instead of encouraging them to unite as one man against their common enemy? Surely he would hang him as a traitor.

In these times when there is such wrangling in the

church, we say a hearty *amen* to Luther's prayer: 'The Lord deliver His church from a vainglorious doctor, a contentious pastor, and nice questions.' Most gospel truths are lost to people whose eyes have been dimmed by the dust of division and disputed questions. I must pity the vile men who have prostituted the gospel to such devilish ends! God's mercy may bring back cheated souls to the love of truth, but as for the cheaters themselves – they are too close to hell for us to expect their return.

Here, then, is the reason why there is not more peace and unity among saints. The gospel which breathes peace cannot be blamed. It is because Christians, the 'gospellers', are not yet perfectly 'gospelized'. And the more Christians actually partake of the spirit of the gospel, the less they will be haunted with the evil spirit of contention and strife. Even the most dedicated saints are in part 'ungospelized' in two areas and this causes all the quarrelings and unkind contests among them.

(a) *In their judgments*

'We know in part, and we prophesy in part' (*1 Cor. 13:9*). Anyone who pretends to know more than this reveals the very thing he denies – ignorance of the gospel. And this defect in saints' judgments exposes them to drink in principles which are not scriptural and thus disturb their mutual peace. All truth is reducible to a unity; like lines which lovingly meet in one center – the God of truth – they are as far from clashing as stones in an arch, which rather uphold one another. The truths of Scripture, then, which agree among themselves so pleasantly cannot possibly teach us to divide.

No, it is the stranger called *error* which creeps in and mars the saint's spiritual health. Wholesome meals do not disturb a healthy body, but corrupt food makes it feverish and out-of-sorts. Then of course when the person gets sick

[341]

his behavior becomes deplorable because of petty pre-judice and selfish trivia. We have seen it by experience. The same people whose lives give out nothing but kindness while they feed on gospel truth become un-usually quarrelsome the very day they take in unscriptural teaching. These men who were once peaceful are now so irritable and sensitive that it is hard to talk with them. Many react with inappropriate behavior at the very mention of Scripture, as if every word made them sick.

But let no one try to blame the gospel for discord among Christians. Paul tells us exactly where to find the father of the bastard called strife: 'Now I beseech you, brethren, mark them which cause divisions and offences contrary to the doctrine which ye have learned; and avoid them' (*Rom. 16:17*). The dividing spirit is contrary to the gospel, and those in its grip never learned it in Christ's school. The apostle tacitly implies that they acquired it elsewhere, from false teachers with false doctrines. 'Mark them,' he warns, as if he had said, 'Look closely and you will notice that they are scorched. They have warmed themselves at Satan's fire and brought from it coals of error which cause the damage.'

(b) *In their hearts and lives*

Because the entire root of sin is not dug up at once, it is no wonder that a bitter taste often remains in the fruit which saints produce. In heaven we will be all grace and all love, with no sin mixed in; but because here our corruptions are still with us, our love is not yet perfect. How, then, can Christians be soldered together in unity, as long as they are not fully reconciled to God in regard to their sanctifica-tion? The less progress the gospel has made in our hearts to mortify lust and strengthen grace, the weaker the peace and love among us.

From the contentions among Christians at Corinth,

Paul concluded that they had not grown in grace beyond the spoonfeeding stage. 'I have fed you with milk, and not with meat: for hitherto ye were not able to bear it, neither yet now are ye able. For ye are yet carnal' (*1 Cor. 3:2–3*): he conceived their behavior to be clear evidence. 'For whereas there is among you envying, and strife, and divisions, are ye not carnal, and walk as men?' But as grace strengthens, and the gospel prevails in the hearts of Christians, love and a spirit of unity increase with it.

We say 'older and wiser' – when children are very young they quarrel and fight, but age and wisdom furnish strength to overcome petty differences. For instance, in the controversy between the servants of Abraham and Lot, Abraham – the elder and stronger Christian – was determined, no matter what it cost him, to have peace with his nephew, who was inferior to him in every way. And Paul is another example. As a Christian who was head and shoulders above the others, he said of himself, 'The grace of our Lord was exceeding abundant with faith and love which is in Christ Jesus' (*1 Tim. 1:14*).

Calvin points out that Paul's faith opposed his former obstinate unbelief as a Pharisee; his love in Jesus overcame the cruelty he expressed against Christians on his persecuting errand to Damascus. He was as full of faith as he had been of unbelief before; and as full of fire-hot love as he had been of hatred. This is what I want you to see – this pair of graces thrive and grow together; a Christian who has abundant faith will also have abundant love.

EXHORTATION TO NOURISH PEACE

You profess to have been baptized into the spirit of the gospel of Christ, but the gospel that makes wolves and lambs agree never teaches lambs to turn into wolves and devour other lambs. Jesus told the two disciples whose anger flared up that they did not realize where the wildfire of their temper had come from: 'Ye know not what manner of spirit ye are of' (*Luke 9:55*). It is as if he had said, 'Such bitter passion does not fit in with the meek Master you serve, nor with the gospel of peace He preaches.'

Now if the gospel will not allow us to pay our enemies back in their own coin, returning anger for anger, then certainly it forbids a brother to spit fire into the face of another brother. When such embers of contention begin to smoke among Christians, we can be sure Satan planted the spark; he is the one great kindle-coal of all strife.

Whenever there is a storm in the spirits of saints, and the winds of their emotions are high and loud, it is easy to see who has stirred up the tempest. The devil practices his black art on unmortified lusts, that enable him to raise easily many storms of division among believers. Paul and Barnabas, for instance, set out in a calm together, but Satan sent a storm to part them in the middle of their journeyings: 'And the contention was so sharp between them, that they departed asunder one from the other' (*Acts 15:39*).

There is nothing, next to Christ and heaven, which Satan begrudges believers more than their peace and mutual love. If he cannot separate them from Christ, and stop them from getting to heaven, he takes sinister pleasure in watching them get there in a storm. He would have them be like a shattered fleet separated from one another, saints deprived of the comfort and help of other Christians along the way. And when the devil can divide, he hopes to ruin also, knowing well that one ship is more easily taken than a squadron.

Now I love clear, calm air; but most of all I enjoy it in the church. I confess I am more aware of the greatness of this mercy when I see the dismal results of divisions that have troubled believers during these last years. What can I compare error to, better than smoke? And contention, than to fire? It is an emblem of hell itself, where darkness and flames meet to intensify the horror. But let me give you three reasons why a believer should give himself to peace and unity.

I. CHRISTIANS SHOULD SEEK PEACE FOR CHRIST'S SAKE

Every time you pray to God in the name of Jesus, you are sure to receive an answer. But how can you in faith use Christ's name as the power to unlock the Father's heart, when at the same time that great name has so little sway with you to move you to obedience for His sake; obedience in this great matter of unity, which He desires to promote among His people?

(a) *Christ's solemn command*

Jesus charged His disciples: 'A new commandment I give unto you, that ye love one another; as I have loved you, that ye also love one another' (*John 13:34*). And notice how He prepared their hearts to open and give welcome to this commandment. He put His own name on it: 'A new commandment I give unto you.' He meant, 'Let this command go under My name. And after I have gone and the fires of strife break out among you, remember the words I am speaking to you now and let them extinguish the flames.'

Again, in this farewell message Christ stressed that His commandment was also a gift; His lips had never spoken sweeter words to them. He saved His best wine till the last. And among other things that Christ bequeathed the disciples in His will, He took this commandment as a father would remove the seal-ring from his finger and gave it to them. Finally, Jesus added the most powerful reason in all heaven and earth for His followers to obey this

[345]

commandment – 'As I have loved you, that ye also love one another.'

Christian! Is not the love of Christ entitled to ask you to do anything – and all things – for Him? If it were to lay down your life for Him who loved you to death, would you deny Him? Cannot His love, then, persuade you to lay down your strifes and divisions? Christ put great emphasis on this, as if His own joy and that of His disciples were locked up together in this one command of loving one another: 'These things have I spoken unto you, that my joy might remain in you, and that your joy might be full' (*John 15:11*).

But we are not yet at the last link of this golden chain of Christ's teaching. He expressed deep love for the disciples, love enabling Him to die for every one of them. Then He boldly told them that they would be His friends if they realized what it was that He was leaving in their hands: 'Ye are my friends, if ye do whatsoever I command you' (*v. 14*). Finally, taking it for granted that they would walk in unity and love as He had commanded them, He further opened His heart to them, keeping no secret back. He invited them to open their hearts to God and be as free with Him as He was with them. And a new intimacy now drew them together: 'Henceforth I call you not servants; for the servant knoweth not what his lord doeth' (*v. 15*) – that is, 'from the time you walk obediently before Me and lovingly to one another.'

(b) *Christ's fervent prayer for this love*

If a minister persuasively pressed a grace or duty upon his people from the pulpit and then entered his closet to plead with God to give this grace to his flock, you would believe he was sincere. Our blessed Savior taught us ministers where to go when we come out of the pulpit, and what to do there.

As soon as Christ finished His sermon He went to prayer for His disciples. Unity and peace was the legacy He wished so much to leave with them, and this was the request He now asked God to give them: 'Holy Father, keep through thine own name those whom thou hast given me' (*John 17:11*). And then He added, '– that they may be one, as we are.' It is as if He had asked, 'Father, has there ever been any discord between You and Me? Then why should these who are Yours and Mine disagree now?' Again, Christ continues to plead hard for the same mercy, not because it was so hard to wrest this blessing from God but because His desire for His people's unity and love was for their sakes. Notice also that Jesus did not speak a word for His own life while He redoubled His prayer for this unity. How can we thus miss its value?

He told His children what they must look for at the world's hand – all kinds of tribulation. Yet He did not pray so much for their immunity from suffering as He did against contentions amongst them. He knew that if His saints could agree in compassion, this heavenly fire of love would quench the flames of their persecutors' fire, or at least the terror of them. In a word, saints who live in strife and contention are sinning against the strong prayers which Christ Himself uttered on their behalf.

(c) *The price Christ paid for peace*

Just as Jesus went from preaching peace to pulling down peace from heaven by prayer, so He went from praying about it to paying for it, but His prayers were not the petitions of a beggar, as ours are. He prayed that God would give Him only what He had paid for. And He was on His way to the place of payment, Calvary, where His blood was the price He willingly laid down for peace. Now this was principally our peace with God but Christ had this other peace in mind also – love among the brethren.

Therefore the sacrament of the Lord's Supper, the commemoration feast of Christ's death, both seals our peace with God and signifies our love for one another.

And now need I show you why our dear Lord followed this design of knitting His people together in oneness of spirit? Truly Christ intended the church to be His house, where He takes rest. But how restful can it be to dwell in a house that is on fire? It is His kingdom; but how can His laws be kept if all His followers argue and fight? Laws are silent when people go to war.

In a word, Christ's church is a people called out of the world to be a praise to Him in the sight of the nations. Peter said as much: 'God did visit the Gentiles, to take out of them a people for his name' (*Acts 15:14*) – that is, a people for His honor. But a jealous, divided people bring no praise to the name of Christ. When Jesus prayed for His people to be made perfect in one, He used the argument, – 'that the world may believe that thou hast sent me' (*John 17:21*). My heart bleeds to hear Christ blasphemed today by so many profane lips. And it is divisions among the saints which have done the most to call forth such evil speaking.

II. CHRISTIANS SHOULD SEEK PEACE FOR THEIR OWN SAKES

(a) *Your relationships call for unity*

Paul says of those who are believers, 'Ye are all the children of God by faith in Christ Jesus' (*Gal. 3:26*) – not only children of God by creation but by faith in Jesus Christ. Because He is the foundation of a new brotherhood of believers, He has set you close to other saints. You were conceived in the same womb of the church, begotten by the same seed of the Word, whereby (as has been said) you became brothers of the whole blood. Joseph's heart went out more to Benjamin than to any of his other brothers because he was his brother by both father and mother. If the body of Christ disagrees, who can agree? Christ has taken great care to remove every occasion for quarreling from the saints; so this makes their dissension both childish and sinful.

Sometimes a child becomes grieved if his parents' affection is given to others rather than to himself; when this happens he envies them and they despise him. But there is no such favoritism in God's family – each one is cherished exactly alike by the Son of God. 'Walk in love, as Christ also hath loved us, and hath given himself for us' (*Eph. 5:2*). Christ in the church is like the soul to the body – every member in Christ has all of Him, His whole heart and love, as if he were the only person to enjoy the Savior.

A natural father often shows great unfairness in the distribution of his estate. Not all his children are heirs, and this sows the seed of strife among them, as Jacob found by experience. But Christ has made out His will so that all are provided for alike, a provision called 'the common salvation' and 'the inheritance of the saints in light' (*Jude 3; Col. 1:12*). Each may enjoy his happiness without disturbing anyone else, as millions of people who look on the same sun at the same time. No one stands in another's light.

Jesus silenced all misunderstanding and preference when He prayed, 'The glory which thou gavest me I have given them; that they may be one' (*John 17:22*). No person can envy another for having more than himself when he sees that the glory is his too. True it is that differences exist in Christians' outward or natural gifts; some are rich in them and others are poor. But are these endowments important enough to wage war over, among those who all wait for the same heaven?

(b) Consider whose territory you are in

Are you not living in the midst of enemies? The rivalry between Abraham's herdmen and Lot's was aggravated by the presence of neighboring heathens: 'And there was a strife between the herdmen of Abram's cattle and the herdmen of Lot's cattle: and the Canaanite and the Perizzite dwelled then in the land' (*Gen. 13:7*). For God's people to quarrel while idolaters look on provides vulgar street talk which dishonors both them and their religion.

Now tell me – who are these people who have been in our land all the time God's men have been scuffling among themselves? Satan's spies have curiously observed every shred of uncomely behavior among Christians and have told the whole world about it. And these carnal ones are equipped with plenty of malicious ability to use this contention for their own ungodly purposes. They stand on tiptoes, in fact, to get on with the work of completely disabling saints who have wounded one another. They sincerely hope to undo us in this way; then they will cure us of our own wounds by inflicting one so deep that it pierces the heart of our life, gospel and all.

O Christians, will you let Herod and Pilate disgrace you? They joined forces in a façade of peace to strengthen their hands against Christ. Are you unwilling to unite against the common enemy of the Lord Jesus? It is a tragic time for shipmates to argue when an enemy is drilling a hole in the bottom of the ship.

(c) Consider the consequences of contention

It is now time for us to examine five major results of Christian contention.

(i) You put a stop to the growth of grace. A person's soul cannot prosper when it is inflamed with strife any more than a physical body can enjoy a fever. Just as this fire in the bones must be quenched and brought down to a

normal temperature again, so must the unkindly fire among Christians be put out.

The apostle Paul shows how men with weak grace can flourish – his cure is a composition of sincerity and love. If these qualities are preserved, the whole body will edify 'itself in love' (*Eph. 4:16*). I pray that in these end times Christians will be lifted from the mire of self-centeredness to the place of 'speaking the truth in love' – or being *sincere* in love. It is Christ's desire that every son and daughter 'may grow up into him in all things' (*v. 15*).

(ii) *You cut off communication with the throne of grace.* It is impossible to go from wrangling to praying with a free spirit. And even if you should be so bold as to knock at God's door you will receive a cold welcome: 'Leave there thy gift before the altar, and go thy way; first be reconciled to thy brother, and then come and offer thy gift' (*Matt. 5:24*). God will not eat our leavened bread – that is, taste any prayer soured with bitterness of spirit. First the peace was renewed, and a covenant of friendship and love made between Laban and Jacob, before 'Jacob offered sacrifice upon the mount, and called his brethren to eat bread' (*Gen. 31:54*).

Even heathens realized that no serious business could ever be transacted by quarreling spirits. This is why Roman senators used to visit their temple and lay down their controversies before they entered the senate floor to address themselves to state affairs. Do we dare approach God's altar and bow in prayer while our hearts are swollen with anger and envy? O God, humble us!

(iii) *You cut off communication with other Christians.* Just as no nation grows everything it needs but must import some goods from other countries, no Christian can live without borrowing from his brothers. There is 'that which every joint supplieth, according to the effectual working in the measure of every part' (*Eph. 4:16*). Truly, Christians' greatest gains come from their mutual sharing of grace, ministry, and power. For instance, Paul told the Christians at Rome that he longed to see them so that he could impart some spiritual gift to them, 'that I may be comforted together with you, by the mutual faith both of you and me' (*Rom. 1:12*).

Divisions spoil all intercourse among believers; they are as destructive to Christian communion as the plague is to the trade of a market town. Communication flows from communion, and a communion which is founded upon union. The church grows under persecution and trial. Believers scatter seed all over the field, taking the gospel to places where it has never been before. But divisions, like a furious storm, wash the seed out of the land.

(iv) *You hazard the decay of grace and growth of sin.* Contention opens the door for more and more corruption to come in: 'If ye have bitter envying and strife in your hearts, glory not' (*Jas. 3:14*). That is, do not think you are such good Christians, for even if you had the knowledge and gifts of heavenly beings, this sin would make you look more like devils than angels. James gives the reason for his statement in the words: 'For where envying and strife is, there is confusion and every evil work' (*v. 16*). Contention is Satan's forge and, if he can heat up the Christian, he can soften him for his hammer of temptation to do whatever it will. When Moses, for example, had an overheated spirit he spoke unwisely. It is no small sin, then, which makes it impossible for a man caught in its snare to do even one righteous act. 'The wrath of man worketh not the righteousness of God' (*Jas. 1:20*).

(v) *Contentions are forerunners of judgment.* A lowering sky forecasts rain; and mariners start looking for a storm at sea when the waves begin to swell with a murmuring noise. Thus judgment is breeding when the faces of Christians grow grim with discontentment like the rumbling of thunder before a tempest. When children fight they can expect their father to come and separate them with his rod of correction. God's prophet 'shall turn . . . the heart of the children to their fathers, lest I come and smite the earth with a curse' (*Mal. 4:6*).

Strife sets people next door to a curse, for God brings heavy judgment on a people when He leaves them. Scripture implies that quarrelsome people cannot expect God to stay among them very long. If the captain abandons the ship we can be sure it is about to sink. 'Be of one mind,' Paul admonished. 'Live in peace; and the God of love and peace shall be with you' (*2 Cor. 13:11*).

God came by Moses to bring great deliverance to the Israelites and, as a token of all the good God would do for them, Moses tried to make peace between two discontented brothers. But his kindness was not accepted and the rejection resulted in many more years' misery in Egypt for the Israelites. 'Then fled Moses at this saying, and was a stranger in the land of Midian' (*Acts 7:29*). After that there was no mention of deliverance for forty years. Have not our rejections of God's healing peace made mercy run away and leave us to groan about the hard times we are having?

III. CHRISTIANS SHOULD SEEK PEACE FOR OTHERS' SAKE

Augustine advised Christians not to despair of the salvation of wicked men, but to give themselves to the peace and unity which would encourage them to seek after godliness. Remember, the only place God has to call His children from is the world. We can pave a way for the salvation of the ungodly by letting them see the truth and ways of God in our love toward our brothers and sisters in

Christ. This, then, is the cumin seed which draws souls, like doves, to the window. It is the gold that overlays the temple of God – the church – to make men love it when they see its beauty.

People are afraid to live in a place haunted with evil spirits. But can hell itself possibly house anything worse than the spirit of division? Christians, agree with one another, and your numbers will increase. The early Christians continued 'daily with one accord in the temple, and breaking bread from house to house, did eat their meat with gladness and singleness of heart' (*Acts 2:46*). And notice what followed their fellowship – they had 'favor with all the people and the Lord added to the church daily such as should be saved' (*v. 47*).

The world was such a stranger to real love that it was probably amused at first and then curious as to what kind of heavenly doctrine could soften men's hearts, plane their rugged natures, and join them into this family of love. And these things helped to persuade many out of the world and into the church. But tragically, the gold dulled – I mean, peace among Christians faded – and gaping holes were seen in the church. These flaws were so obvious that passers-by were afraid to enter it. Here and there Gentiles were almost persuaded to embrace the Jewish religion, but became cautious because of the divisions and offenses embedded in it.

O Christian, do not let such sins as divisions and strifes harden your life! Do you not fear God too much to lay a stumbling-block for men to break their necks over? to roll the stone over a sinner's grave and seal him down in it? Well, even as you keep yourself free of the blood of those who die in their sin, be careful not to contribute to the hardening of impenitent souls through dissensions in the body of Christ.

PEACE WITH CREATION

During his early days of sinlessness Adam was made happy by seeing the beasts of the field coming to receive their names from him; they acknowledged him as lord as he exercised God-given authority over them. But no sooner did man fail in his obedience to God, than every animal forgot about submission and continuously caused problems for its master.

When God and man meet again in a happy covenant of peace, God reverses His wrath against His rebellious children and the war ends between them. 'In that day will I make a covenant for them with the beasts of the field, and with the fowls of heaven' (*Hos. 2:18*). And 'that day' is the one in which God betrothes us to Himself in faithfulness (*v. 20*). So then, peace with creation comes through peace with God.

But I must remind you that, in God's sovereignty, our peace with His creatures is not enjoyed perfectly by the godly. Indeed, the Father is at liberty to chasten His reconciled ones severely, and His creatures often become the rod which He uses. Water, for instance, may drown a saint and fire may consume another to ashes; yet these elements themselves are at peace with believers. God does not send them purposely to hurt His children – He commissions them to act against sinning saints for their good.

God uses the elements of creation against the unsaved as a prince dispatches a general against an armed company of traitors, with authority to take vengeance on them for rebelling against their Maker. But because of the new testament in the Lord Christ's blood this commission changes course and runs in another direction: 'Go, fire, and be the chariot in which a saint is brought home from earth to Me in heaven's glory. Go, water, convey to Me another believer.' It is true that the elements of creation can bring sharp correction at times; but they are ever full of mercies too, and serve the Christian from the good intentions of God's heart. 'And we know that all things work together for good to them that love God, to them who are the called according to his purpose' (*Rom. 8:28*).

3. The Preparation of the Gospel of Peace

WHAT IS MEANT BY THIS PREPARATION OF THE GOSPEL OF PEACE?

We can best understand what this preparation is by considering the part it is designed for – 'the foot,' the only member of the body to be shod. And being the soldier's shoe, this piece of armour is intended more for defense than for appearance. This part of the armour is so necessary that a soldier is disabled for service without its protection during a long march over sharp stones. How long can he walk on a path like this without being hurt? Or, even if the way happens to be smooth, his unshod feet are vulnerable to wet, cold weather and thus possible disease of the entire body. The result is that his lack of preparation will keep him in bed when he should be in the field. In our day almost as many troops die by fevers as by enemy fire.

Now what the foot is to the body, the will is to the soul. As the foot carries the whole body, the will supports the whole man, body and soul alike. We go wherever our will takes us. And what the shoe is to the foot, that 'preparation' – the Christian's spiritual readiness – is to the will. The man whose feet are well shod is not afraid to go through thick or thin, foul or fair, stones or straws; all are alike to him. But the barefooted man, or the one with fragile shoes, shrinks when his feet touch the mud, and shrieks when he stumbles on a sharp stone. Thus when the will and heart of a person are ready for any work, he is shod and armed against any trouble he must go through to complete it.

Some say the Irish move with such agility that they run over quicksand where others sink and die. Prepared hearts can do the same thing; others are unable to walk where these saints run. They do not become bogged down but sing through their afflictions. David, for example, was never more satisfied than when he hid in the cave: 'My heart is fixed, O God, my heart is fixed,' he declared. 'I will sing and give praise' (*Ps. 57:7*). If David's heart had not been ready for a crisis, if it had not had this preparation, he would have been trapped by fear instead of given to singing while his enemies hunted for his life.

WHY IS IT CALLED 'THE PREPARATION OF THE GOSPEL OF PEACE'?

It is called this because the gospel is God's great instrument by which He works into the will of man a preparation for suffering. It is the business we are in, if we preach the gospel, to make a willing people – 'a people prepared for the Lord' (*Luke 1:17*). As a captain beats his drum in the city to call up a company of volunteers to be armed to take the field at an hour's warning and to follow their prince, the gospel calls men to stand ready for God's service, whatever the cost.

The 'gospel of peace', then, brings the good news of peace between God and man sealed by the blood of Christ. It is a rich gift to repenting sinners who have spent their days in 'a fearful looking for of judgment and fiery indignation' from the Lord to devour them (*Heb. 10:27*). As soon as they hear peace by the preaching of the gospel –

and it is confirmed in their conscience by the Spirit – a new life appears in them. And these men who were once so fearfully shy of every minor threat are now 'shod with the preparation of the gospel of peace' and smilingly say – as Jesus did to those with swords and spears, 'Whom seek ye?' (*John 18:4*). 'Being justified by faith, we have peace with God through our Lord Jesus Christ' (*Rom. 5:1*).

Now this gospel peace works so mightily that it makes Christians 'glory in tribulations' (*v. 3*). And we find that these words of Scripture open at least two points of doctrine – first, it is the saint's duty to be prepared to meet any trial; and second, gospel peace readies the Christian to face any trouble which might come.

PREPARATION FOR TRIALS

It is our duty as believers to be prepared to endure any hardship and trial which God lays out for us in our Christian walk. And saints will never be without these trials. As Christ said of the poor, they will always be with us. Augustine said the bloody sweat which Christ felt signified the sufferings which He would endure in His mystical body. Just as Christ's whole body was lifted up on the cross, no member of His can expect to escape the cross now. When it comes to each of us, it will not speak glory for the Savior if we merely yield passively to God's will; we must be ready with an active and holy patience to obey, to be led down into the very chambers of death itself, if that is God's choice.

I heard about an epitaph which should never be engraved on a Christian's gravestone: 'Here lies one against his will.' Paul had the holy mind of Christ when he confessed: 'I am ready not to be bound only, but also to die at Jerusalem for the name of the Lord Jesus' (*Acts 21:13*). Skeptics might think the apostle's boldness flourished only when the enemy was far away, but faded into fear when he had to look death in the face. No, Paul stood on his earlier profession even then: 'I am now ready to be offered, and the time of my departure is at hand' (*2 Tim. 4:6*).

If you listen closely you will hear Paul speaking as if his death had already happened. And he was dead before the stroke was given – not from fear, but from complete resignation to it. A criminal is dead in the sense of the law as soon as the judge speaks the sentence, although the condemned man may survive weeks afterwards. In a gospel sense, then, we say those are dead who have willingly put themselves under the authority of their Father and are ready for death.

Paul's serenity of spirit was even more remarkable if we consider how close he stood to his death. Perhaps he knew he would be beheaded, for he alluded to the pouring out of blood or wine, used in sacrifice. And the sacrifice which he willingly offered up in the service of Christ and His church was like the believers' pouring out their drink offering to God. But now let me give some reasons why we all must be ready for this work of suffering.

WHY CHRISTIANS MUST BE READY FOR TRIALS

I. CHRIST COMMANDS THIS FRAME OF SPIRIT

The yielded attitude is implied in all that God asks Christians to do – it is that which, like the stamp on the coin, makes it current in God's account: 'Put them in mind to be ready to every good work,' said Paul (*Tit. 3:1*). The word in this text implies a vessel fashioned for the use of its master. No one likes to wash a cup and then find it dirty again when he gets ready to use it; he reaches for a clean vessel ready for immediate use. Thus God expects us to keep our hearts pure from the defilement of sin, but with our affections rising to Him: 'If a man therefore purge himself from these, he shall be a vessel unto honor, sanctified, and meet for the master's use, and prepared unto every good work' (*2 Tim. 2:21*).

God calls His redeemed ones to prepare not only for service but also for suffering: 'If any man will come after me, let him deny himself, and take up his cross daily, and follow me' (*Luke 9:23*). These words may be called the Christian's contract sealed by the Spirit of God, for everyone who will be Christ's servant must agree to this relationship before he can call Him Master. The main provision the Lord has made for His servants is for them to suffer in peace. Christ has been careful to reach for the hearts of His servants, for if they love Him deeply they will not merely endure hardships in His service but show their readiness in it. Accordingly, God has included four passages in Scripture for this very purpose.

(a) *The Christian 'must deny himself'*
Christ asks a saint to take his hands off his own will and give it up to Him. From the day he enters Christ's service he must answer the Savior's call with 'I will.'

(b) *Christ gives the believer a cross to 'take up' before He gives him a crown to wear*
He intends that Christians not only 'bear' it – for the ungodly manage to do this against their wills – but to 'take it up.' Of course He does not mean for us to make our own cross and run headlong into trouble, but He does want us to take up that cross He has made for us. We should not step out of the way by any deceitful shift to escape trouble but accept the burden God has chosen as if He were doing us a favor to let us suffer for Him. No one stoops to pick up something that is worthless; but Christ asks His people to take up the cross the way a person takes up a pearl which lies on the ground in front of him.

(c) *Christ wants the saint to take up his cross 'daily'*

Even when there is no burden on a saint's back he must carry one in his heart – preparing himself continually to answer the first call. When Paul professed that he 'died daily,' he meant he was *ready* to die – he did not let preoccupation with present ministries or pleasures make him dread future trials.

God instructed the Jews to eat the passover meal with loins girded, shoes on their feet, and staff in hand (*Exod. 12:11*). And while the Father is feasting the Christian with comforts, he must have this gospel shoe on and remember that he is not just dining at home, but eating as he would do in an inn, ready to travel as soon as he is refreshed a little for the trip.

(d) *The Christian must 'follow Christ' while he bears his cross*

God does not want the saint to stand still and fret or to have to be coaxed to move, but to follow Christ voluntarily, as a soldier follows his captain. Yet Christ is not like a general who drives his men into battle whether they want to go or not. Instead of demanding, He invites: 'I will allure her into the wilderness, and speak comfortably to her' (*Hos. 2:14*). A heart full of grace will follow Jesus into the wilderness of affliction as willingly as a lover goes with her beloved into a quiet garden to enjoy his presence. By His Word and by His Spirit Christ satisfies the Christian, making him want to be with Him anywhere.

II. CHRIST DESERVES THIS FRAME OF SPIRIT

Let us now study two specific reasons, among countless others, why God's Son is worthy of our readiness to sustain suffering.

(a) *Christ endured sorrow for us*

When God called Jesus to be a mediator He found the path covered with much sharper stones than we will ever find on the road mapped out ahead of us. He had to walk on swords and spears, all edged with the wrath of God, and that was the most painful stone of all, yet He took it out of our way. If His feet had not been shod with love for us He might well have turned back and declared the journey impossible.

But it was Christ's choice to suffer for us. 'Lo, I come,' He said to the Father, 'I delight to do thy will, O my God; yea, thy law is within my heart' (*Ps. 40:7, 8*). Jesus responded to God's call like an echo that answers two or three times what has just been spoken. He was so ready to sacrifice His life to save sinners that in the Lord's Supper He sacramentally tore the flesh of His own body, and let His heart break to pour out precious blood, before His enemies ever were able to touch Him. This is why we cannot call His death only the murder of an innocent man; it was a sacrifice freely offered up to God for all believers.

When the time came for the tragedy to take place, Christ walked out to the very spot where He knew the traitor would be and met the dark arms of death. What a shame if we are unwilling to go a mile or two to share the sufferings of such a sweet Savior. 'Could ye not watch with me one hour?' Christ appealed (*Matt. 26:40*). 'Can you not stay with me as I embrace bitter pains of death for your sake?'

(b) *Christ tenderly cares for saints who suffer*
The more gentle a captain is with his soldiers, the more freely they tend to give their lives to his command. Let us turn, then, to some of the mercies Christ holds for each of His saints.

(i) *In proportioning the burden to the back He lays it on.* The same cargo which overloads one ship and threatens to sink her is only a normal burden for another vessel. One saint may sail smoothly under the same suffering which another is not able to bear. Because Christ knows this He personally eases the burden of the weaker Christian by laying more weight on the stronger person. For instance, Paul 'labored more abundantly than they all.' His testimony attested to this fact: 'His grace which was bestowed on me was not in vain' (*1 Cor. 15:10*). God poured out such abundant grace on Paul that it might have been in vain if He had not divided the kingdom work unequally and given him much more than his share. Christ has perfect knowledge of every saint's spiritual abilities and accurately assesses burdens accordingly so that none are oppressed.

The man rich in grace can as easily pay his dollar as the poor man his penny. Paul laid down his head on the block for the cause of Christ as freely as some weak Christians would have paid a few coins from their pocket. He endured death more acceptably than others could have experienced reproach for the name of Christ. Of course not everyone has a martyr's faith and a martyr's fire – this vanguard is chosen from the whole army of Christians.

(ii) *In the consolations He gives to those who suffer.* The part of an army that sees action on the front lines is sure to have its pay – more compensation than those who wait behind in the quarters. I am sure, then, that there is more silver and gold – joy and comfort – in the camp of Christ's suffering ones than in the hearths of prosperity and ease.

God's promises are like strong wine stored up for a time of need: 'Call upon me in the day of trouble,' He says (*Ps. 50:15*). Certainly we can call on God in seasons of quiet peace, but He would have us be the boldest in the 'day of trouble' – no one finds such fast help at the throne of grace as the suffering saint. David testifies to this truth when he says: 'In the day when I cried thou answeredst me and strengthenedst me with strength in my soul' (*Ps. 138:3*).

[363]

We might not welcome a visit from a friend when it is past midnight, but we do not mind if a sick person needs us at that late hour. In such emergencies we gladly go with the messenger who comes for us – and so does God. Peter knocked at the gate of the assembly who prayed for him almost as soon as their supplication knocked at the gate of heaven in his behalf.

The temptations of an afflicted person are great; to him every delay seems like neglect or oversight. Therefore God chooses to show marvelous measures of kindness at these times: 'As the sufferings of Christ abound in us, so our consolation also aboundeth by Christ' (*2 Cor. 1:5*). As man struggles with trouble, Christ supplies comfort. Both tides rise and fall together.

Just as we relieve the poor in their most extreme needs, Christ comforts His people as their troubles multiply. Now tell me, does not our Lord deserve a ready spirit in you to meet any suffering which brings His sweetest grace? And this, when you might expect the pains of severest sorrows to overcome you?

The servant will be cheerful when his master cares enough to bring his breakfast into the field. Christians do not have to wait for heaven to experience joy during their seasons of trouble. Yes, there will be that full supper someday; but there is breakfast now, made of the refreshments Christ brings to you as you serve Him. They are for you to enjoy in the very place where you must endure the hardest trials of faith.

(c) *In the help Christ sends to take saints home safely*
Christ not only comforts us in our troubles but delivers us out of them. There is always a door in the Christian's prison which cannot be seen with the natural eye, but can be opened by Christ's hand for the way of escape. What more can we hope for? What greater security can we want

than the promise of the almighty God who cannot lie? I hope His people will believe Him enough to accept at first sight whatever He brings in exchange for their dearest treasures, life itself not excepted.

Man might, and Satan will, to be sure, leave you in the lurch even after you have diligently done the work he assigned. But know this – if God sends you out He will bring you home safely. You never need to fear a 'You are on your own' from God if it is your faithfulness to Him which has brought you into the briars.

The God who would rather work a miracle than let a runaway prophet perish in his rebellious voyage – he was a good man at heart – will still heap miracle upon miracle rather than let you sink in your duty toward Him. Just do not be troubled if you are thrown overboard before you see the provision God has made for your safety. It is always there, and often very close by, like Jonah's whale; God sent it to ferry him to shore – underwater, with the prophet in its belly – before he knew exactly where he was. The thing which you think has come to destroy you may be the very messenger God has dispatched to bring you safely to land.

Is your shoe on yet, Christian? Are you ready to march as soon as you hear Christ's voice? Surely you are not afraid of dashing your foot against a stone with a sole as thick as this one.

III. THIS READINESS EVIDENCES A HEART FULL OF GRACE
A gracious spirit is an excellent spirit. Flesh and blood have never yet made anyone willing to suffer either for God or from God. The person who can do this has that 'other spirit' which proved Caleb to be of higher stock than this world (*Num. 14:24*). A carnal heart can never suffer freely; Luther said man's will is no more free than it is made free by grace.

[365]

The more flesh in a Christian, the more clumsy he is about coming to God's feet. And where there is nothing but flesh there is nothing but unwillingness to motivate him. But the man who finds his heart gladly warmed at God's command can be sure who has been at work; this is the line which nobody except God can draw in the soul.

The Egyptians reported that Israelite women were so lively that they brought forth their babies before the midwives could get there to assist them. Truly, then, a lively heart of grace is ready to do anything God calls on it to do. The performance of duty does not require the midwifery of lesser arguments and persuasions. The gracious heart has already exercised itself in pure love to God, obedience to His voice, and faith in the surety of His promise so continuously that even a work that is stressful to the flesh is not grievous to the spirit. It looks upward and stands ready to say, 'Nevertheless not as I will, but as thou wilt' (*Matt.* 26:39).

The apostle tells us that surrender to God's afflicting hand exhibits a son's spirit within: 'If ye endure chastening, God dealeth with you as with sons' (*Heb.* 12:6). Notice that He did not say 'if you are chastened' but 'if you endure chastening.' Naked suffering never proves sonship. But to endure it with a full supply of courage, with the shoulder ready to carry it patiently, and with the expectation of future reward – these things show a childlike spirit. And the assurance which comes is especially soothing when the landlord of hell tries hard to use the saint's affliction as evidence to disprove his sonship. Here is the answer to stop the lies of this accuser's mouth: 'Satan, if I am not God's child, why do I so readily yield myself to His family discipline?'

IV. A READY FRAME OF SPIRIT MAKES THE PERSON FREE

Freedom is bought with a price. Birds would rather fly

among the trees of the wood, even in the cold, lean seasons, than live in a golden cage with an abundance of pampering. Some men are so attached to their lifestyle on earth that they soon let it order them about and dictate standards of happiness. Before long they become enslaved to materialism – 'Their heart goeth after their covetousness' (*Ezek. 33:31*); and because money is their master, their hearts wait for it like a dog at his owner's feet.

Others bow to their own reputation; they cannot enjoy anything unless they capture the place of honor everywhere they go. Haman was like this – he was the court favorite who got the king's ring to seal a decree for massacring thousands of innocent persons merely to satisfy his ambition. And it so upset his proud stomach to see one poor Jew refuse to bow that his other achievements did not seem to matter. 'Yet all this availeth me nothing,' Haman said, 'so long as I see Mordecai the Jew sitting at the king's gate' (*Esther 5:13*).

Still a third group are snared by pleasure; everything they do is bound up in having 'a good time'. As the rush grows in the mud and the fish lives in water, these people cannot survive without their fun. If you separate them from entertainment and sports, their hearts, like Nabal's, die like a stone inside their breasts.

Now the freedom of spirit we are talking about breaks all these chains and brings the Christian out of every kind of bondage; it teaches him to accept whatever God sends his way. If prosperity comes he knows how 'to abound' (*Phil. 4:12*). Yet if he is suddenly thrown from the saddle of pleasure his foot will not hang in the stirrup; and his soul will not drag him after it with whining selfishness. Through grace he is a free man and can do without all created things – as long as he can have Christ's company.

Paul stood on this liberty that comes only from the

indwelling Holy Spirit: 'All things are lawful unto me, but I will not be brought under the power of any' (*I Cor. 6:12*). He was indifferent to things of this life – honor or dishonor, abundance or need, life or death. He was persuaded that a servant of Christ should not be so in love with affluence that he could not welcome need, nor have such affinity for earthly life that he runs away from every thought of death. But neither did Paul let himself become so tired of suffering that he wanted death to come merely for his own ease. A Christian rules his life with an excellent spirit if he chooses to face up to and endure unpleasant experiences rather than avoid or escape them.

V. READINESS TO SUFFER PREPARES THE CHRISTIAN FOR SERVICE

A saint cannot serve if he is not prepared to suffer. This is true because all servants have a cross which comes with their calling. If we become offended by the cross how can we serve Christ?

Now prayer is the daily exercise of the saint, but there is no way he can please God in it unless he sincerely says, 'Not my will, but thine, be done' (*Luke 22:42*). Paul was sent out to preach the grace of God to the world and to sustain the wrath of the world for God. The Lord had told Ananias that He had chosen Paul to bear His name before the Gentiles and to suffer great things for His name's sake. If Paul's preaching the gospel – even with his rare art of sweetening it – could not please the ungrateful world, it would be almost impossible for those of us who fall short of his gifts to win the world without some form of reproach, contempt, or downright persecution.

This spiritual shoe, then, must be standard equipment for the preacher's foot that must walk among so many hissing serpents. Who else but a Paul, who overcame both fondness for life and fear of death, would have been willing to preach the gospel in the very den of lions? I mean at Rome, the seat of the cruel Nero: 'So much as in me is, I am ready to preach the gospel to you that are at Rome also. For I am not ashamed of the gospel of Christ' (*Rom. 1:15, 16*).

In a word, it is the duty of every saint to make a free profession of Christ – and often this cannot be done without the threat of danger. If the person's heart is not resolved in this point, the first storm that stirs will make him tie up in any creek rather than venture out in turbulent weather. 'Among the chief rulers also many believed on him, but because of the Pharisees they did not confess him, lest they should be put out of the synagogue' (*John 12:42*). They might have made the attempt had the coast been clear, but they did not have the courage then to face the scorn that threatened.

It does not do any good to confess God if we are not willing to lay everything at His feet. Neither is it worthwhile to set out with Christ unless we mean to complete the journey with Him and not turn back because of a tempest or two.

VI. READINESS TO SUFFER GIVES TRUE ENJOYMENT OF LIFE

It is impossible for a person to savor life unless he is prepared to lose it. Two considerations will quickly unfold this paradox for us.

(a) *Absence of fear*

Where fear is, there is always torment. Even the deer who lives where there is plenty of food is slender because of anxiety. And all who let this vulture continuously feed on them will be spiritually lean as well. Nothing destroys a man's joy like the fear of losing what he already holds – and because of this insecurity he becomes his own worst enemy. Murderers can kill only once, but by meditating on his miseries a man kills himself a thousand times over, as often as the fear of death steals into his mind.

Once the Christian wears this piece of armour called 'the gospel of peace' his soul is prepared for both danger and death. He sits at the feast which God in His providence has now given him and thoroughly enjoys it with no fear of a messenger of bad news knocking at the door. He can even talk about his dying hour and not spoil a crumb of his joy, as carnal men assume it must. To them the mere mention of death in the course of their 'normal' interchange is like the wet cloth that Hazael slapped on to a king's face. The very shock of the subject scatters all the pleasant thoughts which may have dominated the conversation only minutes before.

On the other hand, the saint whose heart is prepared never tastes more sweetness in the comforts of life than when he dips these morsels into meditations of death and eternity. It causes him no more grief to think of losing his life, than it does to have the first serving of food taken away to make room for the main course. David, for example, was so little tied to this world that he could declare 'I will fear no evil' – even in the 'valley of the shadow of death' (*Ps. 23:4*).

And what about Peter? Did he know the secret of peace or not? He slept calmly, bound 'between two soldiers' in a prison on the night before Herod 'would have brought him forth' to his execution. And while these are certainly not the usual conditions for rest, he was so sound asleep that the angel had to strike him on the side to wake him (*Acts 12:6*). I seriously question whether Herod himself slept as well that evening as his prisoner did! No doubt this 'preparation of the gospel of peace' brought Peter to such divine rest. Because he was ready to die he was able to sleep. Why should he worry when the very worst thing

death could do was to usher him into an endless rest in the
arms of his beloved Lord?

(b) *Assurance of God's care*

The more willing a saint is to suffer from God, or for
Him, the more God delights to take care of him. A good
general is most concerned about the soldier who least
values his own life. So the less a Christian values himself
and his interests for Christ's sake, the more careful God
is to keep him from suffering or to keep him in it. Christ
had both blessings in mind when He promised, 'Whosoever will lose his life for my sake shall find it' (*Matt.
16:25*).

Abraham was ready to offer up his son and then God
would not let him do it. But even if the Lord allows the
enemy to strike down his saints to death, severing the
soul from the body, He shows His tender care even
then. The Father gathers up their blood and declares to
the hopelessly cruel world who spilled it: 'Precious in
the sight of the Lord is the death of his saints' (*Ps.
116:15*).

Thus we see that by surrendering ourselves up to God's
will we engage Him to take care of us no matter what
happens. How much more comfortable can life be than to
have our heaviest fear taken off our shoulders and rolled
upon the Father? The poor widow, for instance, never
prospered more richly than when the prophet cared for
her by requiring that she give up all the food she had. And
to reward her faith, God provided a miracle (*1 Kings
17:12–13*). When a person is finally brought to the foot of
God and can earnestly surrender: 'Lord, here I am, ready
to give You all I am and all I have; my will shall be done
when Your will has been done in me,' then the Lord will
oblige Himself to care for that soul.

WHY SO FEW PEOPLE ARE CHRISTIANS

I. GOD CALLS ALL CHRISTIANS TO BE READY TO SUFFER

Genuine readiness to suffer thins out the number of true Christians from the ranks of professing believers; it eliminates those whose walk goes no further than a cheap profession. A person who looks into the crowded sanctuaries of Christendom today and finds multitudes who flock after the Word might wonder why ministers say that this company of Christians is such a small one, and he might think that they who say such things cannot see the forest for the trees. This very situation made one of the disciples question Christ: 'Lord, are there few that be saved?' (*Luke 13:23*). At that time Christ 'went through the cities and villages, teaching, and journeying toward Jerusalem' (*v. 22*). When his followers saw Christ preaching so freely in every town, and people thronging after Him with expressions of hope, it seemed almost incredible to think that only a very few of them would be saved.

Now mark how our Savior solved this riddle: 'And he said unto them, Strive to enter in at the strait gate: for many, I say unto you, will seek to enter in, and shall not be able' (*v. 24*). Christ said His disciples were measuring by a wrong rule. 'If following after sermons and testimonies and excitement were enough to save, heaven would already be full,' He was saying. 'But do not sift the pure from the impure by such a coarse sieve. Strive to enter – fight and wrestle, risk life and limb rather than fall short of heaven.' 'For many shall seek, but shall not be able' – that is, they are looking for a cheap religion through an easy profession.

Almost anyone is willing to walk through heaven's door if he never has to risk his pride in public or hazard his everyday interests by any inconvenience or opposition of the world. But 'they shall not be able' to enter because their hearts are not willing to strive even unto blood. If we take the standard to be *striving*, not merely *seeking*, then the number of Christian soldiers will shrink, like Gideon's army, to a little troop. In fact there are several kinds of Christians – called that in a very broad sense of course – who have never put on this gospel shoe and are therefore sure to falter along the way.

II. MANY REFUSE TO WEAR THE GOSPEL SHOE

(a) *The ignorant Christian*

Sad to say, there are large numbers in many congregations who have no light as to who Christ is and what He has done for them. How, then, can they have enough love to follow this Christ through hardship whom they do not even know? Nabal thought he gave a rational answer to David's servants after they had asked him for help: 'Shall I then take my bread, and my water, and my flesh that I have killed for my shearers, and give it unto men, whom I know not whence they be?' (*1 Sam. 25:11*). He decided the gift asked of him was too much for someone whom he barely knew. It is virtually impossible, then, for the ignorant person to part with the flesh of his own body if he is called to suffer at the command of the Christ.

Paul, however, says his knowledge of Christ was the reason he was not ashamed to suffer: 'I know whom I have believed,' he said (*2 Tim. 1:12*). The Samaritans, a mongrel sort of people in both descent and religion, claimed kinship with the Jews when everything went well with them. But when the church came under affliction they disclaimed it again. Surely there is that same cowardly spirit in the people whom Jesus rebuked: 'Ye worship ye know not what' (*John 4:22*). Christianity has only a loose hold on them because they have no better hold on it than a blind man's hand.

(b) *The worldly-minded*

These people insist on possessing lusts and professing

Christ at the same time; they are a generation who have nothing to prove their Christianity except mere outward observances. There is no evidence whatsoever to show them to be followers of Christ. Can we assume that these men and women stand ready to suffer for the gospel? Of course not, for they will not even wear Christ's yoke, much less bear His burden. Those who refuse to *do* for Christ will certainly never *die* for Him – they are not likely to fight to the blood if they are not willing to lose a little sweat.

(c) *The scheming professor*

This man's fundamental creed is to save himself not from sin but from danger. He studies the times more than the Scriptures and plots strategic moves to shape his course and order his profession accordingly – which, like the hedgehog's house – always opens toward the warm side!

(d) *The covetous professor*

Some men are so full of worldly projects that suffering for Christ seems very foreign to them. You remember what the Egyptians said about Israel: 'They are entangled in the land, the wilderness hath shut them in' (*Exod. 14:3*). And this is even more true of covetous professors. They are ensnared by the world and a wilderness has shut them in. Therefore they are no more fit to follow Christ than a man with his foot caught in a trap can pursue his journey.

Our Savior, speaking of the miseries to come upon Jerusalem, warned: 'Woe to them that are with child, and to them that give suck in those days!' Obviously it would be harder for them to escape the impending danger (*Matt. 24:19*). How much worse, then, the judgment of those who are full of the world when days of persecution come – they will find it almost impossible to escape temptation from life-threatening trials. Actually these people have already made their choices – since their heart is set upon the world they will not be able to leave it for Christ's company.

(e) The conceited professor

Self-confidence is not the right gospel shoe: 'By strength shall no man prevail' (*I Sam. 2:9*). The man who holds an extremely high opinion of himself is far from holiness and humility. During Queen Mary's reign a man vowed that he was so free of his flesh for Christ's sake that he would see his fat melt in the flames rather than fall back into error. But his flesh outlived his commitment, and cowardice eventually made him part with his faith to save his fat. Those who glory in personal valor as they put on the harness, then, will surely put it off in shame. 'The heart is deceitful above all things' – a Jacob that will supplant itself (*Jer. 17:9*). The person who does not know the length of his own foot cannot fit himself for a spiritual shoe.

EXHORTATION TO PUT ON THE SHOE OF PREPARATION

Let all who wear the name of Christ get this shoe of preparation on and keep it on so as to be ready to follow the call of God's providence even if it leads into suffering. Let me share two reasons why you must be prepared.

I. SUFFERING MAY COME SUDDENLY

Sometimes soldiers do not have as much as an hour's warning before they must take the field. And so you, too, might be called out to suffer for God or from Him before you expect it. Abraham, for example, had very little time to deal with his heart and persuade it to obey God by offering his child. 'Take now thy son, thine only son, Isaac, whom thou lovest' – not in a year, not a month or week, but *now* (*Gen. 22:2*). This command came during the night and 'early in the morning' he was on his way to the mountain (*v. 3*).

How could Abraham have handled such a shock had he not already wrestled with his own willingness or unwillingness to endeavor to be obedient to God in all things? Thus God already had His servant's whole heart and all Abraham was left to do was to obey. Sometimes God makes very sudden changes in our personal lives. For example, how would you receive a death bulletin like the one God gave Moses? He did not have the gradual preparation of a lingering illness but heard the message while he still enjoyed perfect health: 'Get thee up . . . And die in the mount . . .' (*Deut. 32:49, 50*). Are we and our feet really ready for a journey like that?

But God can change the scene of public affairs as quickly as He can change personal situations. Maybe authority smiles on the church right now; yet it might frown again soon. 'Then had the churches rest throughout all Judea' (*Acts 9:31*) – it was a blessed time for the saints. But it did not last long: 'About that time Herod the king stretched forth his hands to vex certain of the church' (*Acts 12:1*). In this persecution James the brother of John died by the sword and Peter was thrown into prison. The entire church was driven into a corner to pray in the night; and those who had had rest on every side now were threatened by violent death at every turn.

Weather is far more unpredictable in islands than in continents. Ordinarily we can know what the day will be like for hours at a time; but in islands there is no way of telling what the evening will bring. Summer and winter often crowd into the same day. And all this uncertainty, of course, is caused by the sea which surrounds the islands. Saints in heaven live, so to speak, on a continent where they enjoy a blessed kind of uninterrupted peace. The rest they have today is the same bliss they will experience throughout eternity. But here on earth, Christ's church is like a floating island compassed about with the world as with a churning sea. At times the elements of this world are kind and calm, but often they are relentlessly cruel, as God binds up or looses their wrath.

Now Christians, is it not worth it for you to be ready for suffering, since you do not know from one minute to the next if the winds will favor the gospel or try to destroy your stand upon it? At morning they might fill the sails of your profession with encouragement, but before night falls they may blow a chilling attack in your face.

II. IF YOU ARE NOT PREPARED TO SUFFER FOR CHRIST ON EARTH, YOU WILL NOT WEAR A CROWN IN HEAVEN

'If children, then heirs; heirs of God, and joint-heirs with Christ.' But let us keep reading – 'if so be that we suffer with him, that we may be also glorified together' (*Rom. 8:17*). It is true that not all saints die at a stake; but every saint must have a spirit of martyrdom, a heart prepared for suffering. God never intended for Isaac to be sacrificed, yet he did mean for Abraham to lay the knife to his son's throat. And so then He would have us put our neck on the block and be, as Paul said of himself, 'bound in the spirit' under a sincere purpose to give ourselves up to God's will. Scripture unmistakably issues the call to 'present your bodies a living sacrifice, holy, acceptable unto God' (*Rom. 12:1*).

Just as the Jews presented a living beast to the priest so he could do with it what God had commanded, we are to present our bodies before God both in active and passive obedience. Anyone who refuses to suffer for Christ now is refusing to reign with Him later.

Another Jewish custom was for a man to remove his shoe as a sign of putting off the right of inheritance, as Elimelech's kinsman renounced his estate (*Deut. 25:9, 10; Ruth 4:6–8*). Christian, if you pull off your gospel shoe you disclaim your right to heaven's inheritance. Paul wrote that the persecutions which saints endure for the gospel are 'an evident token of salvation.' Surely, then, denying Christ to escape suffering must be a 'token of perdition' (*Phil. 1:28*). My dear ones, is heaven's glory not worth a few light afflictions?

Naboth's vineyard was no spectacular item of real estate, yet he knew its value as the family's inheritance under God. Rather than sell it at market value or even exchange it for a better plot, the owner chose to forfeit his life by provoking a mighty king. But despite his zeal Naboth lost his life as well as the acre or two of his father's estate. Now there is no comparison between his vineyard on earth and Christians' paradise in heaven, which we will not lose and is infinite in value, but we must emulate him in his readiness to suffer. When your enemies unwittingly do you the favor of robbing you of your physical life they only help you enter into the full possession of your eternal inheritance in heaven.

DIRECTIONS FOR WEARING THE SPIRITUAL SHOE

The question I expect from a true Christian reader now is not how to escape these troubles, but how to get this shoe on so you can wade through them in true peace with cheerfulness. It is right for the Christian soldier to ask for armour so he can fight the good fight; but the coward throws down his protection and asks which way he can run. Now I will give you the best counsel I can in the wearing of the spiritual shoe.

I. EXAMINE THE SINCERITY OF YOUR OBEDIENCE

The same sound motives which take a Christian into Christ's service will guide him through suffering whenever God calls for that to happen. When the children of Ephraim took the field they were fully armed but 'turned back in the day of battle' (*Ps. 78:9*). This seems strange until you read the preceding verse – they were 'a generation that set not their heart aright, and whose spirit was not stedfast with God' (*v. 8*).

Soldiers can wear a complete suit of armour and live in a castle whose foundation is rock and whose walls are brass, yet if their hearts are not right with the prince, the slightest storm will throw open the gate and drive them from their place of duty. Sincerity is the only bolt that holds the gate secure.

We have all seen how honest hearts with very little support from without have held the town, while no walls have been thick enough to defend against treachery and the betraying of trust. Ask yourself why you practice Christianity as you do. If faith's working hand is sincere then its fighting hand will be valiant. The power of faith which enabled saints in days of old to 'work righteousness' – that is, to live holy lives – is evidenced by the sufferings they endured. 'Who through faith subdued kingdoms, wrought righteousness, obtained promises, stopped the mouths of lions, quenched the violence of fire, escaped the edge of the sword' (*Heb. 11:33, 34*).

II. PRAY FOR A SUFFERING SPIRIT

This is not a common gift which carnal church-goers have – it is a peculiar favor which God bestows on only a few sincere souls: 'Unto you it is given in the behalf of Christ, not only to believe on him, but also to suffer for his sake' (*Phil. 1:29*).

It is an amazing thing that a child will often not cry after his falls during playtime. And yet, although the punishment of his father's spanking does not cause half the pain of the accidents, he then cries and refuses to be quieted easily. Thus men bring all sorts of trouble upon themselves – and learn to live with them uncomplainingly. A person can whore away his health, for instance, or shorten his normal life-span by drunkenness – and endure it patiently. If he could have his strength and money back he would do the same thing over again – he does not repent of his lusts but regrets that he does not have the ability to support them continuously. In fact these lusts demand all that he has, down to the last crumb of bread in his kitchen and the last drop of blood in his veins. He is not even afraid of burning in hell, as a martyr for sin. But if you ask this person who is so free with his money, flesh, and soul to lay down his life for a few moments in Christ's cause, he hardens his heart and turns away.

Pray, then, for a suffering spirit for Christ's sake. Saints need to plead earnestly with God for this gift because suffering work does not come into our minds naturally. The flesh loves to be pampered, not crucified. It costs many groaning hours in prayer before we can give ourselves to suffering – but the man who learns to wrestle with God need never fear the face of danger and death.

Prayer brings God's strength and wisdom. And what is too hard for the man who has God on his side? We are told to 'count it all joy' when we fall into temptations – not temptations to sin but *for* righteousness (*Jas. 1:2*). And let me assure you – if Christ leads you into this temptation He stands ready to carry you all the way through it. Therefore 'if any of you' – especially suffering people – 'lack wisdom, ask of God, that giveth to all men liberally, and upbraideth not; and it shall be given him' (*v. 5*).

There are not many masters who would rebuke their servants for humbly asking counsel concerning a dangerous work which they attempt because of love. How much less, then, do you need to be afraid of asking the heavenly Father for wisdom? If you have enough faith to venture out upon the sea of suffering at His command He will find enough mercy to keep you from drowning. If you feel yourself beginning to sink, then cry as earnestly as Peter did: 'Lord, save me' (*Matt. 14:30*). Even if you go all the way under, prayer will buoy you up again.

The proverb is true which says, 'He that would learn to pray, let him go to sea.' But I think it could be more accurately expressed like this: 'He who would go to the sea of suffering – let him learn to pray before he leaves the shore.'

III. MEDITATE ON SUFFERING

The pupil who performs best on a test is the one who has thought a great deal about the lesson before the teacher even gives him the test. In fact, we can discover an important principle when we watch porters carrying heavy loads. They lift them over and over again before they actually take them on their backs. And you can do this, too. In your meditation, lift up the troubles which might come for Christ's sake and see if you can carry them should God require it.

Set poverty, prison, isolation, and fire before you on the one hand, and the precious truths of Christ on the other, along with God's sweet promises for those who will hold fast the word of patience in such an hour of temptation. Suppose you had to choose right now which hand you would take; study this question seriously until your conscience can give a clear answer. Do this often so the self-pity which flesh and blood indulge will not be satisfied, nor the encouragements from Scripture be treated with doubt. You must make sure a promise is true before you stake your life on it.

Augustine summed up the urgency of being prepared before a battle: 'It is hard to find the needed troops during war if we have not sought for and known them during peace.' God's promises are our fortress in times of danger; but it is not easy for us to run to them in a crisis unless we know them in times of comfort as well. A stranger who runs to a house for refuge in the dark night will probably fumble to open the door unless he has located the latch in the daytime – and his enemy may well destroy him while he is struggling to open the door. But one who lives inside that place, or is familiar with it, can get in easily. 'Come, my people,' said God, 'enter thou into thy chambers' (*Isa.* 26:20). He shows us our abiding place in His promises long before sufferings come so we can readily find our way to them in the dark.

IV. ACCEPT GOD'S WILL DAILY

God's will is the lock of the night and the key of the morning; we should open and shut our eyes with the thought of placing our lives in His hands. All resistance to suffering stems from the root of distrust; an unbelieving heart stands on a promise the way a man walks on ice – awkwardly and fearfully at first, wondering if it will crack. Now this daily resignation will bring you into a oneness with God's power, faithfulness, and goodness – and will let you experience the reality of His promises, so that you may rely on them in the future.

Each morning, then, entrust your whole heart and all your ways into God's hand. 'The poor committeth himself unto thee; thou art the helper of the fatherless' (*Ps.* 10:14). And every evening, look back and see how perfectly God has kept you in that trust. Do not fall asleep until you have opened your heart to be flooded with His faithfulness – and purpose to trust Him to take care of you through the coming night. Then if you do experience disappointment, watch for God to fill that emptiness. And again, do not rest until God's name has been fully vindicated in your heart. It is important not to let any dissatisfaction slip into your spirit because of His sovereign decision on your behalf. Instead, keep a close

rein on your thoughts the way David did: 'Why art thou
cast down, O my soul? and why art thou disquieted within
me? hope thou in God; for I shall yet praise him, who is the
health of my countenance, and my God' (*Ps. 42:11*). Once
you have done this, God's blessing will keep your faith 'in
breath' and increase your stamina for a longer race when it
is time for you to run it.

V. MAKE SELF-DENIAL A PART OF YOUR LIFE

What if God asks you to give up everything you own –
even freedom, or your life? Would that seem like an
unreasonable demand? Let us look at three important
considerations to help you decide.

(a) *God is asking you for what is already His*

He has only loaned you life on earth for a short time. Is it
wrong for you to call for money your neighbor borrowed
from you two or three years ago? Of course not – he has
every reason to thank you for it and no reason to complain
about repayment.

(b) *God cannot possibly ask you to give Him as much as He
has given you*

Jesus had more glory and honor in heaven than we can
imagine. He 'thought it not robbery to be equal with God:
but made himself of no reputation' (*Phil. 2:6, 7*). Is it pain
you are worried about? Look at the cross where the Lord
of life hung for our sins. Only then can we take up our own
cross and thank God for making it so light and easy, when
He provided such a heavy and tormenting one for His
beloved Son Jesus.

(c) *God can repay anything you might give up for His truth*

When Moses saw this he ran from riches toward the
reproach of Christ, 'for he had respect unto the recom-
pense of the reward' (*Heb. 11:26*). A natural man will do
without almost anything to get something he wants. He
will, for instance, give up half a night's sleep to plot ways

of showing a profit, and get up early to implement his plan. He is glad to sacrifice nice clothing and fine foods to build up his business – the hope of gain makes up for loss.

Now, Christian, put the gains of worldly men on the weighing scales with what is promised you if you deny yourself for Christ's sake and ask yourself how embarrassing it is to see them so freely give up comfort for an uncertain, temporary goal. All the while, you reluctantly forsake a few short-term pleasures which God will repay more than a hundred-fold here – and inconceivable riches besides, whenever you come into heaven's glory!

VI. LEAVE WORLDLY LUSTS BEHIND

It is the sap in the wood which makes it hard to burn, and unmortified corruption in the saint which makes him slow to suffer. But a heart drained and free of the lusts of the world will endure anything for Christ; it kindles as fast as dried wood. Paul points us toward Christians who were 'tortured, not accepting deliverance; that they might obtain a better resurrection' (*Heb. 11:35*). They did not love the world so much that they wanted to turn back from their journey to heaven – however hard it had become. So be careful not to leave any unmortified lust in your soul; it will never consent for you to endure the smallest suffering for your Savior.

Very few ships sink at sea; they are split by rocks and shallow places in the water. The man who can get off the jagged rocks of pride and unbelief and escape the sands of fear of men and love of the world will pass safely through the greatest storm that overtakes him. 'If a man therefore purge himself from these, he shall be a vessel unto honor, sanctified, and meet for the master's use, and prepared unto every good work' (*2 Tim. 2:21*). If only we could know the heaven in a soul which has been crucified to the lusts of the world!

A man dead to sin lives above all disturbances of carnal passions. And when he comes to communion with God there are no intrusions of rude, sinful thoughts between him and the Father. If he is in prison there is no weeping or lust which hangs on to smother him with self-pity. His heart is free – and prison is welcome if it is the vehicle which takes him to the privilege of testifying to the truth of God.

An unmortified heart, however, is so tightly wedged in by familiar spirits of worldliness that it is impossible to escape their embraces and enter into a willingness to suffer. A traveler who sleeps in a strange inn can get up and leave as early as he wants to; no one begs him to stay a little longer. Yet it is much harder to get out of a friend's house. Like the Levite's father-in-law, he insists that his guest remain one more day, and then another and another.

An aged man once moved from Rome to his country home so he could spend his last years free from the entanglements of the city. As other Romans rode by they assumed he must be the only one of them who truly knew how to live. But did this man really know how to unburden his heart of the world's cares? Many run into the country without leaving the city behind at all; their minds are still in the press of the crowd while their bodies are in the solitude of the wilderness. If this poor man had just known the gospel it could have shown him the way out of the world's confusion in the middle of Rome itself, with all its problems and pleasures. The truth is, only the person who has learned to die to the world knows how to live in it.

GOSPEL PEACE PREPARES THE SAINT FOR TRIALS

The peace which the gospel brings to the heart makes a

saint ready to wade through any trouble that might meet him in his Christian course. And the man who lives in this peace is the only one who stands shod, prepared for every trial. Only Christ can make a shoe fit the Christian's foot so he can easily walk a hard path, because He lines it with the peace of the gospel. Then even when the way is covered with sharp stones, this shoe goes between the boulders and the foot – and obstacles are never much felt.

Solomon tells us that the ways of wisdom – that is, Christ – 'are ways of pleasantness.' But how can this always hold true when we know from experience that some of these paths lead to suffering? Scripture answers: 'And all her paths are *peace*' (*Prov. 3:17*). Because of peace with God and peace with conscience, the righteous man lacks no pleasure. David, for instance, went to bed satisfied when he had nothing for supper but the gladness God had given his heart. In fact, he promised himself a better night's rest than those full of the world's cheer: 'Thou hast put gladness in my heart, more than in the time that their corn and their wine increased. I will both lay me down in peace, and sleep: for thou, Lord, only makest me dwell in safety' (*Ps. 4:7, 8*).

The peace which David's conscience enjoyed comforted his body as well: 'I laid me down and slept; I awaked, for the Lord sustained me' (*Ps. 3:5*). And David had this sweet rest not only when he lay in the stately palace in Jerusalem but also when he fled for his life from his unnatural son Absalom, and may have lain in the open field. It must have been a good pillow that made him forget personal peril when such a disloyal army hunted him from behind.

This gospel peace is so transcendent that it causes the believer to lie down and rejoice to sleep in the grave as well as on the softest bed. Surely you would agree that the child is willing who asks for a nap. Some of God's saints have desired that He lay them to rest in their beds of dust, not because they were tired of trouble as Job was, but because of the strong overcoming peace in their hearts. 'Now lettest thou thy servant depart in peace, according to thy word: For mine eyes have seen thy salvation,' was the swan-like song of old Simeon (*Luke 2:29, 30*). He spoke like a merchant who had finally put all his goods on board the ship and then hailed the captain to hoist sail and steer toward home. Why would any Christian, who is only a foreigner here, want to stay longer in this world, except to get in his full cargo for heaven? Assurance of peace with God is the force which fills the sail and drives that load homeward.

The peace of the gospel and a sense of God's love so empower Christians that the Father often gives a swallow of this strong wine before leading them into the heat of conflict. For example, God called Abram out of his native land but promised to bring his servant's heart to His very foot. Jacob ran to Padan-aram to escape the anger of a brother whose thoughts had already murdered him. But God comforted this pilgrim in a sweet gospel vision by showing to his faith a symbol of Christ and His reconciling work.

So then the sum of all God did for His beloved Jacob was this: 'Your brother Esau hates you, but in Christ you and I are one. Yes, your uncle will wrong you, but do not be afraid of him. I am at peace with you, so through Christ you will have the special care of My holy angels to defend you wherever you go.'

Before the Israelites were ready to march out of Egypt into a desolate wilderness, where their faith would be sorely tried, God entertained them with a gospel feast to prepare them – the passover, which pointed to Christ.

And when the feet of Jesus' own disciples stood by the sea of sorrows which His death would inevitably cause to swell, He invited them to the ordinance of His precious supper. And the pardon of their sins, sealed to their souls in this ordinance, strengthened them to move toward suffering with prepared hearts.

Surely, then, the most important provision Christ made for His disciples was not to leave them a quiet world to live in, but to arm them against a volatile and troublesome world. And He did this by satisfying them with the Father's love – He bequeathed them His own peace and emptied its sweet comforts into their hearts. He promised that as soon as He got to heaven He would pray His Father to send the Comforter. Notice He did not send them out to contest the angry world at first, but commanded them to stay in Jerusalem until they received power which the Holy Spirit would bring. But now let me show you some ways this gospel peace prepares the saint for suffering.

HOW GOSPEL PEACE PREPARES THE CHRISTIAN FOR SUFFERING

I. GOSPEL PEACE LIFTS THE BELIEVER ABOVE DANGER

If a man could be persuaded that he could walk as safely in flames of fire as he could stroll through his garden, he would not be afraid to do one more than the other. Or, if he could wear a secret suit of armour that resisted all blows and ammunition sent against him, he would not hesitate to stand in the midst of the most formidable weapons in the world.

Now the saint who is at peace with God is invested with far more effective protection than this. For whether sufferings come from God, man, or devils, 'the peace of God, which passeth all understanding,' is said to 'keep your hearts and minds through Christ Jesus' (*Phil. 4:7*). The believer is completely surrounded with such blessed benefits that he is as secure as one inside an impregnable castle.

II. A PERSON AT PEACE WITH GOD BECOMES HIS CHILD

Once a Christian experiences God's precious love he does not dread suffering or affliction; he knows the Father will not hurt His own child. I have often wondered about Isaac's peace and patience in submitting to be bound for a sacrifice when he saw the knife so near his throat. We know he was not a mere child because Abraham asked him to carry the load of wood. Some say he may have been more than twenty years old, certainly mature enough to be apprehensive of death. Yet the son had such complete confidence in the authority of his father that he did not struggle, but put his life into his hands. If anyone else had held the weapon he could not have trusted as he did. We must remember whoever may be the instrument of trouble to a saint, the sword is always in God's control. Because Christ saw the cup in His Father's hand He took it willingly.

III. A SOUL WITH GOD'S PEACE IS AN HEIR OF GOD

Kinship to heaven carries this benefit: 'If children, then heirs, heirs of God, and joint-heirs with Christ' (*Rom. 8:17*). Such a privilege lifts the Christian above any fear of suffering he might have had. For example, a few sweet meditations on this truth raised Paul's soul into a place where the troubles of this life could not discourage him: 'For I reckon that the sufferings of this present time are not worthy to be compared with the glory which shall be revealed in us' (*Rom. 8:18*). He refused to let himself or any other Christian undervalue the inheritance or the love of God that settled this glory on him by dwelling on the severity of suffering. It is as if he asked, 'Has God made us

[389]

His heirs, and given us heaven, for us to sit down and moan about a few minor problems in our short lives? How important can suffering be, compared to the vast circumference of eternity that we will spend worshiping at the feet of Jesus?'

A man is confined to a pauper's spirit if he is defeated by one or two petty losses; and it is a miserly Christian indeed who cries and complains about any cross he might have in this life. We must conclude that such a person either is heir to nothing in eternity or that he has little knowledge of what is actually waiting for him.

IV. GOSPEL PEACE MAKES FAITH INVINCIBLE

Nothing is too hard for a saint to believe when he carries pardon in his conscience and peace in his spirit. Because God knew Moses would face insurmountable problems, humanly speaking, in leading Israel into Canaan, He revealed His mighty power in the very beginning of His servant's work. The rod that became a serpent and then a rod again, the leprous hand restored – these were holy demonstrations that God would favor His chosen ones with deliverance in the most desperate crises.

When God commissions a Christian He includes such a testimony of His almighty power and love that the person's faith cannot be destroyed. Pardoning mercy has turned the serpent of the law – with its threatening of stinging the sinner to death – into the blossoming rod of the gospel, which brings forth sweet fruit of peace and life. And which is the greater miracle, after all – Moses' leprous hand made clean, or a sinner's leprous heart made pure by washing in the blood of Christ?

Certainly this miracle of mercy, wherever it is accepted, makes it easy for the believer to trust God in a sea of temporal sufferings and follow Him through a wilderness of distress. Because David's assurance of God's pardoning mercy guided his faith, as a rudder controls a ship, his trust moved right on course through divine deliverance. We find evidence of his peace with God in this testimony of reconciliation: 'I said I will confess my transgressions unto the Lord; and thou forgavest the iniquity of my sin' (*Ps. 32:5*). And notice the heights to which David could now reach with his faith in God in times of invading anxiety: 'Thou art my hiding place; thou shalt preserve me from trouble; thou shalt compass me about with songs of deliverance' (*v. 7*). The larger spiritual deliverance has given him confidence for the lesser ones of this life.

V. PEACE WITH GOD FILLS THE HEART WITH LOVE FOR CHRIST

The Christian's love for Christ catches fire from Christ's love for him. And the hotter Christ's love burns in the person's heart, the stronger the reflection of that love back to Him. Jesus said the person who is forgiven much loves much. And the more love, the less fear of suffering.

Most of us would do anything for a close friend. When Christ told His disciples Lazarus was dead, Thomas wanted to go and die with him. Powerful love is as strong as death. Paul said, 'For a good man, some would even dare to die' (*Rom. 5:7*). How much more, then, will a person full of grace be willing to sacrifice his life for a good God? 'Thy name is as ointment poured forth, therefore do the virgins love thee' (*Song of Sol. 1:3*). Christ's name is poured forth when God's love through Him is shed abroad in the heart. And when this precious box is broken, its sweet savor is diffused in the heart and takes away the scent of even the foulest prison in the earth.

The heavenly fire of Christ's love powerfully beaming on the soul will put out not only the kitchen fire of carnal love but also the hell-fire of fear. What makes the thoughts of death seem so repulsive when it comes toward us in the schemes of persecution? Surely this dread comes from guilt and unacquaintance with all Christ has done to 'deliver them who through fear of death were all their lifetime subject to bondage' (*Heb. 2:15*).

VI. PEACE WITH GOD ENCOURAGES SELF-DENIAL

Self-denial is a grace so necessary to suffering that Christ lays the whole weight of the cross on its back: 'Whosoever will come after me, let him deny himself, and take up his cross, and follow me' (*Mark 8:34*). Some Christians, like Simon of Cyrene, may be compelled to carry Christ's cross after Him only a short way. But the self-denying saint will stoop to his knees and wait for Christ to lay this burden on him. Now there are two ways that peace with God empowers the Christian in the kind of self-denial which prepares him for suffering.

(a) *This peace enables the Christian to deny himself in his sinful self*

Sin may well be called *self* because it cleaves as close to us as our human body. It is as hard to mortify a lust as it is to cut off an arm or leg. Yet when Christ and the Christian feast together with the 'hidden manna' of pardon and peace, He can ask for the head of the proudest lust of all, and take it with less regret on the part of the saint than Herodias felt as she demanded the head of John the Baptist.

There is no other key like love to open the heart. When love knocks at the door and expresses kindness, there is little reason to fear rejection. Esther, for example, persuaded her husband's heart against Haman her enemy as she showed strong love to Ahasuerus at a banquet. And God demonstrates His love to Christians each time He entertains at the feast of His gospel. Surely this is the time He prevails with His children to send the cursed Amalekite to the gallows – that is, lust to its execution.

After Jesus' blessed words of forgiveness fell into Mary Magdalene's grieving heart, do you think she could have been persuaded to leave the embraces of His love and open the door to any of her former lovers and to whoredom again? She would have chosen martyrdom first! That one love which makes the saint deny a lust causes him not to deny a cross.

(b) *This peace enables the Christian to deny carnal enjoyments*

To the same degree the person burns in desire for worldly pleasures, will he tremble in frustration when Christ requires him to part with them. Just as the sweet wines and dainty fare of Capua eventually weakened Hannibal's soldiers, carnal pleasures will weaken the boldest Christian warrior so he can no longer look his enemy in the face.

Gospel peace deadens the heart of the believer to worldly temptations so he can deny the most promising benefits the flesh offers. Paul put it this way: 'God forbid that I should glory, save in the cross of our Lord Jesus Christ, by whom the world is crucified unto me, and I unto the world' (*Gal. 6:14*). His heart was dead to the world, and the cross of Christ was the weapon which inflicted the lethal wound upon his carnal affections.

Now there was a time when Paul loved the world as much as anyone else. But when God's mercy pardoned his sins and received him into favor and fellowship with Himself, he abandoned his lusts to let the heavenly Lord and King reign with peace in his soul.

No one can turn away from thirsting after fleshly enjoyments as fast as the person who has his mouth at the fountainhead – the love of God Himself. A loving wife can forget friends and leave her father's house to follow her husband, even into a wilderness or prison. How much more freely, then, should a Christian say goodbye to life itself and follow Christ, especially when the Comforter spreads the sweet presence of joy along his most lonely paths?

VII. PEACE WITH GOD PROMOTES THE SUFFERING GRACE OF PATIENCE

Suffering is not grievous for a patient Christian. In fact, patience has been called the grace which digests affliction and turns it into healthful nourishment. Weak stomachs prefer bland diets, but strong stomachs never refuse any meat set before them; all fare is alike to them.

There are some things which are hard for the spirit of man to digest – reproach, prison, and death, to name a few. 'When tribulation or persecution ariseth because of the word, by and by he is offended' (*Matt. 13:21*). Usually this kind of hardship will not stay in the stomach of a weak-spirited person, but makes him throw up the most vital food he should strive to keep – his profession of Christ.

The patient person, however, makes his meal of whatever God's sovereignty brings. If peace and prosperity are served up with the gospel, he is thankful and enjoys the abundance while it lasts. But if God replaces these with sour herbs of affliction and persecution they will not make him sick with despair. He simply eats larger servings of the gospel so his bitter herbs go down wrapped in divine comfort.

Christians, then, must rely on consolations that flow from the peace of the gospel if they are to be a consistently patient people. It would be impossible for God's children to endure the persecutions they meet from men and devils without the sweet help of a sense of God's love in Christ which glows at their hearts in inward peace and joy. In fact, the apostle reveals the secret of the saints' patience, hope, and glorying in tribulation: 'Because the love of God is shed abroad in our hearts by the Holy Ghost which is given unto us' (*Rom. 5:5*).

Sin, on the other hand, makes suffering intolerable. A light cart moves over the marsh easily, but one weighted down with a heavy load sinks until it stops. In the same way, guilt overloads the soul and makes it bog down in suffering. But when the cumbersome guilt is lifted, and God speaks peace to the soul, the person who once raged like a madman under the cross will carry it without a whimper. It is worth repeating here – 'The peace of God . . . shall keep your hearts and minds through Christ Jesus' (*Phil. 4:7*).

GOSPEL PEACE AND PATIENCE

I. PATIENCE IN AFFLICTION WITHOUT GOSPEL PEACE

Sometimes we see strangers to this gospel, ignorant of Christ the Peacemaker, who are nonetheless calm and quiet during affliction. If these people had any idea of the seriousness of their spiritual condition, they would not have a shred of patience, realizing that God will throw them into hell before He is through if they do not repent and believe. When I watch a person run over rough stones barefooted without complaining I do not admire his tolerance. No, I pity the man who has so numbed his feet, as it were, by clothing them with dead flesh that he has lost all feeling and cannot sense the pain which signals very real danger.

What good does medicine do in a dead man's mouth? If a person will not be convinced of his critical condition, even the most diligent efforts to restore his health are useless. And if afflictions – the most forceful medicine of all – leave the person oblivious to his spiritual need, there is not much hope left for him.

II. PROFESSION OF GOSPEL PEACE WITHOUT PATIENCE IN AFFLICTION

Inasmuch as the believer has peace from the infallible sense of God's love in Christ abiding within, he can submit to any suffering God might choose for him. This is why we must test our peace and comfort. If you have no heart to suffer for God, but choose a sin to escape a cross, your peace is false. And if you have only limited patience under normal afflictions – if you strain to keep your spirit from murmuring and your heart from sinking – your faith in the promise is precariously weak. 'If thou faint in the day of adversity, thy strength is small' (*Prov. 24:10*).

TENDERNESS OF A CHRISTIAN CONSCIENCE

Keep this peace unbroken and it will keep your heart whole when all the world shatters around you. As long as it rules in your heart you are safe from every fear, in prison or at a fiery stake. But if you allow it to be wounded, your enemies will rush in upon you as Simeon and Levi ambushed the men of Shechem (*Gen. 34:25, 26*). It is a sad thing to go into suffering with a sore, infected conscience. Even a tiny thorn in the traveler's foot makes the smoothest road hard for him to walk; and guilt in the conscience brings severe discomfort to any Christian, especially one who is suffering.

Now if you want to make sure your peace will remain unbroken, set a lifeguard about it. The most beautiful flowers are the ones which require the most care; and the richer the treasure the more we protect it. Surely you will agree that God's cherished peace is worth anything you must do to keep it safe. The Savior taught that worldly goods, such as silver and gold, can be lost in two ways – by thieves breaking in and stealing them, and by rust corrupting them. There are two similar ways a Christian can lose inward peace.

I. PRESUMPTUOUS SINS ARE 'THIEVES' WHICH STEAL COMFORT

When the Christian boldly walks in sinful choices and then thinks he can console his aching conscience with his pardoned state and interest in Christ, he finds the cellar door to God's comforting promises locked fast. Christ has withdrawn and taken the keys with Him. Because of pride, uncleanness, and earthly-mindedness he may even cry out in strong tears as Mary did when she could not find Jesus' body: 'They have taken away my Lord, and I know not where they have laid him' (*John 20:13*).

Be careful, then, to defend yourself against these thieves called presumptuous sins. 'The spirit of man is the candle of the Lord' (*Prov. 20:27*). Has God lighted your candle and warmed your spirit with the sense of His love? If a robber from hell is allowed to touch this candle, your comfort will be snuffed out. Have you fallen into the hands of presumptuous sins which have stolen your peace? Then do not waste any time sending sincere repentance after them and raising a strong spirit of prayer and supplication to God.

As I have already warned, there is no time for delay. The farther you let these sins go without repentance, the harder you will find it to recover your peace and joy out of their hands. Yet know this – as you humbly return to God He is ready to restore to you the joy of His salvation and exact justice upon the enemies of your soul by His mortifying grace.

II. NEGLIGENCE IS THE 'RUST' WHICH RUINS THE STRENGTH OF PEACE

It is impossible for the Christian who is careless in his

walk, infrequent or negligent in his communion with God, to enjoy true peace and comfort very long. Maybe you are not pouring presumptuous sins upon your joy to quench it. Well, you are not to be praised; your failure to feed it the oil of communion with God is enough to eat the heart out of your comfort. You can murder your own peace by starving it as well as by stabbing it.